Born in Saudi Arabia, **Hugh Miles** was educated in Libya and at Eton and studied Arabic at Oxford and in the Yemen. He has written for the *London Review of Books* and the *Sunday Times,* and is the author of *Al Jazeera.* He won *The Times* Young Journalist of the Year award in 2000.

'This account of life in Cairo is sex and the city with a difference . . . Miles opens windows to a little-known side of Cairo . . . His anecdotes are enlightening and along the way he conveys the sense and smell of Cairo, its hustle and humour' *The Economist*

'Miles should be applauded for telling their stories so compellingly, and for giving us such a detailed insight into their everyday lives' *Scotsman*

'An inspiring and moving account of the many challenges faced by women living in Egypt today' *Irish Times,* Books of the Year

'Miles's account of the girls' misadventures is vivid with sympathy and amusement' *New Statesman*

'This book has the feeling of a novel – and a good one at that. *Playing Cards in Cairo* abounds in subtle nuances, and is a book that digs deep into the lives of the ordinary-but-extraordinary women on the front line' *Spectator*

Playing Cards
in Cairo

HUGH MILES

ABACUS

First published in Great Britain in 2008 by Abacus
This paperback edition published in 2011 by Abacus

A CIP catalogue record for this book
is available from the British Library.

ISBN 978-0-349-11980-9

Typeset in Bembo by M Rules
Printed and bound in Great Britain by
Clays Ltd, St Ives plc

Papers used by Abacus are natural, renewable and
recyclable products sourced from well-managed forests and certified in
accordance with the rules of the Forest Stewardship Council.

Mixed Sources
Product group from well-managed
forests and other controlled sources
www.fsc.org Cert no. SGS-COC-004081
© 1996 Forest Stewardship Council
FSC

Abacus
An imprint of
Little, Brown Book Group
100 Victoria Embankment
London EC4Y 0DY

An Hachette UK Company
www.hachette.co.uk

www.littlebrown.co.uk

For Dina

Acknowledgements

This book would not have been possible without the kind help of many people, most of whom do not want their names listed here.

I would like to thank the ladies of Cairo who shared their stories with me. They know who they are. I would also like to thank Clare Alexander, Richard Beswick, Julia Brickell, Amr Mowafak Mosaad, Magdy Eissa, May Abdel Asim from *What Women Want* Magazine, Ahmed Al Awamry, Khaled Mansour, Jon Hill, Ayla Dogruyol, Hossam el-Hamalawy, James Peach, Thomas Jones, Diana al-Shafie, Atia al-Shafie, Oliver Gayner, Peter Behrens, Charles Gillan, Jonathon Clarke, Richard and Hanna Ashcroft, Siobhan Hughes, Hugh Thraves Davis, Sir Derek and Lady Plumbly, Micah Rankin and my family for their support.

The rules of *tarneeb*

There are four players, in partnerships of two. A standard fifty-two-card pack is used, ranking in the usual way from ace (high) down to two (low). The game is played anticlockwise. The first dealer is chosen at random and after each hand the turn to deal passes to the right. The cards are shuffled and cut, and are all dealt out, one at a time, so that everyone has thirteen cards.

Bidding begins with the dealer and continues anticlockwise. A bid consists of a number of tricks and a suit or 'no trumps'. A bid of more tricks outranks any bid of fewer tricks. When comparing bids for the same number of tricks, the five denominations rank in the same order as at bridge: no trumps is highest, then spades, hearts, diamonds, clubs (lowest).

At your turn you can either pass or bid higher than the previous bidder – either by bidding more tricks or the same number of tricks in a higher denomination. The bidding continues until all four players pass in succession. When a bid is followed by four passes the last (and highest) bidder becomes the declarer and the trump suit is determined by the declarer's final bid.

Each partnership's objective is to take at least the number of tricks that they bid and to hinder the other team from doing so. The declarer starts and players must follow suit if they can; a player who has no cards of the suit led can play any card. A trick is won by the highest trump and if the trick contains no trumps, the highest card of the suit that led wins. The winner of a trick leads the next.

When all thirteen tricks have been played, the scores of the two sides are calculated by adding the number of tricks each player won. The game ends when a team equals or exceeds thirty-one points – the team with the highest total score is the winner.

Prologue

The first time I came to Cairo I was seventeen and clueless. It was my school summer holidays and I had managed to wangle myself a placement working as an au pair for a rich Cairene family in a prosperous suburban neighbourhood of Giza.

It was a formative but alien experience. The family were kind and hospitable but since none of them spoke English, and my Arabic was so rudimentary as to be useless, communication during the two weeks was restricted to a few amicable grunts and hoots, as well as sign language.

The family's lavish penthouse apartment was meticulously upholstered in gold and bright white imitation Louis XIV furniture. The father was some kind of industrialist. I never did find out quite what he did, but whatever it was, he was always away on business. I met him on the first day and then never again.

Most of my days I spent in the company of his glamorous and heavily bejewelled wife, who seemed to have nothing better to do than lounge around with me, gossip on the phone and do her eyebrows. Her husband had forbidden her from leaving the house without his permission, so I must have seemed like an exotic distraction from the excruciating boredom of her humdrum daily life. She was an excellent cook and despite our communication difficulties taught me how to stuff dates, bake pitta bread and fry falafel. I still remember with fondness her sweet *Om Ali*, made with cinnamon, milk and nuts, brushed over with melted butter. *Om Ali*, which means Ali's mum, is the queen of Egyptian desserts.

The couple had four children. There was a pair of tearaway twins aged about eight, to whom I was supposed to be teaching English. They were hyperactive and more or less uncontrollable, and I doubt much of what I taught them went in. I struggled simply to stop them drawing on the furniture. Then there was a grungy teenage boy slightly younger than me, who spent his days asleep and his nights loitering with his friends in the car park outside; and finally the eldest child was a beautiful daughter, a year older than me, who always kept a discreet distance. Looking back on it, I realise now she was thrilled to have a boy her age to flirt with in the house that summer, especially a foreign one with whom normal rules did not apply. Her brother, though younger and smaller than both of us, kept a vigilant eye open to make sure we did not get up to any monkey business.

Everyone in the family was very hot-blooded and there seemed to be a row at least once a day, usually between the fifteen-year-old boy and his elder sister. He often found her conduct or dress unacceptable, which would plunge him into a violent temper. If he judged that she had stayed out too late or had been speaking to a man on the telephone, there would be an angry reckoning. He would push her around, call her names and on several occasions slap her face in front of other members of the family. While I sat silent, awkward and English in the living room, understanding little of what was going on, the row would escalate into screams and door slamming until everyone in the family was involved.

I found it novel that a teenager should care so much about his older sister. I did not understand why it mattered to him so much how she behaved or what she wore. It seemed peculiar that he should regard her manners as his personal responsibility. What seemed strangest was that their mother, who often bore witness to their fights, never objected or did anything to stop her son beating his sister, although he was still quite a young man and she easily could have intervened.

Over the weeks I stayed with the family I came to realise that although the boy's behaviour seemed aggressive and overprotective to me, to everyone else it was perfectly normal or even quite affectionate. The mother did not discipline her son because she viewed the way he treated his sister as a sign that he loved her. Besides, it was plain even to me that she often provoked him, letting him catch her on the phone to someone she should not be talking to, or telling him things to his face that she knew perfectly well would upset him. Often I would see her planning ahead for trouble, conspiring with her mother in the kitchen about what she was going to tell her brother when he came home.

Family relationships in the Middle East, I was learning, are different to those in the West. In Arab families a girl cannot up and leave home when she is still a teenager; women are not autonomous individuals who can run their own lives independently of the rest of their family. When the father is absent, a boy must be responsible for his sister. She can be flirtatious and feminine, but it's his duty to play the stern loving protector, because if she erred the blemish would stain the whole family. Honour is too fragile for a daughter to be left to handle alone.

Just because the brother and sister fought, it was not a sign that they did not love each other. In fact they loved each other with a deep and binding love. When they were at peace she could see no division between what was hers and what was his. While she strived to guess his needs and desires in advance, he took great pride in her beauty and comportment. They were bound to each another, like a ship to its mast, for his honour depended on her behaviour and her freedom depended on his mood. While he controlled her physically, her conduct governed his reputation. Loving her meant controlling her; loving him meant submitting to him.

Even after she married and left the home, nothing was going to break the bond between them. One day soon her parents would choose a husband for her, a man she might not even love, perhaps someone who already had other wives and children. But she would always keep her natal name because a husband can be thrown off at any time like a change of clothes. Returning to the bosom of her family, it would be once again her brother's responsibility to look after her. Husbands come and go, but a brother is always a brother, from childhood into the afterlife.

One

The next time I set foot in Cairo was on business ten years later. It was early spring and I was staying for a few weeks in an apartment in Zamalek, an upmarket residential district on a three-and-a-half-kilometre-long island in the middle of the Nile. I was keen to find out as much as I could about the city. I was not looking to fall in love.

Zamalek was uninhabited until the nineteenth century, when the Ottoman governor, known as the Khedive, built a great palace on the island and landscaped the other half into a royal garden. In the twentieth century, during Cairo's land development boom, the royal gardens were partitioned and sold off for development into Parisian-style suburban houses, complete with the latest amenities, like piped water and gas. The block where I was staying, called the Maraspini Building, was one of a pair designed by a Belgian architect in the 1930s. It was a resplendent throwback to a sepia-tinged era when the sun was setting on the British Empire and Cairo swung like one long party for the cast of *Casablanca*.

During the Second World War, the building was home to the wealthiest aristocratic Cairene families. Charles de Gaulle and his government in exile plotted the liberation of France there, although there is some disagreement among the modern tenants as to exactly which apartment the French plotting took place in.

Next door was a newly built neo-Islamic villa that housed a prince and a Turkish sultana and British soldiers dubbed the two buildings 'Elephant and Castle'.

After the war the Maraspini Building passed briefly into the hands of a Chinese nationalist, who sold it to an Italian businessman from whom it was confiscated in the 1960s by President Nasser's Revolutionary Council on their sequestration binge, together with the sultana's palace next door. The captains and kings of Egypt's defunct industries relocated to Paris, Rome or Beirut, leaving proud *fin de siècle* townhouses across Zamalek empty for party apparatchiks to squabble over. The government sold the Maraspini Building to a Swiss insurance company; the palace next door eventually became a ceramics museum. The prince and sultana's possessions were auctioned off by the new regime in a job lot at dime-a-dozen prices.

By the time I came to Elephant and Castle, the truculent French generals had all left and the only traces of the halcyon days of the Second World War were a footnote in the history books and a commemorative blue metal plaque screwed to the first-floor balcony. Twenty-first-century Elephant and Castle had become a luxury block, housing the cream of Cairo's liberal intelligentsia. My next-door neighbour was a movie star; downstairs was a distinguished science professor from Cairo's most prestigious English language university; across the corridor from me lived a representative of the UN; a former member of the Egyptian parliament lived somewhere in the flats upstairs.

I was house-sitting for a banker friend who had leased an apartment from the Swiss insurance company. Since she was always travelling, it was my solemn responsibility to water the plants, keep an eye on the doorman and watch out for any leaks, fires and thefts. Spring was just beginning to bloom as I found myself in this most agreeable position, settling into a beautiful apartment from the *belle époque* in the heart of Cairo's low-rise answer to Manhattan. The weather was getting warmer and each day seemed to bring a thousand new beautiful things.

Cairo is the largest Arab city and the biggest city in Africa. It is one of just a handful of world supercapitals and dominates Egypt. The razzle-dazzle of colonial parties may have faded, but seventeen million people living side by side generate such an abundance of news, it remains a dream location for a writer and journalist. I had come to Cairo to finish a book but was waylaid by the opportunities the city afforded. In the wake of 9/11 Western newspapers had developed such an appetite for stories from the Middle East, I discovered that there was a much more lucrative living to be had working as a freelancer there than I could have doing the same thing in London.

Only the richest and most prestigious newspapers and magazines have enough money to maintain a permanent correspondent in town. Most English-language newspapers and magazines can afford only one Middle East correspondent, who is typically sent to Jerusalem. Every once in a while the unfortunate soul might be given a break to go on a tour of Iraq, but that still left the whole of North Africa and the Arabian peninsula to freelancers like me. Unlike the cut-throat world of London journalism I had left behind, I found stories in Cairo ripened slowly like fat Nile dates until the time arrived for me to trot along from Elephant and Castle and pick them.

And if it was a slow week or I became distracted doing other things, then there was no real cause for concern. While London bleeds money out of you at every step, in Cairo it felt as if you could live on lotuses but get by on pennies. The Egyptian economy tanked badly after 9/11 and only gradually picked itself up. In 2001 the Egyptian pound was devalued twice in six months, devastating tens of millions of Egyptians. But what proved a disaster for nationals has made life extraordinarily cheap for visiting foreigners.

Life in Zamalek ticked along at a leisurely pace. Each morning I walked to my local café to smoke a *shisha* over the paper and enjoy a cup of powerful Egyptian coffee. Mornings were the most peaceful time on the island. On my way I would pass the same familiar sights: clusters of trumpet-shaped jacarandas spilling over garden walls, carpeting the ground in a mass of colour; acacias seeping gum dropping brightly coloured seed pods on policemen snoozing outside embassies; doormen clad in long nightshirt-like gowns known as *galabiyahs*, sipping tea and smoking water pipes, sitting outside dilapidated architectural jewels.

The short walk to the coffee shop took me past the school for refugees in All Saints church, and the leafy streets rang with the shrieks of children playing. Often I would stop and watch the crowds of Sudanese milling around outside the church gates. They were easily distinguishable from the Egyptians, with their long-limbed frames and deep black skin. Fleeing conflicts in Darfur or southern Sudan, they came to Cairo in their thousands, and All Saints church had become a kind of Sudanese community centre, as well as a post-natal clinic, family planning centre, employment office and a point from which many other refugee services of one kind or another had been made available.

Just next to the church lies the Gezira Club, Cairo's most prestigious members-only sporting establishment. Dating back to the colonial era, it was modelled after the Hurlingham Club in Fulham and occupies almost half the island of Zamalek. Carved in the 1880s by the Anglo-Egyptian elite out of the Khedival botanical gardens, it was designed so that off-duty cavalry officers had somewhere to play polo. Golf was introduced a few years later but for decades Egyptians were only allowed to be caddies. After the 1952 revolution in a symbolic act of revenge the course was destroyed and the club reshaped. Nowadays you are more likely to run into a pop star than a dragoon guard, and honking four-by-fours have long since replaced the cavalry horses, but exorbitant annual membership fees ensure the Gezira Club retains its air of colonial exclusivity. Lifetime members today are drawn from the Egyptian ruling elite and early each morning the tough-nut interior minister would have two dozen of his security detail cordon off the Gezira racetrack for his aerobics and jogging routine.

My local coffee shop was on Twenty-Sixth of July Street, a busy thoroughfare that bisects Zamalek, leading at either end to the two mighty branches of the Nile. Twenty-Sixth of July is the anniversary of two momentous events in the history of modern Egypt: the 1952 abdication of King Farouk and four years later the nationalisation of the Suez Canal. When it was too early to talk I would quietly install myself in a corner of the café, in between the other red-eyed men. There I would quietly read a book to the dulcet slurps and gurgles of men drinking coffee and smoking *shishas* over copies of the morning's papers. Curling plumes of sweetly scented smoke would drift out into the street and mingle with the sound of the Koran playing on the radio and the sound of the morning rush hour. Nobody else, I noticed, ever read any book besides the Koran, but sometimes I would see men just sitting silent and motionless, prayer beads limp in hands, simply meditating for half an hour or more.

The coffee shop provided an opportunity for a moment of private introspection, a chance to reflect on the day ahead. Sleepily I would watch the fat black houseflies, as inured to the thick clouds of smoke as the waiters, swarm over the stained wooden chairs looking for traces of last night's mint tea. My thoughts would be interrupted only by the intermittent twittering and bleeping of mobile phones and the occasional pang of what Germans call *Künstlerschuld*: the guilt an artist feels at leading such a trivial existence when all around him others struggle with the daily grind.

All kinds of people dropped by: local businessmen, Arab tourists or the doorman from down the street still wearing his pyjamas. It was a place for men to take time out from their day to chat or meditate a little before they had to go back to the office or their wives. It afforded that most basic of pleasures and the one thing I was missing in Elephant and Castle: the pleasure of human company.

You are almost never alone in Cairo; privacy is a luxury few can afford for any length of time. I had made a handful of friends since coming to town, mostly Western expatriates from the community of some 80,000 foreigners who live in Cairo full time.

With its continental European architecture and year-round river breeze, Zamalek is the favoured expatriate hub and all manner of foreigners can be found pottering around the Western restaurants and bars a stone's throw from Twenty-Sixth of July Street. A cosmopolitan assortment of bureaucrats, diplomats and aid workers rub shoulders with an unending flow of grubby international backpackers. The Egyptians with whom they mingle, in Zamalek's clubs and bars, are drawn largely from the tiny privileged upper class.

For the tourists in Cairo, the halcyon days of pharaohs and polo clubs have never stopped, at least in the oriental comic strip inside their heads. Leaving behind their suburban lives for a few weeks, they step off the plane in costume. Some come as dashing archaeologists intent on unearthing the secrets of the desert; others as belly dancers or secret agents ready to weather a sandstorm. The Egyptians are pretty phlegmatic about all this by now. They are accustomed to the unending hither and thither and nonsense of foreigners. Everyone accepts that they will always be there, are essentially harmless and bring healthy amounts of cash from which they can normally be parted in a fairly straightforward manner.

Most of the foreigners who live in Zamalek do not speak Arabic, but have come to town to work for one of a myriad of non-governmental humanitarian organisations, which draw volunteers from across the world. Typically they are students on a break from a social science or law degree at a Western university. Young professionals far from home feel adventurous and free. Going out is cheap, the weather is good and there are some beautiful Nile-side bars which are perfect for sundowners. For foreigners Cairo is a party town, where everything is available for a price.

Many of the international organisations operating in Cairo are given over to handling refugees, because migration is one African sector that never stops booming. Millions of people flood into Cairo from across Africa, tide upon tide of humanity arriving by bus, by boat or on foot, down the Nile Valley or across the desert. With them they bring dark stories of torture and war. For unknown thousands Cairo is nothing more than a big outdoor waiting room, the biggest metropolitan refugee terminal in the world.

Two

Throwing myself into the murk of Cairo's nightlife, it did not take long before I had fallen in with all manner of expatriates each with a dazzling constellation of stories. Aid workers, diplomats, missionaries, teachers, converts and belly dancers, constantly inventing and reinventing themselves as expatriates are so prone to do, Zamalek's bars saw it all. Some had been in Egypt for years and had embraced Arab life wholeheartedly; others were over for just a few weeks on a contract and were spending most of their free time holed up in their hotel room praying to go home.

My new best friend was a young Jewish-American lawyer I met in a bar. His name was Jerome and he had come to Cairo as an intern, to work for an international aid agency helping refugees in exchange for college credit. Back home he was still a student at Boston University.

Jerome's office was in a leafy English-style suburb in the heart of the capital, which exudes an air of tranquillity. Curving streets are lined with palm, mango and rubber trees. The wealthy neighbourhood formed the backdrop to Olivia Manning's expatriate Cairo saga *The Levant Trilogy*, which traced the fortunes of British refugees in Cairo against the backdrop of the Second World War.

Since the British embassy is close to Jerome's office, there was a constant security presence and the street was cordoned off to all traffic except police trucks. Concrete barriers had been erected to stop suicide bombers and black-clad state security officers with machine guns kept a lazy eye on the line of visa applicants snaking away from the embassy gates. With only pedestrians permitted to pass, on balmy evenings and weekends the street seemed as peaceful as it had done a hundred years ago when the British embassy had been the seat of power in Egypt.

The office was on the third floor of an elegant *fin de siècle* villa. In times gone by it would have been a beautiful family apartment. Large bay windows looked down on treetops and let in a wall of sunshine. Inside business was brisk and all the available rooms were filled to their high ceilings with heaps of documents and files on refugees' cases and identities. Busy international staff with laptops handled long lines of clients looking for a glimmer of hope to take them through the day. Most asylum seekers were from Sudan, Ethiopia and other parts of Africa, but a few came from other Arab countries, and as each week passed more and more began to arrive from Iraq.

Only the dead see the end of war; survivors have to live with its aftermath, and the migrants who came to the sunny office in Garden City had experienced terrible hardship. Depressed, anxious, sometimes suicidal, their wounds were as personal as they were intractable. Each bore the mental scars of persecution and conflict, intertwined with the pain and loneliness of living in a hostile city with no money, no family and no job. Cairo only added to their problems. Racism among Egyptians against black Africans is widespread and even the police robbed them. Nobody cared if they had been recognised as legitimate refugees by the United Nations refugee agency, UNHCR, and issued with the official blue identity cards. Nobody cared if they lived or died.

The senior staff at the office were mainly Egyptians, but the constantly revolving interns consisted of a steady throughput of unpaid foreign volunteers. Like Jerome, most were social workers or trainee lawyers by background, either students on a break from their studies or altruistically minded professionals taking time out from their career to do something different. The office swirled with a heady mixture of daredevils, dropouts and weirdos. It was a comic strip of colourful romantic entanglements as well as of emotionally draining hard work. Naturally there were conflicts. Many of the Westerners seemed to think that coming to Cairo was a bit like going on holiday to Goa, dressing down in beachwear, nose rings and flip-flops. They dreaded their hair and spent each day stoned on cheap Egyptian weed. The more conservative Egyptians spoke about them disdainfully in Arabic behind their backs.

But the friction between Egyptians and foreigners paled in comparison with the dark undercurrent of religious prejudice that divided the Egyptians themselves. An invisible line separated the Coptic Christians and the Muslims in the office. Even when things were calm, tension could be found simmering just below the surface.

The Muslims in the office made their presence felt with regular worship breaks, veils and Internet prayer chimes. The Christians were more subtly identifiable from their names and the small blue tattoo of a cross on their wrists that they were given at birth.

Egypt has more Christian Arabs than the rest of the Middle East put together, but exactly how many there are remains the subject of heated debate. Official government statistics minimise the number, while local churches, basing their counts on baptismal records, claim about 10 per cent of the Egyptian population. Christianity in Egypt differs from that found in other North African countries because it is indigenous. When the Muslims first came to Egypt in the seventh century nearly everyone there was a Christian and the Islamic conquerors used 'Copt' simply to designate the country's indigenous inhabitants. This was a corruption of the Greek word *aiguptioi*, meaning Egyptians, and modern Copts hold that they are the true descendants of the pharaohs.

Relations between Muslims and Christians in Egypt have always been mercurial, and in recent years friction between the two communities has often led to violence and murder. Copts feel besieged in a sea of increasingly angry Islam. A popular Coptic car bumper sticker used to feature a fish, the universal Christian symbol, until Muslims started sporting shark stickers. The message was clear.

As a legal officer, Jerome's primary job was to help asylum seekers prepare for their critical interview with the United Nations refugee agency. The UNHCR interviewed all asylum seekers to determine who was a genuine refugee and who was not. Genuine refugees stood a chance of being resettled abroad whereas economic migrants were not regarded as refugees and so were not eligible for resettlement. Jerome had to try to sniff out who had fled their home country from a well-founded fear of persecution and who was simply looking for bluer horizons in the West. Applicants had to demonstrate that they might be persecuted if they returned home. Interviews took place through an interpreter and an encyclopedic knowledge of African tribes was necessary to tell whether people were who they said they were.

Few of the applicants had ever been interviewed about anything before and rumours spread like wildfire through the migrant community about what would guarantee recognition as a genuine refugee. In a constantly mutating game of cat and mouse, it was common practice for the files of refugees successfully resettled in the West to be copied and circulated so asylum seekers could learn their stories by heart. If someone who had been raped was sent for resettlement, suddenly everyone said they had been raped. If someone maintained the Egyptian police had beat him and stuffed his balls in a plastic bottle, suddenly everyone seemed to have suffered the same thing. They would repeat the same sorry details parrot fashion to Jerome, but in the gruelling four-hour interview often came unstuck.

For Jerome, this was the biggest tragedy of his job. People who had a good claim to refugee status on their own account nevertheless told lies to the UNHCR in an attempt to second-guess the selection process. Discovered, they would be denied refugee status and their file summarily closed, leaving them with the rest of their lives to think about their mistake.

Determining who deserved a new start in the West and who should be left to fester in Cairo involved momentous daily decisions and there was tremendous pressure on the young UNHCR staff. Once rejected, the 'closed files' lived in a kind of legal limbo in an unwelcoming city far from home and family. It was either that or return to whatever hell they had left behind. By way of some kind of catharsis, all the UNHCR and other NGO staff enjoyed discussing work with a gallows humour after hours in Zamalek's expatriate bars.

Jerome lived at the northern tip of the island in what had once been a spectacular family house, but in recent years the building's star had waned. By the time Jerome moved in, the place had fallen into poor shape: the paint on the walls was peeling, the doors and window frames were chipped and battered. His apartment had only ever been half-furnished in the first place, which added to the general sense of deterioration, done up on the cheap out of odd pieces of furniture the landlord's family no longer wanted. Over his year in Cairo Jerome had presided over the apartment's further decay from bachelor pad to ashtray: the stained three-piece suite was covered in newspapers and rolling papers, a well-thumbed guitar stood in the corner and there was nothing in the fridge but beer. A mousy cleaning lady visited once a week, a refugee from Eritrea, but she was too intimidated by the chaos to make much of an impression.

Every night we hit the town, to mingle with the sunburnt foreigners and upper-class Egyptians. As the weather got warmer, we lived at night, trawling through several bars an evening, dancing till the small hours to tight Arab jazz, rock and roll or visiting European DJs mixing electronica. It was only the start of April, but the build-up to a scorching summer had already begun.

At weekends we would check in at Cairo's fledgling rave scene on the outskirts of town, where the network of irrigation channels tapering out from the Nile finally comes to an end and the interminable desert begins. The only buildings that far out of town are farmhouses and the only inhabitants are peasants, tilling the land as they have done for thousands of years. In modern Egypt this is where the Western-educated glitterati go to drink and party unhindered. Children of the regime who spent the 1990s blasted in Ibiza, San Francisco and London have returned home and are now struggling to develop their own rave scene.

In the days leading up to the event the organisers spread the word to the tightly knit party faithful by flyers, email or word of mouth. A villa is hired and the local police paid off. Then late on Thursday evening, the start of the Egyptian weekend, the cars start arriving, big SUVs and swish convertibles winding slowly down unlit dirt tracks which usually only see donkeys and the occasional peasant. The villa might be hard to find in the darkness until you heard the thumping trance music reverberating across the moonlit canals. Then, beyond the high walls, a two-thousand-strong crowd can be found dancing the night away under an indigo African sky, just as fiercely as any underground rave you might find in the West.

By the time the sun came up and it was time to go, we had forgotten we were in Egypt. Making our way back into town, it was disorientating reconciling the edgy hedonism of rave parties with the choking poverty and rigid conservatism of everyday

Egypt. Raves leave no footprint in the national consciousness. Some soap operas on national television run ham-fisted plot lines about goofy teenagers ditching class to party and a state-run anti-cigarette campaign incorporates a clumsy message against dance drugs, but the difference between the parties and normal Egyptian life is so pronounced, it is as if they occur in another world.

Three

Early in the morning, on my way home from the parties, I would often pass by hundreds of bored, unemployed young men, smoking cigarettes and skimming stones, upon the Corniche beside the Nile. You do not need to be a sociologist to understand the scale of the problem the government faces trying to funnel them all into jobs and education.

By 2025 there will be ninety million Egyptians and the already straining economy will need to generate 450,000 new jobs each year simply to accommodate the number of young people entering work for the first time. To accomplish this it has been estimated that the Egyptian economy would have to expand by something like 44 per cent each year – something far beyond the projections of even the most deliriously optimistic economist.

Life for most people in Cairo is hard and the city's infrastructure is stretched to the limit by the sheer size of the population. Unemployment is rife, chronic overcrowding makes daily life a misery and Cairo competes with Mexico City and Bangkok for the title of most polluted city in the world. The average Egyptian gets by on less than a thousand dollars a year and a quarter of the country lives on less than two dollars a day, below the poverty line. Some 98 per cent of Egypt's population are squished in to the 35,000-square-kilometre strip running the length of the

Nile valley, the densest metropolitan population in Africa, and one of the densest in the world. It is an area not quite twice the size of New Jersey but with over nine times the population.

In the real world, away from the rave scene, signs the country was slipping were everywhere and the people were reaching out for the one thing they could be sure of. Beyond our expatriate bubble Islam was everywhere and its ascendancy was clear from the overwhelming number of young women who could be seen wearing the headscarf or veil.

Women wear the veil for many reasons, but by and large it is not because of any urge to follow the Salafi way of thinking. Salafism is a particularly puritanical strain of Islam. Usually girls wear one because they believe that the Koran says they should, or perhaps because that is what they heard from the preacher on TV. Some wear it due to pressure, because a brother or husband forces them to; others think they will not get married without one. Some veiled women are not even religious but simply wear it to look pious and to get along more easily with their neighbours.

There are undisputable benefits to wearing the veil, most obviously that you do not need to worry about your hair. It also helps keep in check Egypt's ubiquitous sexually predatory men and, like a school uniform, it is a leveller that can limit the scope for the rich to show off their jewellery and hair. The full-face veil, or niqab, has the added benefit of concealing your identity. Though still not as common in Egypt as it is in the Gulf States, the niqab's popularity is growing and has recently been the subject of a heated legal battle after university students were found pretending to be someone else to take exams. Several universities subsequently banned the niqab, but in 2007 an Egyptian court ruled that such bans are not binding.

Women have always worn veils in the Middle East. Way back in the time of the Persian and early Byzantine empires, before there were any Muslims, the veil was a social fixture. In patriarchal agricultural societies, where men are fathers and fighters and women are mothers and homemakers, it was a symbol of man's authority and class.

Under the rule of Muhammad Ali in the first half of the nineteenth century, the Egyptian woman's position improved dramatically and many working class women abandoned the headscarf altogether. At the start of the nineteenth century the veil was the fashion mainly among only aristocratic Egyptian women. It was not widely worn again until nearly a hundred years later. It was the British who managed to make the veil an issue. In 1882, with Egypt under British occupation, Lord Cromer banned the veil declaring it to be the 'fatal obstacle' between Egyptians and civilisation, thus instantly ensuring that many more Egyptian women would immediately start wearing one. In one fell swoop Lord Cromer managed to politicise the issue throughout the nation for a hundred years to come. Islamic militancy and women's fashion would henceforth be inextricably interlinked.

In 1899 an Egyptian jurist called Qassim Amin published a book that idolised Europe and Europeans, while pouring scorn on the veil and on Egyptian women generally. Depending on whether they were in favour of British rule or not, Egyptians lined up for and against the veil. Amin's book ensured the veil would become an enduring symbol of resistance to colonialism. Egyptian society was polarising fast.

In the 1920s an aristocrat named Hoda Shaarawi shocked high society Cairo by publicly removing her veil. It was a sign of the westernisation of the Egyptian elite under British rule. At the same time the Muslim Brotherhood, a Sunni Islamist movement founded by a schoolteacher with the credo 'God is our objective, the Koran is our constitution, the Prophet is our leader, struggle is our way' was starting in rural Egypt. The Supreme Guide, the Brotherhood's leader, insisted on women wearing the veil, although he did not oppose women's education and integration in other respects. The veil became an anti-colonial totem and women not wearing it were viewed by the veiled masses as supporters of the colonial occupiers. All the while the British fanned the flames of the debate by asserting that the veil was a sign of backwardness, thus justifying their occupation and so the wheel of resistance turned.

Following what the government of modern Egypt likes to call the 1952 revolution – it was more of a *coup d'état*, since most Egyptians were oblivious to the change of power until they woke up to find the king had been kicked out – the unveiled European look became fashionable again. Nasser came to power in 1954 on a tidal wave of popular support. He was secular and forward-looking and spoke of industrialisation and free education. Suddenly even women could be socially mobile.

By the 1960s the country was thriving and on the brink of major development. Egyptian women were busy working and getting educated and things were going so well even the conservative authorities at Al-Azhar University, the highest religious authority in the land, issued pronouncements in support of Nasser's programmes. For the first time women were competing with men for jobs, salaries and opportunities. Women had careers and rights, not to mention a very high media profile. Unveiled film stars and singers like Om Kalthoum were the living, breathing soul of the new Egypt. The veil stayed off except in the countryside, where peasant women continued to wear it more as national dress than as any kind of religious or political symbol. In the public mind it became an archaic throwback to another era, before the revolution when Egypt was still struggling to throw off the colonial yoke and everything was different.

When the Brotherhood botched an assassination attempt on President Nasser, it furnished him with the excuse the regime had been looking for to crack down and break its power for good. The movement was rounded up and its members jailed, killed or hounded into exile. Religion was knocked out of the picture even further and Islam's influence on women and society in general waned. In its place came new mantras like socialism, Arab unity and Palestine.

Then suddenly it all went wrong. Egypt's calamitous defeat by Israel in the Six Day War cracked the country wide open. Unexpectedly, Nasser came unravelled. The dream was shattered, the emperor was exposed and the hideous, ugly truth came spilling out. Secret prisons, torture, failed economic policies, political unaccountability, corruption . . . The sordid truth of Nasser's regime flooded over the Egyptian public consciousness as though the banks of the Nile had burst. The twenty-five-year dream was over. There was not going to be justice or prosperity for everyone after all. Egypt was as sick as it had been under the king. The regime unmasked, the field was open for the triumphant return of Islam under the Brotherhood's sweepingly defiant slogan 'Islam is the solution'.

Despite the cataclysm the government did not fall, but power passed to Anwar Sadat, another member of the regime. With him came new free-market policies to woo the Americans. Calculating that he could cut a deal with political Islam, Sadat freed the Muslim Brothers from jail or allowed them to return to Egypt from exile. They would be tolerated as long as they behaved. They could issue newspapers and even proselytise on condition that they operated under the guiding hand of the state, but it was to be an experiment that cost Sadat his life. When he returned from Jerusalem after making peace with Israel, Islamic Jihad, a radical offshoot of the Muslim Brotherhood, assassinated him during a Victory Day parade.

The Brotherhood moved into the universities, suppressing the old socialist ideas left over from the Nasser era. They particularly targeted women, politely transporting them to and from college, protecting them from sexual harassment and ensuring that they found seats in overcrowded amphitheatres. But the favours came with a catch – wearing the veil.

By the 1970s the veil was worn by some women throughout Egyptian society, as had last been the case at the end of the previous century under Lord Cromer. Now it was a symbol of resistance against the aggressively secular regimes of Nasser and Sadat and a way of showing tacit support for the largely underground Islamic opposition, a stance that has continued to the present day.

The Islamic revival gained momentum and righteousness became de rigueur on university campuses, in professional organisations and syndicates and among the urban poor. At the same time Saudi Arabia was surfing a tidal wave of petrodollars that enabled it to propagate its own style of Islam around the Muslim world. With missionary zeal, the Saudis poured money into mosques and religious projects and quickly their religious ideology spread.

From the mid-1970s until the mid-'80s, about two million Egyptians went to the Arabian Gulf to find work – about 15 per cent of the labour force. Some villages in the Delta saw two thirds of their men leave, mostly to Saudi Arabia. When they returned home, they brought more than hard currency, white goods and prayer beads. They brought Saudi religious and cultural practices too. Newly rich and successful, with the esteemed title of haji, their wives were not just laden with heavy gold jewellery – they were also wearing the veil.

By the time Hosni Mubarak became president in 1981, he was facing a garden of dragon's teeth that Sadat had unwittingly sown. While tolerating what he judged to be the good Islamists, which meant the peaceful ones, bad Islamists were mercilessly rounded up and destroyed. Mubarak cut the good Islamists a deal whereby they could control what were regarded as the least threatening areas of public life. They could have a newspaper, run some social and educational services, but were excluded from real power. But, as has happened elsewhere in the Middle East, the Islamists made such a success of their limited portfolio that their influence increased far beyond that which the government had anticipated. As Egypt became increasingly capitalist millions of poor were left behind and the Muslim Brotherhood stepped in with social programmes, healthcare and education.

Today the Islamic movement continues to gather strength. With all other political voices silenced, Islam has become one of the only avenues for young people to express their discontent with the avowedly secular Mubarak regime.

From the peasant in the field in her plain black headscarf to the coquettish magazine pin-up in tight Western jeans; from newsreaders and actresses to the idealised woman you see cleaning her loo or washing clothes in television advertisements or on billboards, Egyptian women are wearing the veil. Even the daughters of the regime wear one, much to the amazement of their mothers and grandmothers who threw it off when America still looked like an untainted beacon of progress and Egypt looked Westwards. Above it all sits the President's wife, out of touch and conspicuously unveiled.

Four

Unlike Saudi Arabia or some Gulf countries, Egypt is not totally dry. Al Ahram Beverages, the state-owned drinks company, turns out its own curious brands of whisky and vodka plus some very respectable beer. There are also four varieties of Egyptian wine, none of which I can recommend, although drinking them is fun as the quality varies dramatically from bottle to bottle because since they built the Aswan High Dam the water table has played havoc with the grapes. Local wine is mainly drunk by curious tourists in never-to-be repeated experiments or by expatriates like Jerome and me who do not want to pay the enormous premium slapped on imported liquor. Egyptians themselves account for only about a fifth of sales.

Generally Western expatriates in Cairo like to socialise in five-star hotels. They prefer to drink in comfort, knowing in advance what to expect and at what price. Luxury hotels are also the one place you can always be sure of being served, even in Ramadan. But of all the hotel bars and saloons we caroused that spring, there was none we visited more often than La Bodega, Cairo's expatriate nexus, a drinking joint upholstered in speakeasy 1920s style with a view of the Nile and the finest-looking bar in town. It sucked us in like a black hole.

I quickly discovered that Jerome knew just about everyone in the expatriate community. We could not set foot in a bar in

Zamalek without running into someone he recognised. He was a great lover of women of all shapes and sizes. Tanned and handsome, they loved him too. La Bodega was full of lonely NGO women who had given up on relationships in exchange for a peripatetic career delivering aid in Africa, and for Jerome women like that were the main perk of his job.

But as the new academic year loomed, the time to return to America was fast approaching. 'I don't want to go back,' he would grumble into his margarita. 'At home I would still be clearing snow off my porch.' Sad as he was to be leaving, Jerome was not as sad as I was to see him go. Even though I would be leaving Cairo myself in a few weeks, in the short time we had known each other he had become a good companion. I was going to miss sitting out on his balcony late at night solving the problems of the Middle East, the smell of eucalyptus and lotuses wafting up from the garden below.

One night, a week before Jerome left, we were sipping cool Egyptian beer on his balcony. Above us the stars were twinkling in the inky blackness. Except for the cicadas chirping in the rushes by the banks of the Nile and Jerome gently strumming his guitar, the silence was unbroken.

'I want to introduce you to a friend of mine before I leave,' he said. 'She's a doctor, working for an aid agency here.'

'An old girlfriend of yours?' I asked suspiciously, sipping my drink.

'Nope, never a girlfriend,' he replied dreamily.

I did not fancy the idea of going out with an Egyptian girl. The thought of hordes of nosy brothers breathing down my neck put me off instantly. Besides, a date seemed a slim possibility, since Egyptian girls normally seemed so much more buttoned up than the cocktail-soaked expat crowd we hung out with.

'She's the closest friend I made here in Cairo and she's really open-minded.'

'Open-minded' is code in Egypt, used to describe girls who are unveiled and drink, and men who don't care if women smoke or what they wear.

Despite all his womanising, I trusted Jerome's judgement of character. Making some new friends was just what I wanted, since Jerome was leaving. Otherwise I knew it would only be a question of time until I found myself back in the coffee shop, smoking *shisha* all day.

'So what's her name?' I asked

'Roda.'

A few days later Jerome was having his leaving party at the Semiramis, one of Cairo's five-star hotels. Expatriate life in Cairo is littered with leaving parties as contracts end, leases expire, academic terms finish and people move on. Jerome had booked dinner at the Birdcage Thai restaurant, which is reputed to have the most authentic Thai food in Cairo, and all his colleagues from the office were invited.

As we set off from Jerome's pad in a black and white taxi, the sun was disappearing into the thick haze of pollution over Giza in a blazing orange ball. Neon advertisements up and down the Nile twinkled on in the half-light, and as the cab rattled past the mighty stone lions flanking Qasr el-Nil bridge, tinny pop hits belting out the window, a muezzin cleared his throat like an old blues guitarist and noisily struck up the call for prayer.

Turning over in my mind what Jerome had told me about Roda, the idea of getting to know an Egyptian girl more closely was beginning to seem quite attractive. In the Arab countries I had visited women had always been almost totally hidden. I had seen them walking arm in arm veiled in the street or appearing long-lashed and glamorous on TV talkshows, but besides the daughter of the family I had lived with when I had first come to Cairo as an au pair, I had never had the opportunity to get to know one personally. They were simply a mystery to me.

Pulling up beyond the blast barriers beneath the hotel's giant pillars, we were plunged into a mêlée of international travellers with hotel staff shouting instructions in English and Arabic as they struggled to unload mountains of Louis Vuitton luggage. The lobby was invigoratingly cold and echoed gently to the sound of a noodly jazz band on the mezzanine level. Riding the mirrored escalator to the first floor, we were greeted at the door of the Birdcage by the Egyptian front-of-house, incongruously wearing a black cotton chemise like a rickshaw driver plucked from the streets of Bangkok. His costume did not look adequate for the aggressively cold air conditioning.

'Messieurs requiring a table for two?' he fawned in a thick Egyptian accent.

'We're here for the office party,' replied Jerome debonairly. The front-of-house ran a hairy finger down the register until he found our names.

Shooting us an enormous grin he plucked two menus from under the counter. 'This way, messieurs,' he said, ushering us inside.

The softly lit restaurant had been decorated in red and gold, like the interior of a sumptuous Thai palace. We had stepped momentarily out of Cairo's dusty streets and entered a little slice of heaven, where waiters wearing fishermen's trousers served ineffably elegant diners at perfectly laid tables. Tinkling streams reflected in the smooth black granite walls and the sound of running water echoed all around.

Jerome's leaving party occupied several tables at the back of the restaurant, separated from other diners by a painted bamboo screen. About a dozen of his friends and colleagues had shown up to wish him goodbye, the kind of international *mélange* that quickly becomes familiar after a few weeks in Cairo. Mostly they were girls from his office looking distraught to see him leave: he had evidently been something of a pin-up.

Although I had not met Jerome's co-workers before, they

were instantly recognisable from the rude personal descriptions he had painted of them over the bar in La Bodega. There was the fat American no one in the office could stand; and here was the officious lesbian New Zealander; that must be the pasty English Ph.D. student; the busty Australian lawyer; the suave Frenchman wearing a polo neck; the quietly smiling Sudanese translators. And there, at the back of the restaurant, silhouetted against a tank of slowly circulating black koi carp, was a group of extraordinarily beautiful Egyptian girls.

With her coal-black hair and coppery skin, Roda reminded me of a Nefertiti statue I had seen in the Egyptian Museum when I had first come to Cairo as a teenager. Her beauty and grace stunned me: I did not know that such an exquisite combination of looks and intelligence could exist in a single woman, except perhaps the odd gorgeous physicist in a James Bond movie.

Over carved wooden trays of fishcakes and vegetables cut into the shapes of flowers we all chatted easily about Cairo and the refugee business. The wine circulated liberally, the evening flew past and by the time the bill arrived one of the legal interns was drunkenly putting chopsticks up her nose. Roda and her friends had been delightful company and it felt as if our night had hardly begun when it was time for us to go our separate ways.

We said our goodbyes in the restaurant, the Egyptian girls explaining politely that they had work the next day. As we all elegantly kissed one another goodbye on each cheek, as is de rigueur in the Birdcage, I looked around for Jerome but, finding he had already sloped off with one of the interns, I slowly made my way out of the hotel on my own, past the liveried porters and the mounds of luggage waiting at the main entrance, over the road to the rank where the taxis were waiting in a line outside to take me home. As my cab wound through the night I looked out at the full moon tipped with silver, rising like a dollar in the cobalt sky, and I thought about friendship and travel and how sad it is when someone you know becomes someone you knew. I had only met her that evening, but Roda had made a striking impression on me. I would have loved to see her again, but although I took her number there was no time to meet again because soon it would be my turn to pack up and go. A few days later, saying a wistful goodbye to Elephant and Castle through the rear window of the cab as I made my way to the airport, I was leaving for what I believed in my heart was going to be the very last time.

Five

Sitting in a greasy spoon in Hammersmith, I watched the builder opposite me shovel a fried-egg sandwich into his stubbly chops. The yolk popped out the back of the bread and dribbled in greasy strings onto the remains of the fry-up on his plate.

'More tea?' asked the Thai waitress cheerfully, brandishing a large metal teapot.

'No thanks, love,' replied the builder, briefly looking up from the copy of the *Sun* spread on the table in front of him. Wiping the egg from his hand onto his trousers, he turned, still munching, to the football results.

'More tea?' The waitress looked over at me. I proffered my mug for a refill.

Outside the sun was just beginning to peek out from behind the clouds and dry the streets below. Hammersmith looked so clean and organised compared to Cairo. 'Looks like it's beginning to cheer,' the old lady on the next table said to no one in particular.

Not having anywhere of my own to stay, I had moved in with my brother. Not much had changed since I had last been back. King Street was still full of B-boys in Nike trackies and Reebok Classics bawling inanely at their chav girlfriends. Day-release psychiatric patients from Hammersmith Hospital were wandering vaguely around Lyric Square pestering people for cigarettes.

Single mums trundled baby buggies back and forth to Primark past confused-looking Somali asylum seekers. On the park bench outside the bicycle shop the same group of winos was still harassing passers-by for change. The only noticeable difference was that there was now a large crowd of Polish labourers loitering outside the newsagent, looking for casual work.

It was always strange coming back to the UK after spending a while in the Arab world. I had to stop myself gawping at the scantily clad girls walking past me in the street. Page three girls and semi-naked women on bus shelter advertisements startled me. Homosexuality seemed shocking. I had forgotten how much pointless consumption you find in the West: the tanning salons, the Argos jewellery, the JJB Sports sale at 'wicked prices'. I had forgotten it was not polite to speak to people on the Tube.

Prices astonished me, especially services like dry-cleaning or taking a cab. Even if life in Cairo had sometimes felt like being in a dirty washing machine stuck on spin, I had managed to live like a king. I took taxis everywhere, paid people to fetch, carry and clean for me, tipped them all generously, and still had change from what I made each week to go out clubbing. All foreigners in Cairo lived like that. Discussing where to find the best domestic staff was normal conversation among twenty-year-old legal interns at La Bodega.

A few things were the same. All big cities are alike in some ways. London and Cairo are each a kind of crossroads. In both of them you spend hours travelling around town in a decaying transport system. I used London's to catch up with old friends I had not seen for months.

When you are away you worry that everyone will have moved on without you. When you get back you invariably find everyone still plodding on just as before. With my friends the locus of their social lives had shifted slightly, from nightclubs and bars to dinner parties and summer barbecues, but everyone seemed to be 'doing all right' or 'hanging in there'. One by one they were taking important steps towards determining what kind of people they would be for the rest of their lives: stabilising, taking on mortgages, buying houses and having kids. Only a few were still resisting the steady march towards middle age, choosing instead to lose themselves in shallow New Age philosophies and meaningless sexual connections.

'So how was Egypt?' was the dinner party refrain.

'Fine,' I would say, sipping my wine. But something was not quite right in my heart. There was something about the place that I missed.

I did not dislike being in London. Spring had arrived and I was savouring the simple pleasures of British life that I had longed for, like Sunday morning newspapers, British telly and riding a bike up to Camden Lock. The city's vast reservoir of cultural riches, the concerts, galleries and plays, was so awesome it was almost overwhelming. But while part of me was glad to be back, it seemed that existence in London was somehow pointless, as if no matter how much overtime people put in or how many hours they commuted, they could work their life away without ever finding a purpose for what they were doing. At least in Cairo it was possible to keep your head comfortably above water while doing almost nothing at all. Like rats in a maze, Londoners seemed to me to achieve little either together with all the other rats or on their own. Settling down looked suspiciously like a trap, in which once you had taken the bait, the job and the house, you suddenly found yourself hooked by a cripplingly expensive mortgage. If this was to be my fate, I told myself, I should at least try to delay it as long as I could.

The biggest problem I faced was that competition for freelance work in London is much stiffer than in Cairo. London draws journalists and broadcasters from all over the world and finding original material to write about is a constant struggle. After a month back home I had nearly run out of money but still felt unready to embark on a new job. Listless and reluctant to start the mind-numbing process of scouring the Internet for jobs and sending out CVs, I began to feel like a sullen teenager hanging around the house with a long face.

My brother, a self-made man and the manager of a successful building company, made no secret of the fact he thought I was a bum. There was no let-up in his badgering me to get a job, and not just any job, but a 'proper' one like his, which meant building or the army. Writing, in his view, definitely did not constitute real employment.

'What's your problem?' he snapped at me as I sat slumped on the sofa watching daytime TV.

'I'm watching BBC Parliament.'

'You what?' he replied, making no effort to hide his contempt.

'The parliamentary channel. It's amazing. They've got a live webcast coming out of the House of Commons. I can't believe it.'

'Why don't you get off your arse and get a job?'

'You don't understand. This is the essence of democracy. It's gavel to gavel coverage.'

'Gavel my arse. Get a job, you lazy bastard.'

Try as I might I could not make my brother see that this kind of hi-tech unmediated live coverage, which even came with a caption service and links to an enhanced website, was breathtaking. Coming from a country where the president never had to justify anything to anyone, least of all on television, it was somehow deeply satisfying to see the opposition put the screws on the prime minister.

Irritatingly, my brother was not the only one propelling me into an unwanted career. It was apparently blindingly obvious to everyone but me that my next step was settling down and saving in the hope that one day I might raise enough money to grab hold of the bottom rung of the exorbitant London property ladder. Probably, I reflected gloomily, somewhere out in the suburbs. Friends and family started forwarding me job advertisements and saving newspaper clippings to help me search.

As the weeks grew longer London bled me ever whiter, a problem compounded when my brother thoughtfully decided to start charging me rent. As my spirits slumped I sought solace in television and books, daydreaming about Cairo and Roda while breaking my day with a walk down to the leafy banks of the Thames. Like an explorer trapped inside a pyramid, there seemed to be no way out.

At night, to escape my brother's nagging, I would go to the pub to have a drink and reflect on my predicament. Late one evening I was sharing my problems with an old friend at a lock-in at his local. It was always reassuring sharing problems with Charlie because he was a patient listener and his own problems were always worse than mine, a quality in a friend that invariably makes you feel much better.

'I don't know what the best thing to do is,' I said. 'London is totally doing my head in.' I stared mournfully into the remains of my pint.

'You'll feel better when you get a job,' replied Charlie, drawing smoke from a hand-rolled cigarette deep into his tarry lungs.

'Why does everybody keep saying that? Maybe I don't want a job.'

'Well, how are you going to buy things?' he pointed out, exhaling.

'I guess you're right,' I conceded bitterly.

'You're going to have to get one sooner or later. Why don't you work for your brother?'

'Are you kidding? So he can work me all the hours God sends, like you? No way. I would rather go back to Cairo.'

'Oh yeah?' he replied, looking straight into my eyes.

'You see I met this girl. She's Egyptian.'

'Egypt's a long way to go for a girl. Why don't you come

down the Queen Anne with me tomorrow night? It's a strip pub in Vauxhall.'

'No thanks. Never mind.'

Loneliness is a fact of human existence but it can be hardest to bear in other people's company. I felt so lonely I did not even know myself. Walking out of the pub into the damp night air I wanted to climb up to the pale English moon, kick the ladder away beneath me and so be stranded up there for ever.

Then I discovered that someone had tried to steal my bicycle, badly buckling the wheel in an attempt to break the lock. Cursing crime-ridden, filthy London, I tried vainly to bend the wheel back into shape. After a few minutes I gave up, realising it would be impossible without tools, and wiping the grease and oil from my hands onto my trousers, I began the long slow walk back to Hammersmith, pushing my wobbling bicycle in front of me. It was nearly two o'clock in the morning when it started to rain in fat, penetrating drops.

Trudging past the bright lights of the all-night newsagent on the North End Road I wondered what I was still doing in this town. Why don't I just go back to Egypt? I thought. Although freelancing might not cover a London mortgage, in Cairo it would certainly pay my tab at La Bodega. And there too, of course, was Roda.

Plodding through the rain, the tinkling piano in the Semiramis lobby seemed a million miles away. I closed my eyes and imagined myself back in there, chatting with Roda and her friends as they sat silhouetted against the tank of exotic carp. In my mind's eye I imagined her obsidian eyes and her long black hair like ravens spilling over her shoulder. I wondered what she was doing now or whether she even remembered me.

Where could I find a girl like that in London? I asked myself. For all the people you see each day on the Tube, London is a lonely place where most people are too busy trying to get by to date. The handful of single girls I knew were either highly paid professionals, too focused on their ball-breaking careers to hang out with out-of-work writers like me, or suffered from untreatable personality disorders.

If I went back to Cairo I could at least be guaranteed steady work. I should not count on seeing Roda again, since that, I told myself, would be ridiculous. After all, I barely knew her. But I wanted to see her. Trundling my bike with one hand, I pulled my mobile from my pocket and scrolled through the contact list looking to see whether I still had her number. Trying not to steer off the curb I began to text.

> Bck in Ldn. Cnt stp thnkg abt u.

I looked at what I had written. I might as well send it, I thought. I was not, after all, likely to see her again, so it could do no harm. Hitting SEND, I carried on pushing my bike through the puddles. A minute later the phone rang. Fumbling around in my wet pocket I fished it out.

'Hello?'

'Is that Hugh?' said a voice.

'Roda!' Memories of Egypt flashed before me like pictures from a past life. 'What time is it with you? Did I wake you up?' I stammered, scarcely believing it was really her. It seemed so unreal; suddenly she was here with me on a London city street. 'I was thinking of coming back to Cairo,' I blurted.

'Oh really? Why?' she said coolly. 'I thought you had finished with Cairo.'

'Yeah, so did I. But it's work, you see . . . I have to carry on some, er, very important stuff . . .' I trailed off, not sure if what I had said made much sense.

'That's great! Well maybe we'll see each other again then,' she answered brightly.

'Yeah! I really hope so,' I replied lamely.

'Well let me know what you decide to do.'

'Sure. Will do. Well it's decided actually. I'm coming.'

'When?'

'Soon.'

As I disconnected I looked around at the drizzly street. After weeks of inertia I had finally made up my mind. It felt as if the whole world lay spread before me and what had previously seemed unlikely or impossible was suddenly very close at hand. We are usually too cowardly or lazy to take the chances life offers us to change our destiny. Human nature, like rain falling on the rainforest canopy, takes the path of least resistance towards the forest floor. Over time, that water becomes a stream and then a mighty river locked between two great banks rolling inexorably towards the sea. By the time it arrives there, no one can question why the river flowed the way it did, because it is clear that there could never have been another course.

Exhilarated, I hurried home, switched on my computer and booked my ticket online. The next day I was back in Cairo.

Six

The plants had died in Elephant and Castle while I was away; the summer swelter had killed them a few days after I left. When I returned it was only the beginning of May but the daytime temperature was already firmly set on grill. Being an island, Zamalek is breezier than other parts of town, but the heat of the day still only abated late at night and during the small hours before dawn.

It did not take long for me to slip back into the familiar rhythm. Quickly the greasy spoon in Hammersmith seemed like a faded dream. With Jerome gone, I kept myself busy in the coffee shop, reading books and dreaming up new articles to write for the papers. To fill my days I organised some language classes with a Greek-Egyptian bodybuilder who came recommended on the expat circuit, and I began to speak colloquial Egyptian Arabic in a thick Athenian accent. Each evening I would do my homework in the coffee shop and practise the unfamiliar new dialect on the other customers. Up until then my spoken Arabic had been based on what I had learnt in Yemen, where I had once spent a few months at a language school and it made me sound like a creature out of Chaucer in Cairo.

For men at least *shisha* cafés are one of the great things about Cairo. Like pubs before drinks corporations introduced fancy marketing gimmicks like daylight and menus, Cairene coffee shops are bastions of unreformed masculinity that can be as muted as a library or as rowdy as a locker room after a winning match. My local was just a paved room open to the road, strewn with sawdust to hide the filth and with a collection of rickety wooden tables and chairs crusty with spilt tea and coffee. There was no advertising or branding, it was neither chic nor healthy and the customers only knew the names of the serving staff, not the name of the establishment, if it ever even had one.

Ash-smeared waiters glided between the customers, balancing steel trays of hot drinks or tapping metal tongs together as they serviced *shishas* from a portable brazier of glowing charcoal. Anyone who needed their coals changing could attract attention with just a nod of the head. The waiters shouted orders to an overworked server frantically turning out drinks from behind a grubby plastic screen at the back of the room. 'Two more mint teas out here now for the chief!'

'Yes sir, Mister President,' a voice from within would cry back.

At night the atmosphere got more boisterous, as groups of young men came to play backgammon, dominoes or chess. If there was a football match on, all the chairs would be lined up to face the television and the room would be packed with men, faces lit up by the glare of the screen. If local teams Ahly and Zamalek were playing, than the session could go on afterwards long into the night. When the game was over and the television had been switched off a few customers always lingered, sipping their tea in silence. Dying embers from the brazier lay scattered on the floor lighting the room with a warm orange glow. I would linger too, silently reading my book before the time came to drift off into the night.

I had made up my mind it would be best if I waited a few days before I telephoned Roda. Although I had been the one to get in touch, I still did not want to give her the impression that I had come back to Cairo simply to see her. The memory of our evening at the Birdcage was gilded in my mind, but still part of me felt it would be foolish to chase a girl I hardly knew around the world. I kept telling myself I had come back to Cairo for serious professional reasons, to improve my Arabic, to develop my career as a journalist and to find new things to write about. Secretly I was hoping that Roda might call me – after all I had told her I was coming back to town – but my extremely limited knowledge of Egyptian dating protocol stretched just far enough to know that this was highly unlikely, so after a couple of days irritably circling the telephone I finally gave in and called her.

'Welcome back,' she said warmly.

'Surprised to hear me?'

'You told me you were coming. How was London?'

'Oh fine, fine,' I replied, before adding more seriously, 'I missed you a lot.'

'Really?' Roda asked shyly.

'Really,' I affirmed. There was an awkward pause. 'So when can I see you again? You want to come over for dinner at my place this weekend? I'm house-sitting this beautiful period apartment in Zamalek. Charles de Gaulle lived here. You've got to see it.'

'Come to your place?' she replied, clearly taken aback. 'That's kind, but I don't think I am able to . . . I mean, I can't.'

This sounded final so there was another pause as I struggled to come up with a better offer. Running through Jerome's drinking dens in my mind, they all seemed rather iniquitous for a first date.

'Do you play cards by any chance?' Roda suggested.

'Cards? Are you kidding? I love cards! What kind of games do you play?'

'We play a game called *tarneeb*. It's a bit like bridge, but it's Egyptian. You know how to play bridge, don't you?'

'Yeah sure, of course I do,' I responded instinctively, racking my brain to remember. 'But won't I need a partner?'

'You'll be my partner,' Roda said.

'Right. Of course. Fine.' Dummy, I thought.

'We really need someone to fill in for us. Jumanah's sick.'

'I'm not sure I know how to score,' I added, beginning to hedge, visions of a humiliating defeat at the hands of a gang of lady card sharps beginning to coalesce in my mind.

'That's OK. Scoring is very simple in *tarneeb*.'

'Well er, that's fine then. When are we playing?'

'Are you free tonight at eight?'

Of course I was free – once I had spent the next two hours desperately trying to fix the rickety Internet connection in my apartment in a vain effort to find out how to play bridge. I had played before, but long ago, when I was child, with bored diplomatic wives in far-flung embassies. I certainly did not feel proficient enough to face a gang of seasoned Egyptian lady aces. They would smell my fear the moment I stepped through the door then tear me apart like a boiled crab. Worst of all, if I was Roda's partner I would let her down and she would never invite me to play again.

I was excited to be invited over. I had not been inside many private houses in Egypt and it was far from clear what exactly I had let myself in for. Not many Egyptian women are in a position to invite a foreigner to their house, especially a male one with earrings, and as I brushed up my bridge, it struck me as remarkable that I had been asked at all. I remembered Jerome telling me that Roda lived unusually freely for a girl in Cairo and I hoped that this would be my opportunity to get to know Roda and her friends better, but as I was about to find out it is still not easy for an unmarried Egyptian Muslim woman in Cairo to spend time with a foreign man alone.

Like an amoeba filled with half-digested food, Cairo has many nuclei. Roda's house was in one of them, a huge sprawling suburb called Muwazafeen, on the west bank of the Nile.

Muwazafeen was thrown up in the 1960s and '70s to meet the exponential growth in demand for housing as Egypt's population exploded. It quickly grew to develop its own gravitational pull, voraciously sucking in all the macroscopic detritus of middle class Egyptian life, like American fast-food outlets, plastic-surgery clinics and car showrooms. Its car-choked thoroughfares and concrete flyovers burst with traffic jams around the clock.

Muwazafeen is the home of Cairo's affluent middle class. The name itself means City of Goverment Employees and walking through its streets you might be forgiven for imagining you were in a leafy suburb somewhere in southern Europe. Its residents are English-speaking professionals who live in comfortable apartments, take holidays, walk dogs and have a couple of cars parked outside their detached houses or luxury apartment blocks. But lurking just beneath the surface of this suburban paradise is the teeming working class. In Muwazafeen the poor live a muddy-faced Dickensian existence, eked out from between the cracks of middle-class society, cleaning shoes in the street, peddling vegetables and parking cars. They live hand to mouth under stairs or among the bins in alleyways. They are largely illiterate, struggle to feed their children and own nothing.

When Muwazafeen was built the government still had not grasped the importance of capping population growth. The 1952 revolutionaries thought economic development would take care of population growth and that besides, the bigger Egypt became, the more weight she would carry in the Arab world. They did not know that the multiplying population would derail every other economic or social policy they could formulate and undermine Egypt's future prosperity for generations.

They should have seen it coming. Demographers and social scientists realised in the 1930s that population control was fundamental to the country's success. Trend statistics were available back to 1797, when Napoleon's experts assessed the total Egyptian population at around four million and ten-year censuses have been carried out ever since. By 1932 Egypt had fifteen million people and five years later a conference of Egyptian physicians called publicly for national programmes to curb population growth. Yet the regime resisted the formal adoption of any kind of population policy until 1960 and even then the programme was only vaguely delineated and adhered to. Even after President Nasser, himself the father of five children, recognised in his National Charter of 1961 that high growth rates represented an obstacle to a raised standard of living, no concrete steps were taken to reduce births or increase the spacing between children.

In modern Egypt the Ministries of Population, Health and Social Affairs all have a hand in making population policy. Ministries, committees, commissions and councils make high-sounding pronouncements and the state uses all the means at its disposal, including the media, the religious authorities at Al-Azhar University, four thousand mother and child health clinics and twenty thousand government-controlled mosques, to get the message across.

Policy is imposed on the lower echelons of Egyptian society and along the way passes over the cataracts and filters of what we in the West would term civil society. It faces resistance from religious leaders, who hold that Western conspiracies and a general lack of Islamic values are more pressing national problems than population growth. For most ordinary Egyptians family planning is synonymous with birth control, which amounts to a blasphemous attempt to tamper with God's will. They have faith that God's providence, together with help from compassionate fellow Muslims, will feed and clothe their children.

Since the 1970s the birth rate has slowed a little, but along class and geographical lines. In Cairo people have fewer children, but up in the Delta families continue to have more kids than they can feed. Almost a quarter of the Egyptian population is under ten years old and when parents die possessions are divided between all the children, which means farms become too small to be economically viable. In real terms ordinary Egyptians are poorer than they were in the 1950s.

Seven

The taxi turned off one of the main arteries of Muwazafeen into Istanbul Street, where cars were parked and double-parked as far as the eye could see. I paid the driver through the glassless window of his Lada with a bundle of filthy, torn one-pound and fifty-piastre notes, and as the cab drove away I found myself standing in almost complete darkness. None of the streetlights was working, so checking the address scribbled on my notepad I tried to establish if I was in the right place.

The night was calm and quiet, but my heart was beating nervously at the prospect of seeing Roda again. The Birdcage was a distant memory and I was anxious in case our long-anticipated rendezvous turned out to be a disappointment. I silently prayed that I was not going to screw up at cards. Suddenly, I was startled by a robed figure looming out of the darkness.

'Can I help you, pasha?' the apparition asked with a mouth full of stained brown teeth. His skin was black with grime and he was wearing a dark brown *galabiyah* that made him hard to make out in the gloom. 'Doctor Roda's apartment?' I replied, trying not to flinch.

The apparition was one of the street's self-appointed car-parking attendants. In the darkness he looked more like a revenant from the underworld. 'You have come to see Doctor Roda?' he asked obsequiously. I grunted a yes. I had the feeling he was being nosy rather than helpful and I did not want to give too much away. 'This way . . . pasha,' he crooned, leading me through the glass double doors of a large porridge-coloured concrete block.

In the lobby the air was heavy with the smell of garlic. As I made my way up the stairs I could hear someone tinkling through their scales on a piano, accompanied intermittently by a tuneless male baritone. As if in a doll's house, I could hear two women having an argument, a television soap opera twittering under the stairs and somewhere a child crying.

The doorbell tweeted like a bird. The door opened a crack and a ray of light broke out into the gloomy corridor. Roda looked just as beautiful as when I had last seen her at the Birdcage. We kissed briefly, just an ordinary greeting in London but in the darkness of the stairwell it somehow felt risky, forbidden even. Visiting an Egyptian woman at home and after dark, I had the guiltily exhilarating sensation that we must both be doing something wrong. My heart beating harder, Roda quickly ushered me inside. Then, glancing both ways along the landing, she closed the door behind us.

The apartment was small and cluttered with lamps and furniture. Stylish modern Egyptian art hung on the walls and Arabic and English books and magazines lined every available shelf. I noticed the Bible on the shelf next to the Koran next to a dated row of many bound copies of the *Encyclopaedia Britannica*; insect repellent, half-empty packets of pills, Koranic engravings and spare keys were jumbled together on the side, and in the middle of the room stood a low wooden coffee table covered precariously with teacups and an ashtray brimming with cigarette butts. Between two faded checked sofas a battered television was softly playing Arab music videos. It felt as though the contents of a much larger home had been emptied into this tiny one; there was barely enough space to move.

'Were you looking for something?' I asked, looking around me.

'No.' Roda laughed. 'I am afraid the house is always like this when the three of us are all here.' She blushed.

Taking a seat on a sofa, I felt strangely intrusive and unsure of myself. All the furniture seemed very close to the ground. The place felt homey, but home on a submarine of the 1960s.

Unusually for an Egyptian woman, Roda lived without a male guardian. Her mother was dead and her father lived and worked in the Gulf. By Egyptian standards this meant she and her sisters were in a sense naked in the world. They would never bask in a brother's reflected success nor luxuriate in his protection. Of course they were also free of a brother's control, which from my point of view was to be the *sine qua non* of my relationship with Roda.

As soon as I had sat down, Roda's sisters came in and introduced themselves. Aged just twenty-two, Noha was eight years Roda's junior. Nadia, aged thirty-four, was the eldest. Nadia looked just like Roda. She had the same jet-black eyes and long black silky hair. Her eyebrows were plucked into high arches, making her eyes look wider and her face more arresting than an Old Kingdom wall relief. Kohl around her eyes, extending sideways towards each earlobe, barely concealed signs of exhaustion and she wore theatrical high heels which, together with her make-up, made her look as if she belonged not to the boulevards of Muwazafeen but seated alongside a pharaoh on a barge while a naked slave fanned her with ostrich feathers.

Noha's skin and hair were much lighter than that of her sisters, although she had the same almond shaped eyes, accentuated by the thinnest line of kohl. Like many Arab women her complexion was flawlessly youthful, the result of a lifetime spent covering up from the sun.

We sat together on the sofas and made small talk over tea and biscuits, Nadia and Noha listening politely to the story of how I had come to know Roda through our mutual friend Jerome.

Both knew of Jerome from Roda, and from there the conversation flowed easily as we chatted about our lives in Cairo.

Noha told me that she had recently graduated from university, since when she had been working nights at a local telesales company. Nadia was a doctor, married to a gynaecologist, and the couple had a two-year-old girl called Hind. Nadia worked in the intensive care ward at Qasr al-Aini hospital, a public facility established in the nineteenth century. Although much at Qasr al-Aini was in crumbling disrepair, Nadia explained that the intensive care unit had recently been through a glistening modernisation and refurbishment programme and was now ranked as one of the most modern in the Middle East. In theory the facilities were open to the public, but in reality they were the preserve of Cairo's rich and powerful political elite. Without influence it was impossible to get a bed and the hospital was always full.

Like most doctors in Egypt, Nadia conserved most of her energy and time for more lucrative work in a private clinic after hours. The difference between public and private healthcare in Egypt is substantial and like anything worth having, access is a question of influence and money. Public-sector hospitals tend to be overcrowded and undersupplied and their nurses regarded by society at large as opportunistic petty criminals on a moral par with prostitutes. Their principal vocation is perceived to be extorting as much money out of patients as possible before they check out or die.

Nadia did not play cards because games, she said, were a waste of time and besides her daughter kept her too busy. She preferred to potter, joining in the conversation whenever she saw fit, occasionally logging onto the Internet to chat with strangers online. The cards would start, Roda explained, just as soon as the fourth player, Noha's partner, arrived.

The sisters' warmth was disarming and quickly I began to feel more at ease. While Noha cleared the coffee table and Roda searched for the cards, I sat and drank tea with Nadia, who appeared politely intrigued about what I was doing in Cairo, asking many questions in clipped clear English the way only people who have learnt English as a foreign language are able to do.

'You see, a freelance journalist,' I explained, 'works for lots of different newspapers. One day I might write for a paper in Britain, then next week one in America.'

Nadia looked at me carefully as I spoke, listening intently to every word I said. 'You can work for anyone? Different people at once?'

'That's right.'

'And why did you learn Arabic?'

'Because I am interested in meeting Egyptians,' I replied.

'I see,' replied Nadia, unsure what to make of this, her unblinking black eyes not wavering from mine. Then after a long pause she asked, 'And does the government know what you do?'

'Well, all journalists have to register at the government press office,' I replied.

'And do some people think you are a spy? Most foreigners who speak Arabic people say are spies.'

'Well, I don't know. I don't think so,' I said, breaking into a smile. The floor was strewn with magazines and chewed coloured pencils Hind had spread around.

'You know, I should have married a foreigner, I think,' Nadia said. 'My husband is a doctor too, but he is a gynaecologist. He comes from a town called Qena. Do you know Qena? It's in Upper Egypt and its men are famous for being stupid and macho.'

'They have very hard heads,' interjected Noha, arriving back in the room clutching a deck of plastic-backed cards. 'Upper Egypt is the most conservative part of the country and Qena is the most conservative town there. The men there are the worst kind of Egyptian men.'

'If my husband knew single men were coming around to the

house when he was not there, he would kill me,' said Nadia. 'But I don't care what he thinks any more,' she added crisply.

The doorbell tweeted. For a fleeting second I thought it might be Nadia's husband and was on the point of jumping into the laundry basket or hiding behind the door, like an actor in a French farce. 'It's Yosra!' shouted Roda and Noha in unison.

'Sorry I am late,' said Yosra as she bundled through the door. 'I was having a fight over a parking space.' She noticed me on the sofa. 'Hello. You must be Hugh. I have heard all about you.' She extended her hand for me to shake. 'It is very nice to finally meet you.'

I leant forward and kissed her on each cheek. She squealed and took a step back, making the others all shriek and laugh in delight.

'Hugh, you can't kiss girls here! You are not in London any more,' said Roda.

'I'm sorry, Yosra,' I said sheepishly. 'Just habit, I guess.'

Yosra was at least a head taller than any of the three sisters. Like them she wore no veil, but her skin was paler and her hair was almost auburn, matching her slate-grey eyes. Egyptians come in all shades: they can be light-skinned like Europeans, or dark like the Nubians of Upper Egypt. Outnumbered, I sat back down formally, anxious and slightly embarrassed that I might have done something wrong by kissing Yosra. She threw her jacket down on the couch and unzipped her denim handbag.

'So how do you know Roda?' I asked politely.

Out of her bag Yosra pulled a box of cigarettes and a metal-backed strip of pills. Popping a couple of pills out into her hand she swallowed and grimaced. 'Excuse me, but I need my fix,' she said, sparking up a cigarette. Then closing her eyes with her face turned towards the window, she took several long deep drags of smoke down into her lungs.

'God, I have been wanting to do that all day,' she said blissfully, the stress of the day almost visibly pouring out of her. 'You asked me how I know Roda? Let's play cards and then, if you want, I will tell you the whole story of my life.'

Yosra lived at home with her parents and younger brother, a policeman in a nearby part of Muwazafeen. She had studied marketing at college and now sold health insurance for a multi-national company, counselling drop-ins about the kind of cover that might suit them and how to make a claim in the event they fell sick. She had almost no clients, there were no prospects or benefits and she was not well paid. All that could be said for her position was that it was at least a job, which for a woman in Cairo is no small achievement and meant that she did not have to spend her days in the confined family apartment with her brother, mother and invalid father.

Yosra's solitary office was located in a windowless concrete basement beneath one of Muwazafeen's ubiquitous pharmacies. It was baking hot in summer and freezing cold in winter, there was no heating or air conditioning and the electric wiring hung out of the walls. There were no carpets, nor any furniture besides a sofa and a coffee table strewn with spent pill packets, crumpled cigarette boxes and a faded heart-shaped cushion Yosra had brought from home to use as a pillow.

Over time Yosra had begun using prescription drugs, depending on them until finally she became hooked. Through her network of girlfriends she could easily get hold of whatever she wanted simply by asking. At least five of them worked in pharmacies in Muwazafeen and for a couple of extra pounds they would even have a boy deliver what she wanted to her door. She was never going to quit.

Yosra shuffled in stern silence then split the deck. She clamped her cigarette firmly between her lips and tipped the cards at me. 'Cut!' she commanded. I tapped the deck. I could tell she was a seasoned player and it was making me nervous. She dealt.

'Ready?' Yosra asked Noha, eyeing her partner sternly.

'Ready,' affirmed Noha seriously, diligently putting her cards in order.

'Anyone for tea?' asked Roda. We all said yes.

Cards originated in China but came to Europe from Egypt. Mameluke decks of fifty-two with suits numbered one to ten plus three royals have been found in Spain and Italy dating back to the fourteenth century. The suits back then were swords, polo sticks, cups and coins, and being Islamic no figures were depicted. Europeans added the jack, queen and king, but Islam is the reason that packs from Italy, Spain, Germany and Switzerland to this day often do not have queens.

Roda had told me *tarneeb* was similar to bridge, but I quickly found out it was not as complicated. It is a plain trick-taking game without a dummy, popular across the Middle East and played with two teams each made up of two partners. It starts with a round of bidding as each team tries to guess how many tricks they are likely to take. Once bidding is complete, the pair that bid the highest tries to win at least as many tricks as they said they would. If they make it they score; if they do not, they are penalised.

'I dealt, so you start bidding,' began Yosra.

'Two clubs,' I ventured.

'You start with one. Then you go up to two,' she said, a little impatiently.

'Right.' I corrected myself quickly: 'One club.'

'You don't have to bid a suit. You can bid no trumps if you want,' explained Noha gently.

'Got it,' I affirmed briskly, beginning to feel pressured. 'I'll stick with one club.'

'Then the next bidder can choose either to pass or bid higher, either by bidding more tricks or by bidding the same number of tricks in a higher denomination,' Noha explained patiently.

'And it goes round and round with each person bidding up to the number of tricks they think they are going to win. Up to a maximum of seven,' added Roda.

'I'll stick with one club,' I repeated, concentrating hard as I tried to take it all in.

'One heart,' said Noha. Everyone else passed, so Noha started play.

The rhythm of the game soon picked up and I quickly realised that if I was not to irritate the other three by dithering over my cards, I was going to have pay close attention. The three girls, much more conditioned to what they were doing, soon broke into amiable chatter.

Noha was complaining about her job. She spent her days cold-calling people in the UK, USA and Australia to try to get them to change their telephone service provider. It was a depressing business: nearly everyone hung up as soon as they understood why she was calling and there was little chance of promotion beyond the cubicles on the crowded office floor. Hours were long and the telesales agents were rigorously policed to make sure they did not shirk during working hours. The only thing everyone looked forward to was payday, the first day of each month, when the wealthy owner would push a supermarket trolley around the sales floor, throwing bricks of banknotes wrapped in elastic bands at the telesales staff.

Although the work was dull, from Noha's account it was clear that the telelsales company was a great place for young Egyptians to meet people beyond their usual close network of friends and family. The telesales agents were ambitious and educated with excellent language skills, and came from the best families in Heliopolis and Muwazafeen. The sexes were allowed to intermingle freely and plenty of the girls were there explicitly to husband-hunt. The pay was about £250 sterling a month, which by Egyptian standards was reasonable, and the people who worked there were grateful to have a job, even if they had to take the bus out to a desolate stretch of the desert highway to get to work.

★

'What happened to that guy you were seeing?' asked Roda absent-mindedly, placing a card on the table. 'That guy from the pharmacy?'

'He's stopped coming by,' said Yosra, drawing on her cigarette. 'Thank God.'

'Can I tell Hugh about him?' asked Roda.

'Will he write about us?'

'Will you?' enquired Roda.

'Maybe,' I replied, struggling to remember how many trumps had been played.

'Yosra's having an affair with a diplomat.' Roda chuckled. 'He's African.'

'Had an affair, thank you very much. It's over,' corrected Yosra.

'How black is he?' asked Noha, giggling.

Yosra thought for a second as she pictured him in her mind's eye. 'A little bit blacker than Denzel Washington.'

'That's pretty black!' cried Noha.

'He used to come to her office every day and chat her up,' said Roda. 'But he's in his fifties and married with nine children!'

'Nine children! Yosra, how could you?' shrieked Noha.

'How did you come to know this guy?' I asked.

'He used to stop by my office and we just got talking. He was always very polite and respectable.'

'And what happened?' prompted Roda teasingly.

'And we got to know each other,' said Yosra, a little shy. 'Slowly, over about a year.'

'Got to know each other! He wanted to marry you!' said Roda.

'He can't marry her. He's a Protestant with nine children,' said Noha, relishing the incongruities in this doomed relationship.

'But he said he would convert to marry me,' blustered Yosra, not without pride. '"Please, please let me meet your mother!" he told me. "I want to marry you. I will convert to Islam to have you as a second wife. Your hair is so soft, like a baby goat."'

'A goat?' shrieked Roda and Noha in unison and laughed.

'What was he doing touching your hair? Did you sleep with him?' asked Noha.

'Shame on you! Of course not,' replied Yosra.

'But you did other things, didn't you . . . ?' asked Roda.

Yosra went red. 'Shut up and play,' she said.

Yosra and Noha had bid two hearts, which meant they needed to win two extra tricks – eight out of a possible thirteen – to take the hand. Failing to make it, they were penalised doubly in the scoring. A rubber of *tarneeb* runs to thirty-one points and the girls held the scores in their heads. Roda and I were working well as a team and our eyes locked triumphantly as we beat Yosra and Noha again in the second round.

We played for two hours, stopping only to brew some syrupy mint tea. Yosra made quite sure a brisk pace was maintained at all times, scraping up the cards and passing them authoritatively to the next shuffler with all the panache of a Atlantic City croupier. I slowly adjusted to the rules, a little disconcerted that the order of play was the reverse of what I had learnt in bridge and that in *tarneeb* the dealer deals one hand at a time, not card by card to each player, which to my Western eyes looked suspiciously like cheating. As we played, Arabic pop hits ran ceaselessly on the television in the background.

At quarter to eleven, halfway through our third rubber, play was abruptly interrupted by Yosra's mobile phone bleating.

'It's my father,' she said fearfully. 'Hugh, don't say one word.'

As she answered the phone the other girls laid their cards face down on the table and waited in ominous silence.

'Hello? Baba!' said Yosra, feigning surprise. 'No, I left already. About twenty minutes ago. I am stuck in terrible traffic. No, of course not, no boys. Yes, I am on my way. Yes, I am coming now. Yes, father. See you soon. Goodbye.'

Yosra switched off her phone and stubbed out her cigarette with an air of finality.

'Shit. I have to go, guys,' she said. 'Thanks for the game.'

'Wait, stay and finish!' said Noha.

'I can't. I have to go. My brother is there at home and my father is waiting for me. I told him I left already. I can't be late.'

From the looks on their faces I could see the girls knew there could be no argument. They were aware that when she got home her brother Hassan would be there. Hassan had a reputation as a conservative and spent his time off from the police force practising his detective skills on his sister. He enforced a strict eleven o'clock. curfew and each night when she arrived home made a point of searching and questioning her to double-check her story.

Unsurprisingly then Yosra had never set foot in a nightclub in her life and had scarcely ever spoken at length to any boy to whom she was not related. Her mother arranged the only meetings with suitors she had. She had been engaged once, but when her fiancé had broken off the engagement it had tipped her into her addiction to prescription drugs.

'OK, Yosra, we will see you tomorrow,' said Roda.

'I can't. My mother has fixed up a date for me tomorrow. Do you think I smell of cigarettes?'

'Of course you do. Who's the date with?'

'The son of someone she met at the club,' said Yosra. There was a pause before she added, by way of explanation, 'He's an orthodontist called Khaled and he drives a 2002 Kia.'

'Not bad,' commented Roda.

'Excuse me, I have to go and do my procedures,' said Yosra as she turned and left the room.

The procedures were a thorough hand washing in the bathroom plus some self-administered eye drops, followed by an all-over spray with a can of cheap deodorant – Yosra's attempt to stop her family from smelling that she had been smoking cigarettes all evening. Given the heavy cloud that hung in the windowless room, I doubt it could have been very successful.

As Yosra returned from the bathroom, she popped more pills from the packet into her hand. 'Ugh,' she said as she swallowed them down with a gulp of cold mint tea.

'Are you driving home?' I asked tentatively.

'God willing and then I am going to pass out,' Yosra replied, turning to leave. 'Goodbye, guys. Thanks for the cards. Let's go on a felucca or something this weekend if it's not too hot.' And with that she slipped out the door.

'Is she going to be all right?' I asked Roda, concerned. 'I mean, isn't she a bit loaded to drive?'

'Probably, but she does it all the time,' she replied casually. 'It's the only way she can handle her family. She's a bit depressed.'

The cards over, I began preparing to make my way home. Thanking the sisters for their hospitality, I agreed we should try to find another time to play again soon. Outside in the darkness of Istanbul Street it felt good and somehow natural to have re-established contact with Roda. The truth was I had thought about her constantly since we first met and was excited to have found a way to get to know her better. I also felt privileged to have had the chance to meet Arab women in their home and was eager to find out more about the unfamiliar world into which I had been plunged. Up until now this half of Egyptian society had always been hidden from me.

With that in mind, I had absolutely no idea which direction my relationship with Roda was heading. There were no blueprints to work from and I could think of no role model to follow. I did not know any Western man who had dated an Egyptian girl. All I knew was that I was happy to be back in Roda's company and that when she was not around I missed her. She was, I now understood, if not the only reason why I had come back to Egypt, the most important reason to stay.

Eight

Istanbul Street was lined with sandy-coloured low-rise apartment blocks, each no more than six or seven storeys high. It was a residential neighbourhood, although a few of the ground-floor apartments had been turned into businesses of one kind or another. At one end of the street was a square around which stood a large Orthodox church and the hospital where Roda's mother had been taken when she first fell sick. Most of the day the square was bathed in bright sunlight, but in the afternoon as the sun sunk behind the tallest tower of the medical building a long shadow stretched over the square engulfing the parked cars and the trees, until it touched the church on the other side.

In the middle of the square was a rare patch of greenery amid Cairo's labyrinthine concrete sprawl, but it was only accessible to animals, since the park was ring-fenced by shoulder-high spiky metal railings. The gate was chained and padlocked and the keys had disappeared years ago. Beyond the fence were some wild-looking palm trees and untended knee-high grass, and at one end was an ugly sandstone sculpture that looked like a Soviet attempt at a totem pole that for some reason had never been completed. Every few weeks dirty water seeped up to the surface of the park from broken underground pipes and the ground turned brown and swampy. It was a breeding ground for vermin and on summer nights the chirping of frogs and chitter of cockroaches was audible throughout the surrounding streets.

At the other end of Istanbul Street was Itihad Street, one of Muwazafeen's busiest areas. Each side of this wide boulevard was lined with shops and cafés. The heart of Itihad Street was a looming black tower called the Unification of God and Light Shopping Mall. Inside the tower was a department store selling all manner of clothes for men and women with a conservative Islamic twist. Mostly it was a case of veils, bags, more veils and shoes, and all day it was packed with veiled women shopping. The Unification of God and Light Mall had such an austere reputation for modesty and Islamic righteousness that rumours circulated that Christians had been dragged to the top floor, where they had been made to convert to Islam. When the owner of the store, an ostentatiously religious man, was jailed for having five wives, it did nothing to quench the stories. Sharia law permits a Muslim man to have a maximum of four at one time.

Itihad Street was particularly popular with Arab tourists, who flock to Cairo from the Gulf all year round. In particular they come during the summer months, when the Arabian peninsula is too hot, and during Ramadan, when it is too conservative. At these times the neighbourhood around Itihad Street would never sleep and the restaurants and coffee shops were thronged with tourists from the Gulf enjoying the uncovered women, the cheap prices and the wide availability of alcohol. Cairo's vastness affords Arab visitors delightful obscurity and respite from the claustrophobia of life in the Gulf, where the religious police patrol and everyone knows your family's name. Young men cruise the boulevards of Muwazafeen in deluxe convertibles – roofs rolled back, pop hits belting out – shipped over at vast expense from the Gulf to Suez. After midnight the prostitutes appear, plying their trade in the shadows. Itihad Street is a place of temptation, an Arab Amsterdam, where everything is available for a price.

Passing by at nine or ten o'clock in the morning, you could often see haggard groups of Kuwaiti and Saudi youths making their way home from a long night out partying. Egyptians by and large are contemptuous of their Gulf visitors, who they regard as uncultured and arrogant. 'Buffaloes' they call them, meaning they know nothing. 'The Arabs are here,' they mutter scornfully when a luxury car rolls by.

The following night I cancelled dinner at La Bodega with the press officer from the French embassy to return to Istanbul Street to play *tarneeb* again. This time Yosra was not going to be able to make it as she had a rendezvous with Khaled, the suitor her parents had arranged. She knew little about him except that he was forty-three and single, and that his aunt had met her mother at the Muwazafeen Rotary Club.

Roda managed to persuade her neighbour Reem to partner Noha in Yosra's place. Reem lived with her sister Amira and their mother in the apartment just above Roda and was as close to the sisters as a blood relative. Their mothers had been pregnant at the same time in the same block and had left for the hospital at the end of the street to have their baby daughters together on the same day. Both fathers spent New Year's Eve 1976 sprinting up and down the stairs of the block carrying hot towels, painkillers and baby clothes. Roda and Reem had been together all their lives.

Reem worked part time doing secretarial work for a tourism company and spoke excellent English and German. She was a big girl, unveiled, with a pretty, intelligent face and bright blue eyeshadow. She smiled and laughed often, which made the freckles crowd around her nose and the sparkles shimmer in her lustrous brown hair. She was an odd shape, her legs thin but her arms and torso strangely corpulent, because she had once undergone cosmetic surgery and the procedure had brought about some unexpected consequences.

Cosmetic surgery has been undergoing something of a world-wide boom in recent years and the city has a reputation across the region for quality surgery at affordable prices. This is not an altogether new development: facial operations were performed under the pharaohs more than three thousand years ago and Egypt was the birthplace of reconstructive surgery. In Muwaz-afeen in particular cosmetic operations have become all the rage, although Islamic clerics frown upon frivolous surgery. Such pronouncements do not bother the many prospective patients who travel to Cairo to undergo all manner of procedures. Wives of African diplomats and businessmen regard Cairo's plastic surgeons as one of the chief perks of the post. European tour operators run all-in-one cosmetic surgery package holidays to Egypt. You can order a 'Nefertiti nose' or a 'Pharaoh's tummy tuck' and then spend the rest of your 'collagen replacement holiday' recuperating by the swimming pool in a five-star hotel. Procedures are up to date and doctors quickly mirror the latest developments in enhancement and augmentation on offer in Italy and California.

Virtually everyone in Egypt now has access to satellite TV, exposing the whole of society to the wonders of an American-influenced celebrity lifestyle, and undoubtedly the growing number of Arab celebrities who admit to having gone under the surgeon's knife has served to exacerbate the craze. The gossip pages of the Arab tabloid press rang like bells when talk show host Hala Sirhan, Egypt's answer to Oprah Winfrey, Botoxed her face. When Lebanese singer Nancy Ajram confessed to having had no less than eighteen procedures though still in her early twenties the media exploded in an orgasm of titillation over what – and where – they all could have been.

To compete on the bloodthirsty Muwazafeen marriage circuit it is necessary to look perfectly pert and preternaturally buxom. Cairo's upper classes have adopted the fashionable Gulf practice of taking second, third and fourth wives, which means more pressure on married women to stay looking good. Divorce, easier for women since the introduction of new laws in 2000, means more women are faced with a second start in life and increasingly they turn to surgery to look their best.

Mothers bring their daughters; daughters admit themselves without their fathers' knowledge; employers have been known to reject qualified staff who are not good-looking enough; even Egyptian men have cosmetic surgery nowadays, often with a star in mind whose nose they want to emulate, typically either Ricky Martin or Amr Diab, although increasingly they turn up for their consultation with a picture of a girl.

Reem decided to try cosmetic surgery on the recommendation of her friends. Plenty of girls in Muwazafeen were doing it, apparently with successful results, and the tales of life-changing transformations inspired her. Following long consultations with the bedroom mirror, Reem settled on having the fat drained out of her thighs, since these were, she concluded, her single worst feature. Together with her sister she plotted where to go, scanning the advertisements on the back pages of glossy magazines, looking for 'specialised medical centres'. The advertisements were in Arabic and English, and each was accompanied by dazzling testimonies and full-colour before-and-after photographs of blonde, blue-eyed women. Anything, it seemed, was possible.

When they found a clinic that looked suitable Reem told her mother what she had been planning. She knew she was going to need her mother's help after the operation because she lived at home and it was going to take her months to recuperate. At first her mother tried to dissuade her, insisting that her body was the work of God and that to alter it would be sinful, but with help from her sister Amira Reem managed to bring her mother round, explaining that if she only looked a little thinner she would be more likely to find a husband, and that was all she needed to be happy.

If Reem had read the newspapers, she might not have been so

keen. Had she known that women die every year in Egyptian cosmetic surgery clinics undergoing technically straightforward procedures she might not have decided to go under the knife at all. Surgery clinics in Cairo are unregulated and the market is wide open to cowboy outfits. Barely licensed doctors making crazy claims set up fly-by-night clinics to cash in on girls like Reem at untold risk to their health. Beauty centres in Muwazafeen are locked in a price war over the most popular procedures, which means patients in many clinics are as likely to emerge with a nose job reminiscent of the Sphinx as of Egypt's original beauty queen.

For some time after the painful bruising had faded, Reem actually thought the operation had been a success. Only after a few weeks did she find that her body had simply started depositing fat on her back and arms instead of her thighs. Her top half grew fleshy and misshapen, making her look unnaturally top-heavy. The operation had been a disaster, but she had no legal recourse and could not afford to have an operation to rectify what had happened.

That same year the Egyptian Ministry of Health closed down 1700 unlicensed clinics in Muwazafeen. Most of them quickly reopened. The slap-on-the-wrist fines did nothing to inhibit a trade where even relatively small businesses can make a hundred thousand dollars profit a year.

'One spade,' declared Noha boldly.

'Two hearts,' bid Roda.

'Three clubs,' said Reem, adding lightly, 'Don't worry, Noha. I have a fantastic hand.'

'No cheating,' snapped Roda, before adding for my benefit, 'Reem starts. You go after her.'

'Got it.' I nodded. 'No problem.'

The game began, and it was not long before it was rolling along pleasantly, although not quite as efficiently as it had when

Yosra had been Noha's partner. Reem was rather talkative, and to the gentle frustration of the other girls easily distracted from the matter in hand.

As we played, Reem told us excitedly about her fiancé, whose name was Boutros. She said she had known him for many years, but the couple had only become engaged a few weeks ago after they had found themselves working together at the same company. Reem had been trying ardently to get married for years, and now the prospect had finally arrived she could hardly contain her excitement. With her mother she spent each day planning her wedding with the precision of a military operation, but as she explained, no end of work still needed to be done.

'Where are you going to live after you get married?' asked Noha, straightening the cards in her hand.

'We're going to move to Sweden because Boutros has a Swedish passport,' gushed Reem. 'Isn't that exciting? Have you ever been there? I am dying to see snow—'

'And you're never going to come back to Cairo again?' interrupted Noha.

'Don't be silly! Of course we will. All our friends and family are here. That's why Boutros has to convert first.'

'Convert?' I asked.

'To Islam,' replied Reem. 'Because I am Muslim and he is Christian, he needs to convert so we can marry, otherwise our marriage won't be legal in Egypt. Marriages between Christian men and Muslim women are not recognised under Egyptian law.'

'Civil law in Egypt is based on sharia, and sharia states that a Christian man must convert to Islam before he can marry a Muslim girl,' clarified Noha, seeing the puzzled expression on my face.

'And how does Boutros feel about converting?' I asked.

'Oh, he does not mind,' Reem babbled. As she spoke she jigged her leg and chewed gum ceaselessly, a ball of nervous energy. 'He does not have any strong spiritual convictions about anything. It's just another stupid bureaucratic procedure that you have to do in this country, like military service or applying for a driving licence. But now they're making him take Islam lessons!' she shrieked.

'What a pain,' replied Roda, lackadaisically exhaling cigarette smoke as she placed a card on the smudged glass atop the coffee table. 'Your turn, Reem,' she added with a nudge.

'How long do the Islam lessons go on for?' I asked.

'Weeks. And he has to see three different priests before they let him convert, in case they can talk him out of it.'

'I thought conversion was easy,' I said. 'I thought you just go along to Al-Azhar and see the sheikh.' Al-Azhar University is the centre of Islamic scholarship in Egypt. Once it was the premier Islamic learning institution in the whole world.

'Ha! Boutros would be so lucky. That's what foreigners have to do. If an Egyptian wants to convert to Islam it's much harder. Egyptians convert in a separate part of Al-Azhar after meeting with a priest three times. It's a joke really as I know Boutros loves me and nothing will ever change his mind.'

'Thanks be to God,' interjected Noha sarcastically. 'If only we all had a man like that.'

'My Boutros,' continued Reem, waving a finger in the air, 'doesn't care about religion at all. Only his mother makes it hard for him as she is a really committed Christian, and because he is an only child she has been making him feel bad about convert-ing. But once we get to Sweden, no one will care. Will they, Hugh?'

'No one cares what religion you are in Sweden,' I confirmed.

'Most people in Sweden don't even believe in God, do they?' asked Noha. 'I've forgotten what you call them . . .'

'Atheists?' interjected Roda.

'Most Europeans are atheists nowadays,' I replied.

'So they don't believe in God at all? How can that be? I mean who do they think created the world?' continued Noha, a tone of astonishment creeping into her voice.

'They believe in science and evolution instead,' I replied.

'You mean that we are descended from animals?' Reem sniggered.

'That's right.'

'Weird,' said Reem and Noha together, shaking their heads in amazement and looking at each other.

Since it was the weekend and Reem lived just upstairs in the same block we were free to continue our game late into the night. At three o'clock in the morning the street was still alive with people and sounds, the doorman was mopping the stairwell and traffic was backed up noisily outside. By the time I left to go home, the first pink fingers of dawn were just beginning to appear over the apartment blocks standing around the spiked-fence square at the end of the street.

Picking my way over the broken pavement I made my way towards the junction with Itihad Street, where the occasional cab was still passing by. Dawn was when Muwazafeen was at its quietest, although sleep never came completely. On the corner a pair of sad-looking prostitutes were shivering in Lycra dresses, looking for business. A little way up the street, next to the Unification of God and Light Shopping Mall, a haggard group of Arab tourists made their way home after a long night out, their faces sunken from booze and amphetamines. Somewhere tinny pop music was still playing in one of the *shisha* bars.

As the taxi sailed over the bridge to Zamalek, I watched the early-morning rowers sculling on the Nile and thought about what it might take to bring a revolution to Egypt. History has shown that when sudden change comes it often arrives in disguise, and often small, apparently unconnected events can start a domino effect that no one can control. The first Palestinian intifada was triggered by a car accident. In France in May 1968 a disagreement about dormitories in a provincial French university led to a national strike that swept up two thirds of the French workforce. A cinema fire triggered the Iranian revolution and Ayatollah Khomeini returned from exile on a tidal wave of popular support. No military defeat or financial crisis provoked what happened in Iran; there was no peasant's rebellion or resentful gang of plotting generals. As in Egypt today, the security services were foreign-backed and lavishly equipped.

Arriving back at Elephant and Castle, I plodded up the marble stairs to my apartment past the snoring doorman and imagined how if a revolution were to take place, most likely an unexpected cause and an unknown leader would spark it. What keeps Hosni Mubarak awake at night is not an assassination attempt nor an attack by militant Islamists, but a provincial strike that spreads to infect workers and police across the country, because in the end it is the ordinary working man who overthrows regimes.

Nine

Yosra's date went surprisingly well. Khaled, a successful ortho-dontist, with his own clinic in Heliopolis, was well mannered and polite; he listened to what Yosra had to say and twice mentioned how much he was looking forward to having children one day. At forty-three he was a little older than Yosra had hoped for but still within what she considered acceptable limits. Her only concern was that he still lived at home with his mother, but when she quizzed him about this, he replied that he had lived away from home in the past. He had been married once before, although the union had lasted less than a year and he had no children. Since his divorce, Khaled said, he had seen no reason to move out.

The only thing Yosra failed to ascertain on the date, which was of key importance as far as she was concerned, was how open-minded Khaled was. This she regarded as particularly important, as what worried her more than almost anything else was marrying a man who wanted to impose restrictions on her and curtail her freedoms the way her brother did. Khaled did not seem overly conservative; he did not have the telltale *zabeeba*★ on his head or a Brotherhood-style beard, although he had mentioned that his sister was veiled.

★ A *zabeeba* – the Arabic word for raisin – is a brown mark caused by contact between the head and ground when praying. It is a flamboyant sign of faith since it is perfectly possible to pray without acquiring one – no women do.

All in all, Yosra concluded, the brief hour they had spent together was probably one of the most successful dates she had ever been on. Having explained all this and more to Roda at considerable length on the telephone, the two friends resolved that Yosra should arrange to meet Khaled again as soon as possible, before some other girl snapped him up like a must-have bargain in August's City Shopping Festival.

Normally after a blind date in Cairo it is customary for the man to take the lead in establishing contact again if he would like to take things further. But on this occasion Yosra was so eager she broke with protocol and telephoned Khaled herself the very next day, intent on arranging another meeting. She was taken aback when his mother answered the phone.

'I'm sorry. Khaled can't come to the phone right now,' Om Khaled said tersely. 'He has a tennis injury.'

'Since yesterday?' blurted out Yosra incredulously, before quickly correcting herself: 'I'm so sorry to hear that, Auntie. I hope it's nothing serious?'

'He hurt his knee last night playing with some friends at the club,' his mother replied curtly. 'I'll tell him you called.'

Khaled's mother's message sounded off-key to Yosra. Khaled had not mentioned anything about playing tennis. He did not look like the sporty type. Besides they had met in the early evening and he hadn't been dressed for tennis. What time of night, she wondered, could his tennis practice begin? In any case, even if what she had said was true, she could see no reason why a knee injury should stop him speaking on the telephone.

Angry with herself that she had called so impulsively and frustrated that it had been his mother who had come to the telephone, she was at a loss as to what to do next. Uneasy about calling again lest she seem too pushy, she had left herself no other choice but to wait and see if Khaled would call back. But no call came, not later that day nor that evening nor the whole of the next day.

For three days Yosra waited impatiently for the phone to ring, turning over the details of the date in her mind. She could not understand what had happened; they had seemed to get along so well. Baffled and increasingly depressed, she sought solace in drugs, coming up with a million reasons why Khaled might not have called her back.

For a little over two years Yosra had been a habitual drug user. She took just about anything that passed under her nose: cough syrups containing codeine were the cheapest and most easily available, but her penchant was for amphetamines, diet pills and Valium, Xanax and Rohypnol, the date rape drug or 'the cross's father' as it is called in Egypt because the pill has a little cross on it. From time to time she would get her hands on stronger, more addictive morphine derivatives like Tramadol, anti-epileptic drugs such as Rivotril or, most notorious of all, Parkinol – street name 'cockroaches' – a popular recreational drug in Cairo that is so named because when you come down you feel as if insects are crawling under your skin.

Yosra took chemicals every day – to sleep, diet or simply avoid the depressing reality of her humdrum existence. She was thirty-three and knew that the clock was winding down on her marriage prospects. When she was not on drugs, to cheer herself up she would embark on fridge-emptying food binges, making her fatter and so inevitably less likely to get a boyfriend, which was the main reason she was depressed in the first place. It was a vicious circle.

The collapse of her engagement had sparked her habit but in truth Yosra had been miserable all her life. As a child her earliest memory was trying to prevent her mother repeatedly jumping off the kitchen table in an effort to abort her unborn child. After forty-five days the village sheikh had judged that the embryo was now alive and to continue to try and abort would now be sinful. That foetus went on to become her brother, and had Yosra known how miserable he was going to make her she probably would not have tried so hard to stop her mother aborting him.

Yosra's mother Salma was a big-hearted, loving woman who liked to spend her mornings in the market sniffing bunches of herbs, knocking on watermelons and haggling for the best pigeons. Afternoons she spent in the kitchen cooking recipes she had learnt at her mother's knee back in the village. Yosra had studied at university, but like many Egyptian women of her generation Salma had left school as a teenager, and although the two women loved each other dearly the differences between them often resulted in complications and misunderstandings.

Salma had married Yosra's father when she was eighteen in an arranged match. Suleiman was forty-eight, divorced, with a middle-ranking position as a government administrator at the Department of Culture. Coming from a reputable family he looked set to provide Salma with a decent standard of living and a new life in Cairo. Only after they married did Salma begin to learn of the colourful life her husband had led before they had met, of which he seldom spoke. She tried as best she could to discover what that life had been like, but many important details remained obscure, as if she were assembling a complicated jigsaw with most of the pieces missing.

Yosra felt by turns contemptuous and pitiful of her mother's ignorance. Salma regarded her daughter as pointlessly ambitious and worried constantly that she had not brought her up to be sufficiently obedient, or a good enough cook to keep a husband. She saw nothing wrong with telling her friends that she preferred her son to her daughter, who she often said had wasted her life on education. Hassan, on the other hand, was indulged in every way.

When she was not busy cooking or socialising with her friends at the club, Salma took a keen interest in her daughter's love life and it saddened her to see Yosra so upset. In particular she was alarmed to note that her daughter was off her food, because Salma was a generous and talented chef who expressed her love for her family through her prodigious cooking. She was not used to her food being rejected, and the huge portions she served came with too much guilt for Yosra normally to be able to refuse.

Since she had helped arrange the date with Khaled in the first place, Salma felt responsible for her daughter's predicament. As the days passed, sick of watching Yosra mope around the house, she tried to think of ways she might intervene to help resolve the situation. Never a slowcoach when it came to social engineering, Salma hatched a plan to contact Khaled again, believing that probably he had never received the message Yosra had left with his mother to call back.

So as not to risk Yosra losing yet more face, it was agreed that this time Salma would call Khaled's house. In order not to miss any of the conversation, as Salma dialled from the hall Yosra listened in on the second phone next to her father's bed, her hand over the receiver to muffle his snoring.

'Is that Khaled speaking?' asked Salma as brightly as she could.

'This is Khaled's mother speaking,' came the stentorian voice. In Yosra's stomach butterflies were beating a tattoo.

'Why hello, my dear!' exclaimed Salma. 'This is Salma, Yosra's mother.'

'How lovely to hear from you, Salma!' replied Khaled's mother with exaggerated warmth.

The two women then embarked on the kind of ritualistic greetings characteristic of two socially conscious women of a certain class who do not know each other particularly well. Once these had been expressed at some length, Salma began enquiring about Khaled's family, every member in turn whose name she was able to remember.

'And how is Khaled's Uncle Muhammad?' Salma cooed.

'Thanks be to God, Muhammad is fine. His cold is almost completely gone.'

'And how is Muhammad's wife?' she simpered.

'Thanks be to God, she's fine. Still expecting.'

'Thanks be to God. That's wonderful news. God is generous.'

'Yes, it is good news, isn't it? It will be their first.'

'What God wills, what God wills.'

'And how is Khaled's Uncle Rida?'

'Thanks be to God, Rida is fine too.'

'Thanks be to God.'

'And Uncle Mamdouh?'

'Thanks be to God, Mamdouh is fine too . . .'

And so it went on for several minutes while Yosra held her breath, until Salma had mined the small talk just about as thoroughly as anyone could, quite exhausting the health and whereabouts of all Khaled's closer relatives. Eventually, Salma came to the point.

'So, tell me, my dear, is Khaled available to come to the phone?'

'I am afraid Khaled is praying,' replied his mother firmly.

'Praying?' Salma replied, scarcely able to hide her disappointment. Yosra's heart sank.

'Yes, praying,' repeated Khaled's mother unwaveringly.

'Will he be long?' Salma asked haltingly.

'I really could not say . . .'

'Of course not!' Salma giggled, at a loss, for once, as to what to say next. 'Well I do think it's absolutely wonderful when one's son says all the prayers. And it's been wonderful talking to you.'

'Simply wonderful!' echoed Khaled's mother.

'And I have taken up more than enough of your time . . .'

'Think nothing of it, my dear! I will have him call you back just as soon as he is finished.'

After a few more minutes of circuitous social gymnastics Salma extricated herself from the conversation and put the phone down. In the other room Yosra breathed a great sigh of relief and replaced her receiver. She was satisfied with her mother's limber performance, even though she had grave doubts that Khaled really was praying. At least, the pair congratulated themselves, they had managed to wring a promise out of Khaled's mother that he would call back. Now there was nothing more that could be done except wait.

Ten

We played cards all summer long. Through long hot nights, over cigarettes and endless cups of syrupy tea, I listened to tale after tale of bullying husbands, overprotective brothers and a litany of sexual harassment by strangers. Roda and her friends would gossip, rant and celebrate life until a mobile would ring and a curfew would call one of them home. Whenever we gathered to play, the television would be tuned to one of the many Arabic twenty-four-hour music channels and every now and then the rhythms would prove just too irresistible, the cards would be thrown down and the girls would all jump to their feet and begin belly dancing and clapping along to the beat.

Typical card table conversation revolved around marriage and sex, contraception, fertility and virginity. We talked about back-street abortions and what to feed your husband to make him horny. I learnt where a woman can go for a cheap hymenorraphy from a reliable doctor and colourful new expressions meaning to grope someone in a crowd, to stick one's finger in someone's butt when travelling on public transport and to grab a woman's breasts as she crosses the road and turns to look for oncoming traffic.

Most of the issues we discussed were the kind of things you might find inside an issue of *Cosmopolitan*, except that Egypt is a conservative country and such racy magazines are not easily available, so women are obliged instead to turn to their friends for answers to life's most important questions. Besides friends, religion supplies the framework by which most people make their important decisions in life. For many Egyptians, Islam is often the solution. Except, frustratingly, the Koran is not specific enough to provide guidance for every dilemma of modern life because things have moved on since the seventh century, which is why online Islamic chat rooms are filled with questions like, 'Is it OK to pray wearing nail varnish?'

Many young Muslims expect Islam to supply a complete practical guide to how to live their lives, guidance which if followed closely will provide the key to happiness and success. They are not satisfied with spirituality and ritual. The problem is that Islam is so fragmented no single religious authority can provide such detailed guidance, so Muslims tend to pick the interpretations and individuals that they admire or that fit the situation they find themselves in at any given time. Parents, imams, newspaper commentators, TV stars and the Internet all provide interpretations and advice. Some brandish impeccable religious credentials; others, like the wildly popular lay preachers on television, are enticing but entirely unqualified. Questions of authority and authenticity abound. Who is the real teacher, the old sheikh everyone switches off when he comes on TV or the dashing young preacher with no religious credentials who can attract an audience of millions?

The media has become the ideological battleground on which social norms and truths are established and in recent years has served to consolidate the power of Islam in Arab society. Unlike in the West, where relationships and sexual issues are hotly debated, in the Arab world there is one universally understood gold standard for moral behaviour and by Western standards it is very conservative. Although this standard is rooted in religion it is not exclusively Islamic, because despite their antipathy towards one another in Egypt Copts and Muslims live by a very similar moral code.

Religious recordings and books are a sprawling industry in the Arab world; the Web is littered with Islamic chat rooms and at the Cairo annual book fair I found that over half the publishing houses deal exclusively with Islamic-oriented literature. It seems strange that contemporary arts and literature should be so conservative since the current editors, publishers and gallery owners are largely from the revolutionary generation of the 1960s who once struggled to overcome censorship themselves.

The government looms menacingly over the arts, particularly over Egyptian literary life, but out of a misplaced sense of national pride rather than to censor it. Bearing in mind that half the Egyptian adult population is illiterate, you might have thought the state would concern itself more with what was broadcast on television than published in books, but fierce debate rages over what is acceptable reading material. In reality the few Egyptians who do read books usually choose ones they think are useful, which typically means either the Koran or a computer manual. The range of foreign books available in Arabic is pitiful, and if the West ever wanted to make a sincere and significant difference to the average Arab's world view, a good way to start would be by mass-translating dozens of liberal classics into Arabic and distributing them as freely and widely as the Koran.

The most popular radio station in Egypt is the Holy Koran, with well over half the population tuning in each day. Similarly, since the end of the 1990s, religious television has come to the fore, although ironically these channels are owned by the same millionaires who control the sexually provocative music stations.

One kind of religious programming in particular has achieved massive success in recent years – Islamic televangelism. For millions of Arabs, the cranky old sheikh droning on from the pulpit about fire and brimstone is a thing of the past. Islam today issues from youthful preachers wearing coloured headgear or designer suits, speaking on MTV-style sets. The new face of Islam is young, attractive and starkly at odds with the government's hard-forged myth that all Islamists are atavistic violent lunatics. Society wives invite the most fashionable television preachers to evangelise during special afternoon salons in their holiday homes.

If while we played cards a curfew was transgressed then it was never long before a husband or brother would call to find out what had happened to his missing wife or sister. The cards would immediately stop and I would be instructed to stay absolutely silent while a friend fielded the call. 'She's having her hair cut.' 'I am alone in the library.' 'This is a wrong number.'

Family pressure to conform to impossible rules had turned all the women I knew into polished liars years ago. It was the only way to cope with the massive gulf between their private lives and the face they were obliged to show their families and the rest of society. The girls covered for each other artfully and usually successfully, but if a man's voice could be heard in the background no amount of explaining would save them from a severe punishment when they got home, like grounding or even a beating. 'The day I let you come home at two o'clock in the morning is the day I leave for ever because I am not having the neighbours think I am a pimp!' screamed one irate father. We all had a good laugh about that one.

When one of the players had to leave, the card circle would collapse and everyone would go. Before dispersing, scent would be sprayed and oranges peeled, to remove the smell of cigarettes from hands and clothes. Then, in a cloud of fruity perfume, each went her separate way, always by car so as not to be harassed, flashed at or groped on public transport, as happens almost daily to women travelling alone in Cairo at any time of day or night.

Unencumbered by a curfew, I could linger behind when the other girls had gone home. Sometimes I would stay for hours, just drinking tea and chatting with Roda and her sisters. All the time our relationship was steadily developing, and as the weeks passed I found myself spending less time in the coffee shop and more in the little apartment in Istanbul Street instead.

Then one evening Roda called me breathlessly, asking if I could stand in at the last minute for a colleague who had let her down. There was a concert at the Cairo Opera House for the UN annual day, a dressed-up affair where a folk orchestra would be playing traditional rural songs. Naturally I jumped at the chance to spend more time with Roda and our first date turned out to be a star-studded event. The Cairo Opera House is the city's flagship cultural centre and it hosts some of the finest national and international artists. Opened in 1988, it is situated in the middle of the exquisitely groomed Gezira Exhibition Grounds in the heart of Zamalek. The building's modern Islamic design obscures the fact that it was actually built by the Japanese.

The original Opera House, like many of the most beautiful buildings in Cairo, was erected on the instructions of the Khedive Ismail. Designed by Italian architects Avoscani and Rossi it took fewer than six months to build, opening to great acclaim in 1869 to celebrate the completion of the Suez Canal. Before it was even finished, Ismail had commissioned Giuseppe Verdi to compose the music for the inaugural performance. The Khedive wanted something to reflect ancient Egyptian history, something heroic and romantic, so he commissioned French archaeologist Auguste Mariette to write a synopsis of Egyptian history, which he passed on to Antonio Ghislanzoni to use as the basis for his libretto. The result was *Aida*, one of the most loved and performed operas of all time. Unfortunately another piece by Verdi had to be performed on the opening night because the Franco-Prussian War was raging, France was in turmoil and the costumes and scenery did not arrive from Paris before the curtain went up.

Over the following decades the Opera House went on to become the finest venue of its kind on the African continent, playing host to world-famous orchestras, until one early October morning in 1971 the building was razed to the ground by fire. Nothing could be salvaged except for a pair of statues.

The new Opera House opened seventeen years later. It took

nearly three years to build and opened with a Kabuki show. The night Roda and I went, we were too engrossed in one another to pay much attention to the performance, although over canapés at the reception afterwards I remember people telling me that they thought it lived up admirably to the Khedive's vision. The dazzling white lobby glittered with the stars of Egypt's stage and screen: there were one or two I recognised, as well as a galaxy of others I did not. Roda pointed them out to me and explained who was who, but I regarded them all with a glazed indifference.

Being our first date, I was slightly apprehensive about what going out with an Egyptian was going to be like. As it turned out, it was much like dating a Westerner. There was just one striking difference. The concept of honour may mean little nowadays in the Western world – and many people might regard that as a good thing – but the notions of personal honour and reputation still carry great weight in the Middle East. A woman in Egypt must be seen to behave properly at all times since it is not only her name at stake but her family's too. This decrees where she can be seen, what she can wear and how she may behave in public – whether, for example, she can drink alcohol or smoke. Roda drank alcohol – about half the girls I had come to know did – but very few of them would do so in public and none in front of a male relative.

Thankfully, Roda did not have any close male relatives other than her father, and with him in Kuwait she was unusually free to run her own life. Nevertheless, though it may have seventeen million inhabitants Cairo's well-heeled classes rotate through a remarkably small number of nightspots and you never know when you might run into an inquisitive cousin or someone's aunt. Not much stays secret for long. So conversation and behaviour in public is guarded and care must always be taken in order to maintain a veneer of piety and sobriety, regardless of what goes on in one's private life.

★

There were occasionally other male visitors to Roda's apartment. A distant relative of Yosra's, named Dwayne, was the most familiar face. He would swing by at all hours of the day and night partly because, like Noha, he worked odd hours in the telesales company and partly because he was perpetually stoned and kept only rudimentary track of time at best.

Although he had only just turned twenty-one, Dwayne's solid build and strong jawline made him look several years older. When he was eighteen he had enjoyed an affair with a divorcee from Liverpool who had come to Hurghada on a package holiday so he spoke excellent English with a slight Liverpudlian lilt. Now he was in love with an Egyptian girl called Layla he had met at work, but because her father and brothers did not approve the relationship was progressing only haltingly and mostly in secret.

Dwayne's real name was Muhammad, but his bosses at the telesales company guessed that an Arabic name might compromise his sales potential with American customers so they rechristened him – so to speak, as of course Dwayne had never been christened in the first place. The ruse worked well, the name stuck, and soon everyone except his mother was calling him Dwayne.

Dwayne did not play cards but he enjoyed stopping by at Istanbul Street to savour the female company. A natural salesman, talkative and funny, more than once he had managed to win the largest monthly sales bonus by peddling more shoddy phone lines to foreigners than anyone else. He liked to joke about how easy it was and he would often regale us, complete with authentic impersonations in realistic accents, with tales of who he had encountered on the phone that day, in Nebraska or New York.

As long as he had some hash in his pocket, Dwayne seemed to have not a care in the world. Like a Frenchman sampling fine wine, he smoked with the refined appreciation of a connoisseur.

Most Egyptian men I knew did – sometimes it seemed that inertia brought on by smoking hashish all day was the only thing preventing a revolution in Egypt. Being a devout Muslim Dwayne never touched alcohol but claimed to be able to identify exactly where every piece of hash he smoked originated from simply by tasting it. Taking a long slow draw on a joint, Dwayne would exhale wisely proclaiming 'Ahmed Fahmi – 100 per cent definite' or some such. Since it was quite impossible to know whether he was right or wrong with any of his pronouncements, the girls sensibly attributed about as much credence to them as if he were reading their tea leaves.

The only thing that seemed to ruffle Dwayne's laid-back lifestyle was a long-running struggle with the Egyptian police over his military service. This is compulsory in Egypt and has a notorious reputation as an intensely degrading experience. One year is the minimum enlistment for conscripts. Officers get a better deal but are required to spend three or four years studying at military college first. Although the Egyptian army is generously subsidised by the United States, most of the cash seems to disappear into certain important people's pockets or goes to finance elite units. Ordinary soldiers are dismally equipped, routinely going without shoelaces and eating food months or years out of date. Dysentery is a way of life and over the year of conscription everyone experiences drastic weight loss.

Typical training activities include diving from a great height into a trench of raw sewage, walking from Cairo to Alexandria through the desert or lining up in the infamous 'sun queue', where soldiers stand facing the blazing sun from dawn till dusk, without moving or drinking water, sometimes for several days on end. Conscripts from Cairo spend most of the year in remote desert locations earning pennies each day far from the comforts of home. Potable water in the desert is in constant short supply and in summer often too hot to drink until the heat of the day begins to subside. If the water supply truck is late soldiers have no choice but to drink black water out of cars and trucks once the silt has settled and the worst of the oil has been skimmed off. Accidental death by heatstroke or during live firing exercises is commonplace. The military regards fewer than one in four men killed in training as an acceptable fatality rate. Many men refuse to discuss what happened to them in the army for years afterwards. Enduring psychological trauma is normal. Many soldiers also leave with large debts, run up by bribing their poorer comrades to do the really dirty or dangerous jobs for them.

Certain fortunate categories of men are not conscripted. Naturally the rich and well-connected can normally wriggle out of it, as can some other less privileged individuals who fit government criteria designed to make the draft more humanitarian: men with neither brothers nor sisters and men whose fathers are over sixty are not obliged to go, for example. Dwayne had been entangled for several years in a tedious bureaucratic struggle for exemption on the grounds that he had knock knees and flat feet.

He needed to have his exemption papers completed and stamped by his next birthday or he would pass a legal deadline, which meant if he had still not been officially excused he would be in trouble with the law. In the meantime he was forbidden to travel because Egyptians need clearance from the Ministry of Foreign Affairs before they can leave the country. Graduates need their academic documents stamped and if they are male have to prove that their military service has either been completed or deferred for a good reason. Military service status, done, excused or pending, is clearly emblazoned on a man's passport right next to his religion. Being stuck in Egypt bothered Dwayne considerably because, like most of the staff at the telesales company, all he really wanted in life was to move to the United Arab Emirates to find better-paid work there.

Dwayne and Noha would sit and chat for hours about their dream of starting new lives in the Emirates. Many of their friends had already gone. Above all, they dreamed of Dubai, with its famed economic horizons so much bluer and wider than those in Cairo. Just as importantly, the Emirates were renowned for being a proudly Arab and Islamic success, built on business acumen rather than just oil money. Unlike President Hosni Mubarak, Abu Dhabi's late ruler Sheikh Zayed had been genuinely loved and admired.

Every little thing that happened in Dubai made waves at the company. When Giorgio Armani opened a new restaurant in a five-star hotel, telesales was alive with comment for a week; when a girl in accounts came back with photographs of herself on the Olympic-sized ice rink in one of Dubai's super-malls, the rest of the office turned green with envy. Tales of the fortunes one could make there circulated like rumours of gold in the old Wild West.

Unlike in Cairo, where Nasser's promise of a job for every graduate had long since turned to dust, everyone it was said was guaranteed a job in the Emirates. The best jobs were in technology and the best technology jobs were in Dubai Internet City where the starting salary was said to be about £750 sterling a month, about three times what Dwayne and Noha earned. All the biggest names in software and computers could be found among the hundreds of international companies operating there. As everyone in telesales well knew, the project had become so successful so quickly that by the second half of 2005 applications to locate companies there had to be delayed because the available office space had been exhausted. A backlog of wealthy foreign companies was building as everyone waited for the immigrant labourers to finish construction. Noha, Dwayne and their friends would have given anything to be part of it all, but until a precious visa could be arranged it was just another deliriously successful Emirates miracle to salivate over on the Internet when the boss was away.

★

Dwayne had a complicated family life about which he spoke little. His father was abusive and a drinker and had a poor relationship with the rest of the family. By day he worked in an overstaffed government office, but like many Egyptian state employees his minuscule salary had long ago pushed him into a second career. By night he moonlighted in a human trafficking business.

Each evening after work Dwayne's father would stop at the family house in Heliopolis only long enough to change into a black leather jacket and some gold jewellery. Then he would head straight back out to a bar or a nightclub, where his other, more lucrative business affairs were conducted. He was part of a gang running cheap labour and prostitutes into the Gulf. His clients were pimps and gangsters known as 'snakeheads' and the late-night meetings were when he would collect orders for entry visas. Visa prices varied, depending on age, sex and nationality, from a few hundred to several thousand dollars a head. Young unskilled women were expensive; a man in his mid-twenties who had finished school was cheaper. Dwayne's father and the snakehead would haggle, and once a price had been agreed, the snakehead would have his associates send over a few dozen passports together with the agreed amount of cash. Dwayne's father was the middleman, calculating the price and collecting the money, before passing the passports along to his contact inside the Emirates interior ministry. He never met with any of the migrants himself.

Once all the paperwork was in order, the visas would be issued with a photocopy of each attached to the corresponding passport. Then they were returned to Dwayne's father, who handed them back to the snakehead, who passed them in turn to the criminal gangs in the migrants' country of origin. By the time the migrants arrived a few weeks later, the original visas were ready and waiting for them to be collected. The Emirates' immigration authorities granted each migrant a three-month visitor's visa, which spelt three months lucrative prostitution or other illegal work. At the end of their stay the migrants returned to their home country for a break and a holiday, before beginning the process all over again.

It was a risky business and it made for a complicated double life for Dwayne and his family. His father badgered Dwayne to join the business, even promising him a visa to Dubai himself if he helped him out with his work, but Dwayne had always resisted, preferring instead to try to make his own way in life. He rarely spoke about his father, but the brand-new BMW motorbike parked outside the family house indicated that whatever he was earning did not come solely from working overtime in the office.

Several times a week, when his father was home, Dwayne would drive over to the little apartment in Istanbul Street from Heliopolis on the other side of town. Careering up to the door in his dilapidated white Renault in a haze of hash smoke with Pete Tong's *Essential Collection* pounding on the car stereo, even above the noise of the street we could hear him coming a way off. It was a pleasant change to have another guy around, especially such a good-natured one, although I noticed his presence muted the conversation. Roda and her sisters may have come to trust him, but most of the girls who passed through to play cards were wary about discussing their personal lives with an Egyptian man present, even only a young stoner: careless talk might come back to haunt them later. Sensing this Dwayne rarely stayed long, and after an hour or so would politely make his excuses and leave to visit his many other friends' houses in Muwazafeen.

One night Noha, Roda, Yosra and I were playing cards when Dwayne stopped by, looking uncharacteristically glum. Slumping down on the sofa, he began irritably picking a hole in his counterfeit Nike trainers.

'Man, life sucks,' he announced despondently.

'What happened?' I asked. 'No hash?'

'No. I asked Layla's dad if I could marry her.' He turned to look straight into my eyes. 'He said no.'

'Dwayne, that is terrible news. Why did he say no?'

'Because I told him I was not going to take any financial support from my dad.'

'Why don't you want to ask your dad for any money?' I asked.

Dwayne shot me a penetrating look. 'You don't know my dad, man. We don't get along very well . . . Let's just say I'm closer to my mum.'

While Dwayne's father pursued his second career, Dwayne's mother spent her days in the beauty salon or playing *tarneeb* at the Heliopolis Rotary Club.

'I told Layla's father I would support his daughter financially,' Dwayne said, his voice rising in anger, 'but he didn't take me seriously. It wasn't just the no that bothered me. It was the way he said it.'

'How did he say it?' I asked quietly.

'He asked me how long it would be before I thought I was going to be financially independent. I told him two years – maximum. But he laughed in my face.'

'That sucks,' I said as sympathetically as I could. It was clear his pride had been badly bruised and I did feel genuinely sorry for him. But at the same time Dwayne was young and penniless, so I could understand why Layla's father had refused.

'But Dwayne, you are only a telesales operator,' I said as soothingly as I could, 'even if you are a really good one. If I was Layla's father, I doubt I would let you marry my daughter either.'

'I'm looking for jobs!' rejoined Dwayne, obviously hurt. 'I'm not going to be in telesales for ever! I even told him about my plan to open a coffee shop in Heliopolis renting out computers to play PlayStation. I've got a great location right next to the Emerald Square mall!'

'Well maybe when that is up and running you can ask for his daughter's hand again.'

'That's what he said,' replied Dwayne dolefully. "'Come back in five years!'" he snorted, contemptuously echoing Layla's father's words. Then, a louring expression on his face he added, 'He'll see. He'll regret it.'

There was nothing unusual about Dwayne's problem: I had heard this kind of story many times before. At least he had a job; he was one of the lucky ones. Officially Egyptian unemployment is about 9 per cent, but in reality about 25 per cent of young men and as many as 59 per cent of women are without work. No work means no money and no money means young people cannot afford to get married. Since marriage is the only legitimate way to obtain sex that means frustration, particularly because Cairenes, like the rest of us, now live in the information era, and despite Islam the daily bombardment of erotica has never been more intense.

Egyptian tradition dictates that when a young Muslim man wants to get married, he starts by buying his fiancée a furnished apartment before showering her with lavish gifts like precious stones and jewellery. Given the country's depressed economic situation, this is little more than a fantasy for most young Egyptians. Like Dwayne, they live at home with their family and struggle to scratch enough money together to look after themselves, let alone anyone else. There are seven million women over the age of twenty in Egypt who have never been married, half of whom are over the age of thirty-five. There are also eleven million unmarried men. But now an increasing number of young people are turning to a controversial Islamic practice. They have what is known as an *urfi* marriage, a contentious but legally and religiously recognised institution that opens the door to sexual relations.

An *urfi* marriage is a special kind of union between a man and woman, a bit like a common law marriage, permissible under Sunni Islam. Unlike a regular marriage, it can take place in private and need not be registered at a government office. In fact the state is not involved at all. The couple need only marriage contracts, which they can draft themselves, an imam willing to perform the ceremony and two friends (who must be Muslim men) to act as witnesses. Typically the witnesses are close friends of the groom and no parents are informed. After the ceremony the contracts are exchanged and the bride and groom each keep a signed copy as proof that the wedding actually took place.

Urfi marriages are much cheaper and therefore within reach of young people, but they are not as socially binding. Frowned upon by Egyptian society, they are generally secret and entered into either by young people who want to have sex, men who want to marry a second wife without their first wife knowing or couples denied a regular marriage by one or both sets of parents. Conservatives decry them as a harbinger of the demise of traditional Egyptian society and when a respectable parent in Muwazafeen finds out their daughter has had a covert *urfi* marriage, it is about as big a domestic disaster as one can imagine.

In extreme cases *urfi* marriages can even be a way for poor families to sell their daughters into prostitution under the guise of marriage. There need be no official record of the union and if the girl is over sixteen no crime has technically been committed. When the man wants to move on, the pair can easily divorce.

The problem is that since Islam sanctions *urfi* marriages, they cannot easily be outlawed. As long as young people do not have the means to get married conventionally, with all the gifts and the gold and the parental consent, *urfi* marriages will continue to exist as the only institution providing a veneer of respectability to a young Muslim couple who want to have sex.

Urfi marriages were shoved into the public eye when a court case occurred involving a twenty-four-year-old Egyptian movie star and his attractive twenty-seven-year-old costume designer. After meeting on the set of *When Daddy Returned*, the pair had an *urfi* marriage that left the costume designer, whose name was Hind el-Hinnawy, pregnant. Her lover, Ahmed al-Fishawy, refused to acknowledge paternity, so in what was to become a landmark case she decided to sue him. What made the case a sensation from the outset was el-Hinnawy's remarkable candour in a society that is not known for its sympathy towards women in domestic disputes, while until the scandal broke her lover, who came from a famous acting family, had been a great public moralist who liked to make a show of his painstaking adherence to Islam. He fronted an Islamic programme for youth on television and had once quit a sitcom citing religious reasons.

The salacious details of the case were almost drowned out by the noisy public debate about whether *urfi* marriages could or should be banned, but not quite. To the general amazement of the Egyptian public, rather than abide by tradition and swiftly abort, have a hymenorraphy then quickly marry someone else, el-Hinnawy went ahead and had the baby and then filed a paternity suit. Since a woman's testimony is worth only half that of a man's in a sharia court, el-Hinnawy took al-Fishawy to a civil court instead, where a man and a woman are valued equally.

The case broke new legal ground and shattered some major cultural taboos: it was the first time DNA evidence had been demanded in a paternity suit; el-Hinnawy admitted she had deliberately waited until it was too late to abort the child before she told her parents she was pregnant; and perhaps most controversially of all her father chose to stand by her. El-Hinnawy claimed that when the baby was conceived the couple were in an *urfi* marriage. Al-Fishawy denied that the baby was his or that there had been a relationship between them at all. The problem was that el-Hinnawy did not have her copy of the marriage contract. Al-Fishawy had asked to have a look at it one day, she said, and then omitted to give it back. He claimed caddishly that there was no contract and that the case was merely a ruse for el-Hinnawy to get her hands on his fortune.

Throughout this long-running saga which gripped the Arab world el-Hinnawy maintained that what she wanted above all was legal recognition of her daughter's paternity so that the little girl might be issued with a birth certificate. Without a birth certificate, you have a major problem: you cannot get an identity card, and without an identity card effectively you do not exist. A child without a father also legally has no religion, a crucial omission which leaves it stranded in a bureaucratic and legal limbo. If the future of an illegitimate child is bleak, the future of its mother is even bleaker. Egyptian single mothers are unlikely ever to marry and face ostracism, ridicule and even sometimes death at the hands of relatives intent on restoring family honour.

Eventually, al-Fishawy conceded the pair did have a relationship after all, but denied that they had been married and denied paternity of the child. The whole of Cairo immediately set about debating the rights and wrongs of the case. Even Al-Azhar's grandest imam was sucked into the tabloid debate. Could paternity be decided on evidence from the mother alone? What should be done in the absence of any legal documents if the father denied the marriage? Should a man be obliged to marry a woman just because they had an illegitimate child? Did a child deserve to have a legal father if it was born out of wedlock? Muslim scholars raced to come up with religious guidelines for when it would be suitable to use new medical technology, like DNA testing, to determine paternity. What, they asked one other in desperation, would the Prophet have done?

Many blamed el-Hinnawy for having sex outside a regular marriage. Many more blamed her family for having brought their daughter up badly in the first place. Some condemned al-Fishawy for not taking responsibility for the child he had fathered. Others condemned both parties as equally repugnant, choosing instead only to root for the baby, whose name was Leena. The case was generally regarded as a moral tragedy and sad proof, as if it was needed, that sex scandals and moral turpitude were not the exclusive property of the West.

El-Hinnawy lost the paternity suit because al-Fishawy refused to provide any DNA and nothing in law could force him to do otherwise. The judge ruled that it was the task of the plaintiff rather than the accused to submit evidence and that a marriage, even an *urfi* marriage, needed witnesses to be legitimate under Islam. Courageously, el-Hinnawy went on to challenge the verdict in the appeal court and this time the judge found in her favour. He overthrew the initial ruling on the strength of statements from eye witnesses who had seen the pair enter and leave her apartment block together. These witnesses, the judge ruled, were sufficient to render the marriage legal, which in turn made al-Fishawy Leena's legal father. El-Hinnawy broke down in tears when she heard the verdict; the baby took al-Fishawy's name; the case was closed and women's rights in Egypt took another small, painful step forward. There were about fourteen thousand other paternity cases handled in the Egyptian courts that same year, mostly stemming from *urfi* marriages or from non-conjugal love.

Eleven

On 7 July 2005 a series of coordinated explosions hit London's public transport system during the morning rush hour killing fifty-two commuters plus the four suicide bombers, and wounding hundreds more. At a press conference soon after, the British police stated that they would be interested in speaking to an Egyptian chemical engineer named Dr Magdi al-Nashar to help them with their enquiries.

As Scotland Yard and the FBI began poring over al-Nashar's life, it was only a matter of hours before the international press pack landed at Cairo airport, eager for any details they could unearth about the mysterious young doctor, his friends and family. Dr al-Nashar, it emerged, had come to know the bombers through worshipping at a Leeds mosque. The explosive used in the attacks, acetone peroxide, aka the 'mother of Satan', was particularly volatile and required a high degree of skill to assemble. Dr al-Nashar, an accomplished biochemist as well as a devout Muslim, had left the UK shortly before the attacks but not before lending the gang the keys to his apartment. All this made Dr al-Nashar look rather suspicious.

The story created on the ground in Cairo an instant demand for Arabic speakers and drivers, and I swiftly enlisted as a fixer with the British tabloid press. Together with about fifty other journalists and cameramen we settled down with tea and falafel

sandwiches on the doorstep of the fifth-floor apartment belong-
ing to the beleaguered al-Nashar family in a run-down tower
block in the impoverished neighbourhood of Basateen, some-
where on the southern edge of Cairo's urban sprawl.

Unplanned and unloved, Basateen is the kind of slum that
never makes the tourist maps. Its unpaved broken streets are
pockmarked with dark puddles of sewage water, there is little
infrastructure or garbage collection and most of the thorough-
fares are too narrow and clogged with people and animals
for motorised vehicles to pass. Many of its inhabitants are
African refugees and a Sudanese street gang called the Lost Boys
is headquartered in a slum nearby. The Lost Boys are locked in
a bitter and pointless war with another refugee gang, the
Outlaws, who live in the vast suburb of Ain Shams. Both gangs
have a bad reputation for knifing and defenestrating people.
Unemployment is high, expectations are low and it was not
hard for the assembled journalists to imagine how someone
who had had the misfortune of growing up in such a place
might feel so angry with their lot they might be driven to
violence.

The press corps washed through the neighbourhood like a
tidal wave, swarming over anyone who entered the al-Nashar
family's featureless concrete tower block, snapping their picture,
recording their opinions, then playing it all back at the top of the
hour. The bemused residents of Basateen, who up until this point
had been generally ignored by the world at large, took to the
stage only rather suspiciously, confounding the media with their
vagueness and refusal to speculate over such key issues as whether
the doctor might have been a recruiter for al-Qaeda or whether
al-Nashar might really have been his code name. In general the
local residents were broadly supportive of the al-Nashar family,
who had resided in the area for years and enjoyed a respectable
reputation locally as modest pious people who had never been in
any kind of trouble before.

Shortly after Scotland Yard announced its interest in speaking to the doctor he was scooped up by the Egyptian secret police in a Basateen mosque after Friday prayers. Under interrogation the doctor confirmed that the bombers had indeed had a set of keys to his apartment but insisted that beyond that any apparent connection between him and the bombings was nothing but a series of unfortunate coincidences. The doctor claimed he had simply been trying to help out fellow Muslims he had met at the mosque and had no idea that he had in fact befriended a ruthless suicide squad.

After a day or two Dr al-Nashar was acquitted of any involvement in the bombings and, to the great satisfaction of the Egyptian press, released. The international press corps had hardly got itself comfortable on the doctor's doorstep. When the British announced soon after that they too had no further interest in speaking to the doctor, the news hounds camped outside the block reluctantly packed up their cameras and microphones and skulked off. Meanwhile the real ringleader, along with our story, disappeared somewhere into the badlands of Pakistan. Bored, disappointed and wishing they were in Pakistan, the press retired to drink beer and sunbathe by the pool of the Nile Hilton, trying to dream up some other stories they could cover while they were in Cairo.

'So this chemist, he turned out to be totally innocent in the end?' asked Roda, sounding satisfied.

'I can't believe it,' said Yosra. 'I can't believe what has happened since 9/11. Everybody is out to get us Arabs! Even Britain!'

Fresh back from Basateen I was playing cards again, partnering Roda as had become usual. Yosra was partnered with Roda's sister Noha.

'If you even look like an Arab you can get locked up nowadays in America,' complained Noha. The other girls clucked and nodded in agreement. 'There are no human rights any more. Just because he is a Muslim and a scientist everyone thinks he has to be a terrorist. It's very racist actually,' she added.

The Egyptian press had given solid coverage to the saga of Magdi al-Nashar as it unfolded, from the moment his name was first mentioned in Britain to his speedy vindication and release. It was presented on the front page of every newspaper as a great nationalist struggle: an Egyptian scientific success story hounded by a vindictive Western regime with its foot on the neck of the Muslim world community. To most Egyptians al-Nashar's arrest fitted with what was understood by now to be an established anti-Islamic pattern in the West.

'You have twenty-one points; we have fifteen,' said Noha, tallying the score up in her head. 'You're getting better at this. Yosra deals.'

'Hey, Yosra, any word about that dentist?' enquired Noha.

'You mean Khaled? The orthodontist? He never called back,' Yosra replied gloomily. Her eyes looked like glazed grey dinner plates. The pupils were tiny dots.

'Didn't his mother promise he would?'

'Yeah, she did . . . but it doesn't matter. I had forgotten about him anyway.'

'What an arsehole,' commented Noha sourly.

'Hey, let's go away next weekend,' suggested Roda. 'A friend of mine from medical school is having a party on the north coast on Friday and everyone is invited. We can all stay the night.'

'I can't go,' said Noha. 'I have to go to a birthday party for a girl from work at the Cairo Jazz Club.'

'I can't go either,' said Yosra gloomily. 'My brother will never let me.'

'Tell your mother he has to let you go because you have a date,' said Roda.

'I don't think it will work,' replied Yosra. 'She won't let me stay overnight.'

'Come on!' encouraged Roda. 'You have to give it a try. Just ask her. Please?'

'She might say yes,' I speculated brightly.

'If she says yes, it is only because she is sick and tired of me hanging around the house and because she thinks it is shameful having a thirty-three-year-old daughter who is still unmarried.'

'Well that can be your excuse to go then,' reasoned Roda.

'She just wants to get rid of me,' Yosra said miserably.

'Didn't she help you try and get in touch with Khaled? She just wants you to be happy,' I replied, trying to sound cheerful.

'I wish that was true,' said Yosra despondently, her dead eyes fixed on the floor.

Yosra seemed to be slipping deeper into depression. Her inane job, her spying brother, her miserable home life, all conspired to pull her down. She was using tranquillisers every day now to insulate herself from the pain, but while the drugs had once made her seem relaxed and happy, now they served only to encase her in a detached numbness. She dealt the cards robotically as if only vaguely aware of the conversation happening around her.

'Your brother is really terrorising you, isn't he?' I probed.

Yosra took a deep drag of her cigarette and thought about this for a moment. 'He's a man, I guess.' She shrugged. 'He does what he has to do. He knows what I am like.' She took another drag and shaped the cigarette smoke into a grey ring with her thickly glossed lips then exhaled, sending it cruising across the room.

'You really haven't done anything wrong.' I persisted. 'He could go a bit easier on you.'

'It's just how Egyptian men are,' stated Yosra indifferently. 'They're all like that.'

I knew Yosra loved her brother and accepted the asymmetry of power between them even though he was younger than her. She never objected to the strict regime he imposed on her and would always rather blame herself than find fault with him.

Suddenly a thought struck me. 'Does he know where you are now?' I asked anxiously, thinking that in her state it might have slipped her mind that she was supposed to be at home already.

'Don't worry about him,' she replied breezily, cracking a smile. 'He's away all week. They sent him to work in a prison in Helwan full of Gama'a al-Islamiyya.'

'What's the prison like?' I asked. Egyptian prisons have a reputation for deprivation and cruelty. Gama'a al-Islamiyya is the militant Islamist organisation that struggled throughout the 1990s to overthrow the Mubarak regime.

'It is very tough but he likes working there a lot. He says most of the guys in jail are really decent and well-educated people, not like ordinary criminals at all. Most of them are from our class.'

'He likes them because they pray all the time,' observed Roda.

'Well, that's true. He says they are religious, just like his friends in the police, actually.'

'What kind of crimes did they commit?' I asked. 'Are they terrorists?'

'Oh, I don't think many of them have actually committed any crimes. It's just a precaution.'

'A precaution? So how long do they stay in jail for?'

'God knows. Five years? More perhaps . . .' Yosra trailed off. 'What are trumps again?'

Thousands of Islamists rotate through Egypt's hellish prison system. Many are never charged with a crime, nor even referred to a court or prosecutor's office. Often inmates are declared innocent and officially released a dozen times, but still remain in prison, sometimes for years, while they wait for the cogs of the glacially slow bureaucratic machine to align and release them.

The prison cells where the Islamists are kept are concrete and barely two metres square, without windows or ventilation, except a spyhole in the roof about ten centimetres in diameter through which guards monitor the five or six inmates in the cell below.

There is no electricity, water or sunlight and to make life as miserable as possible the walls are kept soaked in kerosene, which contaminates the air and eats away at the prisoners' lungs, causing lifelong respiratory problems.

Torture using electricity, passing a current through the urinary tract or under the tongue for long periods, is common. There is nowhere to urinate or defecate, except on the floor or into the same plastic bottle in which water is provided, so if prisoners want to use the bottle they first have to finish the water. Sometimes a prison guard takes pity on them and gives them a plastic bag, which they share for days. To try to avoid all this prisoners fast for days on end, which inevitably leads to dehydration and then kidney problems and infections of the urinary tract. Food is served on the floor, upon which the prisoners also sleep and pray. Every four days they are allowed out for a few seconds or a minute, just long enough to reach the tap outside their cells where they can wash their faces and refill the bottle with water.

Over two decades this brutal regime combined with intelligence from a network of prison informants has taught the Egyptian regime how Islamist groups are formed and structured. While Western nations struggle with Islamic terrorism, Egypt has successfully faced down the worst of its extremists. The ruthless prison system helped drive Islamic Jihad out of Egypt and broke the back of Gama'a al-Islamiyya, which called a ceasefire from its prison cells in 1998. Today the Egyptian government cautiously regards its measures as successful, even though Islamic Jihad in exile has joined forces with al-Qaeda, providing invaluable expertise and personnel to Osama bin Laden.

Egypt's fabled prowess at tackling Islamists has ensured its prison system has become an attractive destination for the American military, looking for somewhere suitable to interrogate Arab and Muslim captives taken during their 'war on terror'. Believing the Egyptians could crack even the hardest nuts, in 1995 America began extraditing its own terror suspects to Cairo for interrogation in a controversial process known as extraordinary rendition, which the American government maintained was completely legal. The Egyptians were happy to help since many of the suspects were their own nationals and they often wanted to get their hands on the same people.

After 9/11 the CIA dramatically stepped up the number of prisoners undergoing this process from dozens to hundreds. The partnership between the CIA and the Egyptian security services became so close that CIA counterterrorism experts liked to boast that they could give the Egyptian interrogators questions for the detainees in the morning and by the evening would be getting their answers. There were only two problems: they were not always the right answers and no one knew what to do with the detainees afterwards. Such prisoners can never be brought back into an open court system either as witnesses or defendants because of what they might say. In addition, with human rights groups on their case, it can be difficult to kill them too, although several suspects extradited to Egypt have 'disappeared'. When Colin Powell laid America's case for war with Iraq before the UN in 2003, his 'proof' of a relationship between Saddam Hussein and Osama bin Laden was based on the confession of an al-Qaeda leader, extracted under torture in Cairo.

'The funny thing is,' Yosra continued, 'I know lots of people who would blow themselves up if there was a chance to kill some Americans or Jews. A lot of people were thrilled when the towers came down.'

'Even if that meant killing civilians?' I asked. 'And women and children? I mean, 9/11 was not exactly self-defence.'

'I think people are generally sad if Muslims get killed, but at least they know they all went to paradise, so they don't mind too much.'

'But even if you don't mind, what about the family you leave behind?' I persisted.

'Dying does not matter to Muslims,' Yosra continued dreamily. 'Our bodies and our families and what we have here on earth, they are only with us now in this physical world. You belong to God and when you die you return to Him. Life is God's will and if God wants you to be a suicide bomber then that is what you should do.'

'And what about the London bombings? Do your friends support them too?'

'Most people say they never happened. It was just a trick by Tony Blair to make an excuse to declare war on Muslims.'

'Of course they happened! Are you crazy? My sister was on the bus behind the one that blew up. Everyone saw it happen!'

'Well you say that . . . but what about the weapons of mass destruction in Iraq? Wasn't that an excuse too? And weren't the British police doing an anti-terrorist exercise that very same day?'

'What about the pictures on TV? You saw the bus with the roof blown off, right?'

'If it had been blown up, why was it not blackened and burnt? Why was it still red and why did we not see any pictures of the trains which they said were blown up?'

'Because it happened underground!'

'That's what you say,' said Yosra defiantly.

Conspiracy theories are the bread and butter of the Arab world and you hear them everywhere you go. I had heard stories so outlandish I wondered how anyone could take them seriously, even for a second. I had lost count of the number of times people told me that no Jews died in the twin towers on 11 September because they had been warned in advance not to turn up for work that morning. A group of lawyers I met in a coffee shop once even tried to convince me that it was the CIA killing American soldiers in Iraq.

No plot is too improbable, no ruse too far-fetched for many Arabs, who believe the key to understanding events is a cunning

Zionist–American stratagem to subvert the Muslim world community and restructure the Middle East. But no matter how often I heard them, these theories always jarred. When the television was still saturated with pictures of the devastation in London, they seemed doubly depressing.

'Look, I am not interested in politics,' said Roda, quickly peacemaking. 'Are you going to ask your mother if you can go away next weekend or am I going to have you kidnap you?'

Twelve

The next morning I met up with the British tabloid reporters still kicking their heels by the Hilton pool. Frustrated by the premature demise of the Magdi al-Nashar story, I found them irritably pacing up and down between the sunloungers like caged predators, chain-smoking cigarettes, applying layer after layer of sunblock, pondering where they might uncover some fresh meat to serve up to their bloodthirsty editors impatiently waiting their call back in London.

Since they had arrived in Cairo, the reporters and snappers from the *Daily Mail*, the *Mirror* and the *Sun* had struck up an uneasy alliance, agreeing to pool resources and information as long as they were all looking for the next story. Despite pleasantries at breakfast it was plain to see that it was a fragile coalition: each journalist would have slit his own throat for a chance to scoop the others on the next story. Over a buffet breakfast by the pool I helped out by scouring the morning's newspapers. Since no one had a better suggestion, we had decided to search the Egyptian press for a story to reproduce from a British perspective for the papers back home.

'What about this one?' said the man from the *Daily Mirror*, pointing lecherously at a picture of an attractive brunette in dark glasses. 'She's gorgeous. Who's she?'

'Let me see,' I replied, obediently checking the caption. 'She's an actress who tried to divorce her husband, but when he found out, he divorced her first.'

'Bloody useless,' interjected the *Sun* man, pulling on a cigarette. 'It needs balls. Can't you find something with terrorism in it? What about that one then?' he suggested, pointing to a double spread of text on the middle pages. 'What's that all about?'

'It's about the high prevalence of hepatitis in Egypt,' I read, scanning the page. 'As many of 20 per cent of all Egyptians suffer from hepatitis C, an untreatable, chronic debilitating liver disease. Most of them contracted it in the 1960s and '70s when the government immunisation campaign against bilharzia repeatedly reused needles, infecting huge swathes of the population.'

'Daft monkeys,' said the tattooed *Mail* snapper in a thick cockney accent, not bothering to hide his disappointment. 'If it had happened today they would have contracted HIV too.'

'Isn't there anything a bit juicier? Bombs, murders . . . some preacher making crazy statements?' the *Mirror* grimaced.

'Or anything with a British angle?' asked the *Mail*.

'I think the al-Nashar story is over,' I replied.

'Total bloody waste of time,' muttered the *Mirror*, extinguishing his cigarette in a Hilton croissant. 'I knew I should have gone to fucking Pakistan.'

'What about Kifaya and the democracy movement?' I suggested brightly. 'There's going to be a big demonstration today outside the Ministry of Justice downtown, next to Ramses Square.'

There was a moody silence.

'I don't think our readers really give a shit about demos,' eventually admitted the *Mail*.

'Unless you think someone's going to get killed?' the *Sun* added hopefully.

I shook my head glumly. 'I doubt it.' I had a feeling I was beginning to feel more at home around the card table with Roda and her friends than I did with other British journalists.

'OK, I've got a better idea,' I suggested, thinking laterally. 'I've heard that some Egyptians still don't believe the London bombings ever happened. What about if we got someone on record saying that?'

'That's not a bad idea,' reflected the *Daily Mirror* man. 'How about it?'

'Nah,' said the *Sun* dismissively. 'Forget it. No one's interested in that.'

A few hours later at home my mobile rang. It was the *Sun* reporter.

'I want to go after that thing you suggested at breakfast.'

'Which thing? I didn't think we had any good ideas.'

'Getting someone to deny the London bombings – it's a good idea for a story.'

'So why didn't you say so this morning?'

'Are you crazy? In front of the others?'

Bloodhound instincts had told him at once that finding someone important to deny the London bombings would make a tremendous tabloid spread. The question was, who was crazy enough to say so, while also familiar enough to the great *Sun* readership? Naturally, the tenacious *Sun* man had the perfect solution.

'Listen,' he told me furtively. 'I came to Cairo right after the 9/11 attacks to interview Muhammad Atta's father. You know Muhammad Atta, the lead hijacker on one of the 9/11 planes? Well, surprise, surprise, his dad is a complete wingnut too, and if we could just get him on record again, this time denying the London suicide bombings ever took place, it would make a great headline.'

It made perfect sense. It was exactly the kind of family horror saga the *Sun* did best. 'I think it's a great idea,' I said. 'How can I help?'

The reporter explained that he had left Atta senior his card and promised to stay in touch in case he needed any more hateful and small-minded comments from him in the future. There was only one problem.

'I've forgotten where his bloody house is. If you could help me find it again and we managed to get something good out of him, I would make it worth your while.'

Unlike Dr al-Nashar, who had defied the odds to crawl out of the slums and become a successful British-educated chemist, Muhammad Atta's upbringing was comfortably middle class. Before he became a terrorist he had been a student, ironically enough of urban planning. Students from his college in Hamburg remembered him as being diligent, respectful and polite, an apparently normal guy. His student thesis had been decidedly progressive: he had argued that contemporary urban planning in Aleppo should reflect the long-standing coexistence of Muslims and Christians in Syria.

In the wake of the attacks his fellow students recalled that Atta junior had not struck them as an extremist. He had supported the Islamist movement in Egypt and on several occasions had criticised the Egyptian government generally and the Mubarak family in particular. Most likely it was Muhammad Atta's life in Egypt rather than anger over issues like Palestine or the Gulf War that drove him to lead the worst terrorist attack in history. He would not have been alone in feeling this way. Egyptians have played a decisive role in al-Qaeda's strategy at every step, from its inception through the planning and execution of the 9/11 attacks and later in the Iraqi bloodbath.

Suicide bombers are often presented as exceptional in some way, insane killers without conscience or reason. Western observers have hypothesised that if he was not crazy, Muhammed Atta might at least have been some kind of sexual deviant, citing testimony by one of his female teachers who remembered him appearing uneasy during their lessons together. Arab governments feed into this stereotype, painting Islamic extremists as illiterate fanatics drawn from the working class. But the reality is quite different: the shocking truth is that they are actually quite ordinary people.

Suicide bombing is also not a religious phenomenon. Some of the most prolific suicide groups, like the Tamil Tigers and the Kurdish PKK, are secular. The urge to become a human bomb stems from how people are recruited and trained, not from religion.

A hundred years ago French sociologist Emile Durkheim said that there were two kinds of suicide – egotistical and altruistic. Egotistical suicide happens when an individual feels too disconnected from society; altruistic suicide happens when integration is too strong. Muhammad Atta and Muhammad Sidique Khan isolated themselves from their friends and loved ones through their fundamentalist habits; the jihadi network became their new family and they then resolved to kill themselves.

Islamists of all stripes tend to be educated, often to a postgraduate or doctorate level. Like Yosra's brother, typically they are drawn from the middle classes, since these are the people most frustrated with the political stagnation and endemic corruption of Arab societies. Without influential links to the regime or ruling family, they are the ones who suffer most under the status quo. Bin Laden himself is a bilingual expert in Islamic jurisprudence who holds three academic degrees – in civil engineering, business administration and economics. Ayman al-Zawahiri, his right-hand man, is a physician, author and poet, and speaks fluent French and English as well as Arabic. Ahmed Omar Sheikh, who decapitated the *Washington Post* journalist Daniel Pearl, was a championship chess player and studied at the London School of Economics.

Palestinians with twelve or more years of education are more likely to become suicide bombers than those who cannot read. Hezbollah fighters are more likely to have a secondary school education, and come from richer homes, than their contemporaries who do not fight. The leaders of Hamas all have undergraduate degrees and many have masters' qualifications too.

Islamists in Egypt are strongest within professional associations: they control the Bar, the hospitals and the guild of engineers. Extremism can be found anywhere you find clever doctors, dentists, architects or lawyers. Technological expertise and religious absolutism are perfectly compatible: in fact a technical education untempered by the arts but combined with religious dogma is a recipe for extremism. Despite apparently insurmountable contradictions regarding the nature and origin of the universe, you can even find fundamentalist Islamic scientists.

Seldom found are Islamists with a background in the liberal arts. Subjects like literature, music and drama lend themselves badly to extremist interpretation. Unfortunately, in much of the Arab world these subjects are viewed as a waste of time. With the Middle East driven by the mantras of progress and development, the liberal arts have come to be regarded as somehow extraneous.

The truth is that Muhammad Atta was an unexceptional man. Thousands of educated, frustrated Egyptians from the 'generation of peace' would do what he did if they had the chance.

Finding the Atta family house turned out to be easy. Since the 9/11 attacks many international journalists have visited the sandy-brown tower block in search of colourful comments from the notorious terrorist's father. The eighteen-storey block, a couple of miles from the great pyramids of Giza, has become something of a media landmark.

Muhammad Atta senior is a lawyer still registered in Cairo, now in his seventies. When we arrived, we found his tired-looking Mercedes parked outside next to the local supermarket. As we entered the block, a surly doorman stopped us beside the lift, demanding to know who we were and who we had come to see. When we explained we wanted to interview Atta, the doorman instructed us to call his apartment on the intercom before he would allow us up. Pressing the buzzer in the cool of the foyer, we waited to see if anyone was at home.

'Hello?' a disembodied voice crackled over the speaker.

'Mr Muhammad Atta? We would like to talk to you. May we come up?' I asked.

There was a long pause. The intercom hissed so we could tell he was listening.

'Who are you?' said the voice.

'I am a journalist from the *Sun* newspaper in Britain,' interrupted the reporter in English. 'My name is Brian. You met me in 2001. We had a cup of tea together. Maybe you remember me? Can we come up please?'

'I am not interested in talking to you. Go away.'

'Mr Muhammad, we just wanted to hear your thoughts on what happened in London. Can we come up please, just for a moment?'

'Go away,' said the voice. 'I am not interested in meeting you. You can all go to hell.' Then he hung up.

The next day we discovered that CNN had beaten us to the story anyway. They had visited the same block just a couple of hours before we turned up, but unlike us had managed to persuade Muhammad Atta senior to let them come upstairs for a proper interview. It turned out to be a good story. Not only did Atta passionately curse the West, he also expressed strong support for the London bombers, proclaiming the attacks the start of a fifty-year anti-Western onslaught. Speaking beside a prominently displayed photograph of his dead son, he told viewers he would do everything in his power to encourage more such attacks, adding that should CNN ever want another interview, next time he would charge them five thousand dollars for the privilege and give the money to terrorists. CNN told him they did not pay for interviews.

Big news stories happen all the time in Egypt and the press pool did not have to wait around long before the next headline exploded on their doorstep. The following weekend a series of suicide bombings rocked Sharm el-Sheikh, the town Egyptians call the 'city of peace', and suddenly the foreign journalists were back in business. Determined not to miss another scoop, the correspondents still in town after chasing Dr al-Nashar flew like hungry condors down to the Sinai coast, where the tourist season had come to an abrupt and bloody end. I arrived with the rest of the tabloids just in time to find the local dogs cleaning up the last of the human remains.

The Sinai coast – dubbed the Red Sea Riviera by the Egyptian tourist board – is an otherworldly slice of paradise and the site of the world's first mineral mines. Lying at the crossroads of Asia and Africa, the peninsula is triangular: the north coast faces the Mediterranean Sea; the east coast stretches the length of the Gulf of Aqaba from the Israeli–Jordanian border in the north to Sharm el-Sheikh in the south; and the west coast stretches the length of the Gulf of Suez, from Sharm el-Sheikh to the mouth of the Suez Canal in the north.

Sharm el-Sheikh is on a promontory overlooking the Strait of Tiran. Its strategic location has ensured its transformation in modern times from a sleepy fishing town into a major port, naval base and the administrative capital of the Sinai region. Breathtaking landscapes, year-round sunshine, long natural beaches, coral reefs and clear calm waters have turned the city into a foreign oasis, where European tourists frolic at lavish five-star resorts and dive at a plethora of world-class scuba sites. At dusk, schools of dolphins pass by within sight of the coast and the warm water teems with hundreds of species of brightly coloured exotic fish.

Upon our arrival in Sharm el-Sheikh, we were greeted with a scene more reminiscent of the lower reaches of hell than a heavenly paradise. Eighty-eight people had been killed in three massive explosions which had occurred in packed public areas in the heart of the resort town at around one o'clock in the morning when the streets were still thronged with families. Much of the downtown district had been totally devastated. Two of the bombs detonated in the central shopping area, ripping through shoppers and spraying debris and body parts over a wide area. Cars had been reduced to twisted metal, masonry blown off buildings, and windows and glass shopfronts shattered for hundreds of metres in all directions. A suicide driver ploughing into the front of the Ghazala Gardens Hotel delivered the most destructive bomb. The explosive-laden car detonated in the lobby causing part of the hotel to collapse in on itself. By the time we arrived the Egyptian police had completed their haphazard forensic work and journalists and locals were picking their way through the still-smoking ruins taking care not to tread in the sticky puddles of human gore.

The bombings were the worst terrorist attacks in Egypt since 1981. It was such a big story the foreign press ran with it for days. First came the interviews with the survivors together with pictures of bag-laden tourists queuing up to leave the shell-shocked resort. Then came the gruesome business of identifying the dead together with the sombre arrival of families looking for loved ones. Next came the search for the culprits, alleged to be Sinai Bedouin by the Egyptian authorities although al-Qaeda claimed responsibility. Then finally, a week later, came a review of the damage to Egypt's tourist business together with a survey of al-Qaeda influence in the region. The attacks had been a direct assault on one of the bulwarks of the Egyptian economy. Tourism is the nation's principal source of foreign exchange and valued at eight billion dollars a year.

For the Egyptian government the bombings were a terrifying reminder of the war they thought they had won when Gama'a al-Islamiyya laid down its weapons in 1998. The police reacted as they had done then, rounding up thousands of suspects in a massive security dragnet that stretched across the Sinai. Suspects were carted off in droves to the notorious Tora prison outside Cairo, where they were detained for weeks or months without charge amid widespread reports of torture. Quickly the authorities moved to allay the concerns of foreign investors and travel companies, assuring them that they had solved the case, that the perpetrators had been caught and that Egypt was now safe for business again. Without a trace of irony the Ministry of the Interior pointed out that unlike in the West there had never been a terrorist attack in Egypt that had not been solved, usually within a few weeks.

For me and many other local journalists the bombings meant a lucrative summer, working as fixer and translator for a variety of British and American newspapers. Bilingual journalists with their own car were earning £250 sterling a day, more than a consultant in an Egyptian public hospital gets in a month.

Thirteen

'What kind of job is it that makes you chase bombs?' Roda shrieked, opening the door of the apartment. 'Are you trying to drive me crazy already?'

Seeing Roda was the first thing I had wanted to do since I had got back from Sharm el-Sheikh, but from one snatched telephone call on the way from the airport I had already guessed that she was not happy with me rushing to the scene of terrorist attacks.

'He's a journalist. What do you expect?' Reem's voice called from inside the apartment.

'You'll drive me mad! I can tell!' Roda continued to yell, slapping her face with her palms.

'Shut up and sit down!' Reem said. 'Deal the cards.'

The little apartment was tidy and airy. The carpet had been freshly vacuumed; the washing-up done and put away. Baby chaos was conspicuously absent.

'Where are Noha and Nadia?' I asked.

'Noha is working nights and Nadia and Hind have moved back in with Muhammad,' Roda explained.

'But we are here!' chorused Amira and Reem, smiling on the sofa. 'So let's play *tarneeb*!'

I had never met Amira before, although I had heard all about her from the other girls and several times while visiting Roda's apartment I had tripped over her shoes. Like her sister, Amira was pretty, with wavy brown hair stretching far down her back, but she was slimmer than Reem and her body, undamaged by surgery, was a more natural shape. Svelte and cat-like, she wore heavy make-up and played cards sitting with her legs beneath her as if practising yoga.

Amira had an *urfi* marriage with a boy she had met at medical school. Her husband was training to be a doctor and still lived with his family elsewhere in Muwazafeen. He had resisted getting properly married because he had made a promise to his father that he would hold off until after he had finished his studies. He had also vowed to Amira that he would marry her properly as soon as he was done studying. Neither set of parents knew about the relationship.

Even though she lived just upstairs from Roda, Amira kept going-out clothes and shoes in a suitcase in a corner of Roda's bedroom so that in the event of a rendezvous with her husband she could excuse herself from home, explaining that she was just popping downstairs to see Roda for a few hours. Stepping out of the apartment in her robe she could change downstairs before slipping out into the night. Amira was so afraid that her mother would find out what she had done she had given Roda her copy of the marriage contract for safekeeping.

By day Amira worked as a brand manager for a well-known American designer label in Cairo's most palatial shopping mall in Heliopolis. The mall was called Emerald Square and the licence to distribute the brand had only recently been issued, so she had not been in the position more than a few days and was still ecstatic. Getting any job in Egypt is a cause for excitement, but for a girl to secure such a well-paid position dealing with an American luxury brand was a terrific success, especially if she had managed to get there without being sexually exploited in the process. Her parents, blissfully ignorant of their daughter's *urfi* marriage, naively hoped it might improve her chances of finding the right husband.

Amira had first heard of the vacancy at the new store through a friend in the government department responsible for issuing import and distribution licences. Like most jobs worth having it had not been advertised; only posts with multinational companies operating according to international standards ever are. Demand so far outstrips the number of vacancies, if a job is advertised it is not uncommon for several thousand young people to send in their CV in the space of a week.

Each year more than seven hundred thousand new graduates chase an estimated two hundred thousand jobs. Even students from Cairo's most prestigious colleges struggle to find employment when they graduate. The state is the largest non-agricultural employer in the country, providing about 40 per cent of job opportunities, and the more educated you are, the more likely you are to work for the government. The best most young Egyptians can hope for is a position in an overstaffed and unproductive public sector company, Egypt's disguised welfare system. The state-owned sugar, textile and steel businesses are some of the biggest employers. So heavily protected are these industries from market forces it is quite normal to find three or four people doing one man's job. It is a system that destroys ambition, in which pay and working conditions are often appalling, but the presumed social cost of doing away with it is too high for anyone in power to contemplate.

Many young unemployed choose to go into further education in an attempt to break the cycle of poverty. This is such a familiar story in Cairo that a young person trying to juggle study and work commitments has become the standard plot for Egyptian TV soap operas. Young Egyptians care more about getting a job than almost anything else, certainly more than they care about democratic reform or the Palestinians. For the lucky few who do manage to get jobs, pay is still torturously low: a teacher or a policeman for example can earn a salary of less than £70 sterling a month.

*

'This is my bad-hair month,' said Amira.

'You say that every month,' said Roda, shuffling the cards.

Reem lit a cigarette and ran her fingers through her sister's long brown hair. 'You should wear a headscarf. It gives your hair more lustre,' she said.

'Fuck that,' said Amira. 'Why don't you wear one?'

'One heart,' I said, organising my cards.

'Does it say in the Koran women should wear veils?' I asked Amira.

'Nope,' she replied, 'at least not unequivocally.'

'The word "hijab" is mentioned seven times in the Koran, but never in the context of a headscarf,' explained Reem, clearly accustomed to this debate. 'And the word "hijab", the modern word for veil, can also mean a number of other things, including a curtain, divider or screen.'

'So if the Koran does not say it is required, why do women wear the hijab?' I asked, perplexed.

'There are plenty of instructions in the texts for both women and men to dress modestly,' explained Roda. 'The Prophet's wives wore veils and many people think it is best to do as they did.'

'But the Prophet's wives were a special case to whom special rules applied,' interrupted Amira assertively. 'They were also forbidden to marry after the death of their husband, for example, and besides no one said they should be imitated.'

'Muslims should think and judge for themselves.' Reem tapped on the table as she spoke. 'To insist that women are always veiled is an embroidery of God's rules.'

This sounded like a sensible compromise to me. As a non-Muslim, I had always found it hard to understand why people should imagine that God took such a keen interest in women's headgear. It seemed strange that God, in His wisdom, did not let women decide for themselves what was appropriate to wear.

Although no one said it, we all knew that there are many Muslims prepared to die and kill to ensure that women remain covered up. In 2002 riots in Nigeria sparked by the Miss World pageant resulted in around two hundred dead. In the same year fifteen people died when religious police in Mecca refused to allow schoolgirls to leave a burning building because they were improperly dressed.

As I counted out the cards, I noticed the television was quietly playing an old Egyptian movie from the 1960s. It was bawdy, like the British Carry On series from the same era with the same kind of low-budget look and terrible sexual puns. The women had those big fleshy tits and large arses that made the men's eyes roll around and which seemed to disappear from the screen for ever at the end of that decade. It was a reminder that the Egyptian movie business had once churned out innumerable raunchy comedies each year. Egypt, like Europe and America, had experienced a sexual revolution in the '60s, but while the West had moved forward (in a manner of speaking) into the soft-porn era of the 1970s, Egypt's revolution had stalled then petered out. The local stars of that generation had either long since died or reinvented themselves as social conservatives, and many actresses from that era are now veiled. Only a select few, like ageing sex symbol Yosra and the indomitable comedian Adel Imam, continue to fill the screen with boozing, double entendres and slapstick sexual humour.

'One diamond,' announced Amira confidently, starting the bidding.

'Two hearts,' snapped Roda, catching my eye with a smile. By now we had played enough cards together to give any of her friends a run for their money.

'I'll play on that,' said Reem, laying a card on the table. 'Hit it.'

We played cards without a break into the small hours. The game ebbed and flowed; tea was served several times; at midnight Reem braided her sister's hair; several text messages were sent and received and countless cigarettes were smoked. At ten minutes past three a key turning in the lock of the apartment door interrupted our game. Alarmed, we sat bolt upright, wide-eyed, as the door swung open, wondering who it could be. Nadia, carrying a large soft bag over one shoulder and her sleeping daughter in her arms, entered the room. The girls' faces sank.

'What are you doing here?' asked Roda, bracing herself.

'Good evening everyone,' replied Nadia wearily.

'Where have you come from? Why are you here?' Roda repeated. Nadia unshouldered her heavy bag onto the apartment floor with a sigh, saying nothing.

'Are you OK?' Reem added.

'Thanks be to God,' muttered Nadia, flumping down on the sofa. She kept her eyes trained on the floor and held her hand up to shield her face, saying nothing more. In the light from the table lamp we could see that the thick black kohl around her eyes was smeared, her cheek was red and swollen and there were bright red fingermarks on her neck.

'He beat you up again!' exclaimed Roda angrily.

'The bastard! He's lower than a razor blade lying on the ground,' spat Reem. 'What are you going to do now?'

'I don't know,' replied Nadia, her voice strained.

'Why don't you ask him to divorce you?'

'Ah, I don't know. Everyone has problems. What would I do for the baby?'

There was an uneasy silence. All the girls knew that if Nadia wanted a divorce she was faced with an unappetising choice. Under Egyptian law there are two types of divorce a woman can seek. Either she can ask for one based on her husband's faults, which if successful means she stands to win full financial rights. Or under a law introduced in 2000 a woman can divorce unilaterally. To prove her husband is at fault, a woman must produce substantial evidence of harm, evidence that usually needs to be supported by eyewitness testimony. The unilateral method is faster but incurs a financial penalty that lasts for life. If she successfully divorces this way, she must return her dowry and surrender all financial claims including alimony.

Either way she needs to go to court, to face a complicated and bureaucratic legal battle in an environment overwhelmingly officiated by men. There are only about a dozen female judges in Egypt. A man can divorce his wife simply by saying 'I divorce you' three times in front of two Muslim male witnesses without so much as setting foot in court and without any legal need for a mediator. He does not even need a reason. As a result, a divorce happens every six minutes in Egypt. Once a woman is divorced, if she has no children or if her children are above the legal age of custody she can also be expelled from her home – after she has spent three months in her husband's house, a mandatory requirement in both sharia and Egyptian law, to ensure that she is not pregnant.

As in most north African countries, Egyptian men are entitled to total obedience and complete power in the home as long as they provide financial support for their wives. If a woman leaves her husband before they are officially divorced, he can file charges against her under the Disobedience Laws, which remove her right to financial support. Such a legal system condemns many women to a lifetime of abuse.

'Whether you go to court or not, you can't let him treat you like this,' said Reem sympathetically.

'What about the baby? What happens if you do get divorced?' I asked.

'The courts awards custody of the baby to the mother, unless she remarries in which case custody reverts to the father,' explained Roda.

'Unless the court has labelled him a bad parent,' Nadia added portentously. 'For example if he has been to jail.'

'That's what you should do,' urged Roda. 'You should land that bullying Saidi★ bastard in jail. That would teach him a lesson.'

★ 'Saidi' is the name given to people who come from Upper Egypt.

'I don't know,' sighed Nadia sadly, and as she sighed our hopes deflated too. 'No relationship is perfect. I was complaining about him at work to this nurse and you know what she said? "Don't tell me about your problems. My husband never makes love to me any more, so all I do for sex is masturbate from my anus"!'

The girls all shrieked with laughter. 'And she is totally veiled!' added Nadia.

'Why her anus?' Reem asked.

'I think she only ever had anal sex so that is what she is used to.'

'She must be from the Gulf,' said Roda.

'Why would she be from the Gulf?' I asked.

'Because women in the Gulf often only have anal sex because they don't want to lose their virginity.'

'A girl I work with – she's got an elastic hymen,' interjected Reem.

'Wow! The lucky bitch,' chorused the girls in astonishment. 'But how can that be?' they asked each other wide-eyed.

'It just does not break,' explained Reem, 'no matter how many times she does it.'

'Wow!' everyone repeated, awestruck.

'That's amazing!' said Amira.

'I did not know such a beautiful thing could exist in this world,' said Roda mistily.

It is remarkable that something so biologically useless has come to carry such a burden of bridal purity and family honour, but the reverential way the girls spoke about this membrane, the exact anatomical function of which scientists still disagree over, underlined just how important it is for women in Egypt to bleed heavily on their wedding night. If they do not, divorce or worse may ensue.

It is difficult to know how many murders in the name of honour are committed each year, but an Egyptian report in the mid-1990s ascribed 52 out of a total of 819 murders to honour killings. Almost certainly this figure was a gross underestimate. What is clear is that having an intact hymen reduces a woman's chances of being murdered on her wedding night. Over the years women have come up with any number of ruses to avoid this potentially terminal threat to their honeymoon. From applying animal blood in the bathroom to lacerating their genitals with razor blades, there are many tried and tested country remedies for this problem, none of them very pleasant or reliable.

Of course just like anywhere else in the world premarital sex happens all the time and plenty of people are no longer virgins by the time they get married. But it is a severe case of double standards: if a boy loses his virginity it is something smugly to brag to his friends about the next morning; for girls it is an unforgivable transgression that can cost her everything.

When an unmarried Egyptian girl loses her virginity, no matter what her lover might tell her the next morning a black cloud of despair descends that lasts for months or even years. It is a secret she can share with no one, not even her sisters or mother. She can only hope they will guess to save her the shame of having to admit to what she has done. Typically she convinces herself that she has committed a dreadful sin and that her life is now damaged beyond repair. Her best hope for the future is a miserable life as a spinster or a quick death to end her suffering, since this is what she now deserves. Depression sets in and she withdraws from family life, feeling guilty at the dishonour she has brought upon her loved ones. Quite likely the only thing that prevents her from drinking poison to end it all is the fear of an afterlife filled with eternal pain.

Despair may be allayed by a surreptitious visit to a doctor with a reputation for abortions and hymenorraphies. After examination an unscrupulous doctor may inform her that her hymen is still partially intact and that some part of her virginity can be salvaged. All she needs is one operation. A hymenorraphy, hymen replacement surgery or revirgination as it is euphemistically known in America, is a simple surgical procedure taking no more than half an hour. The doctor sews the ruptured hymen back together, using skin from the vaginal wall if necessary, with the patient under general anaesthetic. It is an absurd practice, not least because checking hymens for virginity or looking for blood on the wedding night are flawed procedures anyway. Fewer than 50 per cent of women bleed the first time they have sex and the hymen's condition is not a reliable indicator of whether a woman past puberty has lost her virginity.

Until 2007 hymen replacement surgery could not be performed legally in Cairo, although it has long been widely available on the black market for the equivalent of about £300 sterling. A more popular bargain hymenorraphy is also available, costing around £50, but the hymen only stays intact for three days so the operation needs to be performed shortly before the wedding night. If bleeding heavily is an absolute must, deluxe variations are also available. A gelatine capsule filled with a blood-like substance can be placed inside the vagina before the doctor sews the hymen up. On the wedding night the capsule bursts messily, the bloodied sheet is ceremoniously paraded around for all to see and the revirgin breathes a great sigh of relief, silently thanking her surgeon for saving her life. In the modern world, no matter where you come from often it's a surgeon that is a girl's best friend.

Which means of course that in modern Egypt when a woman bleeds on her wedding night the groom is left wondering whether she has just had a hymenorraphy. Ironically, the surgeons who perform the operation, whether for cash or out of some sense of solidarity with the woman's plight, are doing more to perpetuate the significance of the wedding night sheet than anyone else. Expectations are raised which girls who cannot afford expensive operations cannot meet and Egyptian society remains as fixated on the cult of the wedding night sheet as ever.

Fourteen

The weekend after the Sharm el-Sheikh bombings, Roda, Dwayne, Yosra and I took a trip to the north coast, where a friend of Roda was hosting her party. Her parents' beach house had been generously stocked with crates of Egyptian beer and wine courtesy of a relative working at the state alcohol company. Dozens of people were invited; a hundred were expected. We travelled up in Roda's car.

Because Yosra's brother Hassan had refused Yosra permission to stay out overnight, the girls concocted an elaborate cover story about a wedding at their friend Jumanah's house. Jumanah's cousin, they told him, was marrying a Lebanese boy and the wedding was expected to go on late into the night. With a wedding as an excuse, the girls calculated that Yosra would be allowed to stay out until at least four o'clock, giving them enough time to make it safely back to Cairo. The drive back from the north coast took about three hours if there was not much traffic. Jumanah was fully briefed on the plan so that in the event of questioning their stories would match.

Every weekend during the baking summer months thousands of Egyptians head north out of Cairo for the coast near Alexandria, Egypt's second city and largest seaport. From June until October the public beaches beside the famous Corniche are spotted with thousands of shirtless men and heavily veiled women carrying parasols. Crowds of Egyptians stand in the white-tipped waves beneath circling seagulls, eating ice cream or simply savouring the breeze. The sea air is the perfect antidote to the toxic cloud that hangs over Cairo all summer long.

Beyond the Corniche, Alexandria itself is crumbling and given its glorious history a bit of a disappointment. Earthquake subsidence dumped the ancient city's royal and civic quarters beneath the harbour long ago and behind the modern-day library and the ribbon of whitewashed period houses facing the seafront the streets are strewn with rubbish and rubble. Contrary to what one normally expects in a beach town, deep religious conservatism prevails: many of the men are bearded and almost all the women wear veils of one kind or another. Unlike in Cairo, the Wahhabi-style full-face veil, or niqab, complete with black gloves and a burka, is common. In recent years religious sentiment has run so high tension between Copts and Muslims has bubbled over into violence.

Since Alexandria is so crowded during the holiday season with tourists from across the Arab world, well-to-do Cairenes rarely hang around in town for longer than it takes to fill the car up or have a meal and they certainly never deign to visit one of the crowded public beaches. Muwazafeen's moneyed classes head straight out to one of the many tourist villages strung out along the coast. These 'luxury hospitality areas', as the Egyptian tourist authority has branded them, are the heart of the domestic tourism business. Advertising blurbs refer to the 'Egyptian St Tropez', but in truth most of the concrete houses are cheap and characterless. Thousands of identical apartment blocks and holiday homes, for sale and for rent, become cheaper and grottier the further back from the sea and into the desert you go.

Next to the war graves of El Alamein, inside gated, walled communities that stretch miles along the coast, rich Egyptians make like they are in Europe, wearing bikinis and chugging beer. Beautiful greenery and fake lakes, malls, cinemas and the odd golf course characterise this part of Egypt. But such is the demand, at the height of summer even the most exclusive tourist villages are stuffed with Cairenes, the swimming pools clogged with families and screaming kids. Nothing deters the hordes of weekenders from Cairo, who take solace in the thought that at least they are jammed up against people of their own class.

Roda's friend's party was in a whitewashed seafront villa in an exclusive gated community, at one of the chicest tourist villages on the coast. The house next door was owned by a relative of Suzanne Mubarak and just a short swim away lay a sandy peninsula covered with large villas where various government ministers maintained exclusive summer hideaways. From the living room window along the Mediterranean coast the twinkling lights of Alexandria were just visible in the distance. Further away, out of sight, the shore curved north around the Nile Delta, past the Suez Canal and along the Sinai Peninsula until finally it curled around to the Gaza Strip.

By half past eleven the party was filling up with the beautiful people of Muwazafeen. The French windows leading out from the living room had been thrown open, the music was pounding and the revellers spilled out into the garden and onto the beach beyond. Beneath stars like pinpricks in the cloudless night sky, Roda, Yosra and I danced, watching the boys drinking beer by a bonfire on the beach watching the girls belly dancing barefoot on the sand.

Disaster struck at midnight when Yosra's phone rang: it was Hassan insisting that she come home at once. Her father Suleiman had fallen sick and she was required at once to look after him. When Yosra refused, explaining that she was at a wedding, Hassan grew angry and instructed her fiercely not to move as he would be coming at once in his car to Jumanah's house to collect her. As he pressed her for directions, Yosra panicked, made some electronic static noises as if the connection had been lost, then hung up.

Around us people were still laughing and dancing, but as Yosra flipped the phone closed we could see that she was terrified. 'I have to go right now,' she said urgently above the music. 'Right now.'

'What are we going to do?' Roda replied. 'It will take at least three hours to make it back to Cairo from here.'

'I am dead,' said Yosra in a low voice. It was all she could muster; her face was drained of blood. 'When he finds out I am at a party with boys, he is going to kill me.'

She looked like she was dead already her face had turned so pale.

'We had better go,' I said. 'Find Dwayne and tell him we are leaving.'

As we were scouring the party for Dwayne, Roda's phone started ringing. This time it was a call from Yosra's house phone.

'What shall I do? Shall I answer it?' Roda asked fretfully.

'No, just leave it,' replied Yosra, struggling to regain her composure. 'We can tell him the music at the wedding was too loud and we didn't hear the phone.'

We found Dwayne sitting on the stairs, rolling joints and listening to Bob Marley with a group of guys. 'Dwayne, we have to go right now,' commanded Roda. 'Yosra is in trouble.'

'Take a hit on the zagazig, man, and say hello to the kingdom of heaven,' said Dwayne, exhaling a huge cloud of smoke. 'This shit turns your brain ceramic.'

'Dwayne, you cretin, we have to leave right now. Yosra is in trouble.'

'Don't be such a downer, man, we only just got here,' replied Dwayne, proffering the joint.

'Right now,' repeated Roda angrily.

Dragging the reluctant Dwayne from the stairs, we bundled out of the villa and into the street, where a cool sea breeze was gently rustling the slender palms along the beachfront. As we tried to remember where we had parked the car among the identical villas and chalets of the resort complex, there was no let-up in Dwayne's moaning.

'People are still arriving,' he kept repeating. 'We only just got here.'

'Look, it's a straight choice,' snapped Roda. 'Either get in the car and come back with us or find another lift.' The car finally located, grudgingly he got in.

Throughout the journey back, the girls' phones never stopped ringing. Calls came alternately from Yosra's house phone and Hassan's mobile. Deciding it would be better not to answer again, barely a word was spoken as we drove fast through the night, the desert air whistling through the open windows. In the passenger seat Yosra was quietly and fearfully reciting what she could remember from the Koran, her face illuminated by the light of the dashboard clock. In the back, next to me, Dwayne snored noisily.

Except for the occasional long-distance lorry wobbling along with no lights, the road at that time is almost empty. The police speed radar on the Alexandria desert road does not operate at night, so Roda kept her foot on the floor until two and a half hours later, when the car drew up under the sodium lights at the final toll station on the outskirts of the capital. Within the city the traffic thickened into its usual dull viscosity. Although it was late it was the weekend and the streets were still humming, so rather than waste more time travelling across town to drop off Dwayne at his house in Heliopolis and me at Elephant and Castle, Roda turned us out at a convenient junction with instructions to take cabs home. What happened next, I heard from Roda later that night, when she called to give me a blow-by-blow account.

The two girls circled back round into the heart of Muwazafeen, cutting through the late-night traffic as fast as they could, making for Yosra's home. As the time approached for Yosra to face her family, her face grew ever more ashen and her prayers steadily louder. All the while they drove, their phones never stopped ringing.

By the time the car finally drew up at the front door of Yosra's block in Muwazafeen it was half past three in the morning and Roda had fifty-five missed calls on her phone; Yosra had sixty. Although already inexcusably late, the pair sat quaking in Roda's car while Yosra tried to summon up the courage to face her brother and the inevitable storm.

'I can't face it. I don't want to go inside,' said Yosra.

'You have to. Where else are you going to go?' replied Roda.

'He is going to beat me. I know it. I would rather never go home again.'

'Don't be silly. He's not going to beat you if you talk to him. I'm sure you can make him understand. Haven't you done worse before?'

'Not when father is sick. God forbid anything serious has happened to him.'

From the car window the block glowed in the moonlight. Stray dogs were sniffing around a pile of trash on the verge by the gate beneath a rubber tree. All the lights in the ground-floor apartment were on.

'You had better go,' said Roda.

'Don't leave me,' Yosra suddenly pleaded, plainly terrified. 'Stay the night. He is less likely to do something if you are there.'

There was nothing Roda wanted less at that moment than to walk into a row with Yosra's policeman brother, but at the same time she was unwilling to abandon her friend. It would certainly be easier for Yosra if she came too. Without her there was no telling what Hassan might do.

'OK, I'll do it,' said Roda. 'But just remember, we were at a wedding. The music was loud. We did not hear the phone. Got it?'

'Got it!' said Yosra with grim determination.

'I'll talk to him. He'll understand,' said Roda, steeling herself as she swung open the car door.

'Thank you, thank you,' said Yosra, checking her face one last time in the rear-view mirror before she opened her own door. 'I owe you for this,' she added.

Padding up the garden path, Yosra slowly turned the key in the lock. For one magic second it seemed as if everyone inside had gone to sleep and the row would be postponed until the next morning but then heavy footsteps sounded and the door was yanked open to reveal Hassan, still wearing his policeman's trousers and a vest, his eyes straining in a face flushed with anger.

'Where have you been? What time do you call this?' he bawled.

'We were at a wedding,' said Yosra.

'Don't lie to me,' he snapped back through gritted teeth, veins protruding from his neck like cables. 'Why aren't you wearing wedding clothes then? Tell me where you were!'

'The music was loud, we did not hear the phone . . .' protested Yosra.

'What is *she* doing here?' he raged as Roda stepped through the door.

'Sleeping over?' ventured Roda meekly.

'I was not talking to you!' he yelled, spittle stringing between his lips. Turning back to Yosra he shouted, 'You . . . you . . . I have not even started with you yet.' Grabbing her by the arm, he began to pull her across the living room.

Stumbling over the edge of the sofa, Yosra yelped in pain as she knocked her shin. 'Let me go! Let me go!'

'Don't hurt her!' yelled Roda. 'It's my fault! Let her go!'

'Over my dead body you come home after midnight! You think I want people saying that my sister stays out late? You think I want that? That I am proud of you? You think I like that?'

'Don't hurt her!' shouted Roda, throwing herself on Yosra as Hassan dragged her towards the door. 'Leave her alone! We were at a wedding! It's not her fault! It's mine.'

'Shut up! I don't want to talk to you,' Hassan yelled back, twisting Roda's grip from his sister's arm. 'I can't stand hearing any more of your lies.' Pushing Roda violently back onto the sofa, Hassan wrenched Yosra through the door by her wrist and slammed it shut behind him.

'Your father is in hospital and this is how you behave? I am going to teach you a lesson you will never forget!' his voice continued to boom from the other side.

'God have mercy on me!' sobbed Yosra.

'If you behave like a bitch you get treated like a bitch!'

'Don't hurt her!' cried Roda as she collapsed breathless and sobbing on the sofa. But no one was listening.

Fifteen

Yosra's father Suleiman spent two nights in intensive care, desperately thin and weak. Years of cigarettes and *shishas* had taken a terrible toll on his body. He had endured diabetes, emphysema, a heart attack and lung cancer. More than once he had pulled back from the brink of death and for over a year he had been permanently confined to bed. His voice had become almost inaudible, his skin was like paper and his hair had all long since fallen out. Lying in hospital with tubes sticking out of him at all angles, he was a pitiful sight.

His spirit however remained remarkably undaunted and whenever he was awake he kept a sharp eye on his family to make sure they never usurped his authority or otherwise tried to take advantage of his condition. His wife kept a constant vigil by his bedside, holding his skeletal arm in one hand and a tissue in the other which every now and then she touched against her nose with a sniff. She was determined not to leave him to the nurses.

Being his only daughter, it was expected that Yosra should take responsibility for her father. Since her disgrace she had been grounded indefinitely and so had no choice but to resign herself to nursing her father in hospital, working at the office and staying at home. Yosra telephoned Roda to let her know that she would not be available to play cards for a while.

The night Yosra arrived back from the north coast Salma had tried to intercede on her daughter's behalf, but such had been Hassan's fury there was no deflecting him. This was not the first occasion on which Salma had intervened to protect her daughter. When Yosra was nine, Salma had whisked her away to Cairo to stop her paternal relatives in the village where she was born from circumcising her. The fashion had changed since Salma was a girl; clitorectomies were now usual only in rural Egypt. Of course Hassan had still been circumcised. He was six and on holiday when his father told him that the village barber wanted to take a photograph of his penis. Proud that someone should take an interest, he willingly made his way to the barber shop at the centre of the village. Yosra went with him and stood outside, and the screaming she heard that day was etched in her memory. When it was over, the family threw a party to celebrate, but Hassan never forgave his father Suleiman for lying to him.

Salma had been circumcised too, when she was nine, in the days when female circumcision was still universal in Upper Egypt. She had looked forward to the operation for months because the other girls in her village, who had already been cut, used to tease her about not yet being a woman.

'All the girls have had it done except me,' Salma would say, pestering her mother. 'What about me? When am I going to be a woman? I want to grow up.'

'You are becoming an attractive girl,' her mother would say. 'Soon you will have the operation and then you will be a woman too. But for now be patient.'

Eventually the day came when one of the women in the village removed her clitoris with a razor blade. She scraped it out like she was hollowing out an aubergine. There was no anaesthetic and Salma bled for days afterwards. Later in life it never appeared to particularly bother Salma that she had been circumcised. She just accepted it because she knew no different and because all her friends had been.

Since she was eighteen, when she got married, Salma had lived in Cairo, but she still remained in touch with her relatives back in the village where she had grown up, and would try to visit them at least once a year. Salma had recently made up her mind that the time had come to seek professional advice on the parlous state of her daughter's love life. The inspiration for this decision had come from a relative back in the village whose advice Salma would often seek, an elderly aunt to whom she had been close all her life. Her aunt, a source of wisdom on matters of this nature, had suggested that Yosra should pay a visit to a certain mystic healer who had acquired an enviable reputation on the Muwazafeen social circuit for treating women of a certain class for a variety of emotional and psychological ailments.

Several of Salma's friends had already seen the healer and the word on the Muwazafeen grapevine was that he was not just a highly skilled practitioner of white magic but also very handsome and single. Operating under the sobriquet 'the Sheikh', the mystic ran a kind of spiritual welfare clinic out of a dilapidated 1970s bungalow in Haram, just a short drive from the Pyramids. Salma arranged an appointment for Yosra with the Sheikh one evening.

Egyptians believe that the jinn are all around us, even if we cannot see them. An invisible race of spirit-like creatures, they are held accountable for all manner of maladies ranging from schizophrenia to infertility. They have a long history in Middle Eastern mythology and art. Their exact attributes are unclear: some say they can shape-change or inhabit the bodies of animals. Others believe they grow old and have families like human beings.

The Sheikh was a devout Muslim well versed in Islamic lore, but his clients did not come seeking religious counsel. They were drawn instead by his reputation for communicating with the world of the jinn, a gift bestowed by God which allowed him to see things forbidden to other men. Since jinn feature prominently in the Koran, the Sheikh and his clients saw no contradiction between his activities and his faith. He took no money for his work, believing it to be his sacred duty to help people in need.

'I guess this must be it,' said Salma a little doubtfully, squeaking open the wrought-iron gate and walking apprehensively up the concrete path to the front door, with Yosra close behind.

'You won't regret this,' she said reassuringly to her daughter. 'He has a wonderful reputation.' Taking a deep breath she knocked firmly.

The Sheikh swept the door open in a kaftan and a cloud of incense. Slim and handsome with a white beard and intelligent languid eyes, he greeted them in a booming voice. 'I have been expecting you, Yosra!' he said dramatically. 'Peace be upon you both and enter!'

'Peace be upon you too,' replied Salma. Yosra and her mother exchanged glances, taking care to step over the threshold with the right foot, as is the custom when entering holy places.

In the dimly lit entrance hall, modern Islamic art hung on the walls and a thick rug covered the floor. A polished brass chandelier decorated with inscriptions from the Koran hung from the ceiling. 'You can tell this is the house of a real mystic!' whispered Salma excitedly, running her fingers through a wind chime.

The Sheikh led Yosra and Salma through an interconnecting door at the back of his bungalow into a converted garage, which was where, he explained as he strode ahead, he conducted all his spiritual operations. Inside the garage several drizzling candles burnt on side tables and on a large crate in the corner of the room covered in a stained white sheet. The Sheikh closed the door behind them and drew the curtains tight to blot out the bright sunshine outside. Then, directing Yosra to a wooden stool in the centre of the room, he began preparing himself. Salma stood in awed silence by the door, clutching her handbag to her breast and wondering what mystic powers were about to be unleashed.

Prowling around Yosra's stool in the centre of the room, the Sheikh then began making strange shapes in the air with his hands.

'Speak to me, my daughter,' he commanded in a deep portentous voice, 'and tell me what has brought you here!'

'It's my love life,' said Yosra. 'My mother suggested I come and see you because I don't seem to have much luck with men. I have been trying to get married but . . . it hasn't worked out.'

Taking hold of her chin between finger and thumb, the Sheikh peered deep into Yosra's slate-grey eyes. 'Now close your eyes,' he said, running his long bony fingers across her face. 'And open them!'

'I . . . I can't,' stammered Yosra. 'My eyelids feel too heavy.'

'Aha!' snapped the Sheikh knowingly, continuing to circle. His tall robed silhouette threw strange shadows around the garage. 'Do you have trouble sleeping, my child?' he asked. 'Do you have bad dreams?'

Now, Yosra often had strange dreams passed out on the sofa in her office. She took so many benzos she had even brought her own pillow to work. The only time she could be said to be even half conscious was on the road between the office and her house, and even then she was often not sure whether she was awake or dreaming.

'My sleep is very disturbed,' said Yosra, 'and I often have bad dreams.'

'What are your dreams about?' asked the Sheikh.

'I can't tell you – I am too ashamed,' replied Yosra shyly.

'There is a jinn who is in love with you,' boomed the mystic. 'A small black goblin who follows you everywhere.'

'No!' gasped Yosra and Salma at once.

'He is invisible to people who cannot see jinn,' continued the Sheikh. 'He fell in love with you seven years ago and ever since he has prevented other men from falling in love with you because he is so jealous.'

'Protect us from the jinn, o Lord!' cried Salma, breaking into a stream of prayer, wide-eyed at this terrifying diagnosis.

'The nightmares you have been having are caused by the jinn having sexual intercourse with you in your sleep.'

'That's right!' exclaimed Yosra. 'Sometimes I dream about sex and it feels like there is a man with me when I sleep!'

'Hovering above you?' asked the Sheikh, before announcing without waiting for a reply, 'That is him! That is the jinn who has been making love to you!'

Suleiman was discharged from the hospital a few days later. He was still bedridden but preferred to convalesce at home rather than take his chances with the nurses. For the next few weeks he was going to need round-the-clock help: he could not feed himself or even go to the bathroom alone. For several days he could not even summon enough energy to lift the telephone receiver by his bed to eavesdrop on his daughter's telephone conversations. Dutifully Yosra tried to cut her days at work short to spend as much time as possible caring for her father. She showered and washed him, changed his sheets and made his meals. Her brother, when he was not working, meticulously monitored her detention.

When Salma told Suleiman what had happened when Yosra visited the Sheikh, he was alarmed but relieved to know that at least there had been a proper diagnosis and that the problem was now in the hands of an expert. He instructed his wife to make another appointment at the garage clinic as soon as she could so that the process of liberating Yosra from the amorous jinn might start at once. The next meeting was scheduled, on the Sheikh's advice, for the day after Yosra finished her next period.

When Hassan heard the news about the Sheikh's diagnosis his face became ashen. 'Yosra, I must tell you that I am seriously concerned that your virginity might have been compromised,' he told her gravely. 'It's possible the jinn could have opened you up, and if he has it's possible you might no longer be a virgin.'

'What can I do?' replied Yosra fearfully.

'Check your underwear for blood spots,' he advised, 'read a chapter of the Koran and every time you come across the word "strength", read ten supplementary *Fatihas*. Is that understood? It's better that we know now what has happened.'

The only perk of her restricted circumstances – and for Yosra it was a very substantial perk – was that her nursing duties included taking her father's handwritten prescription to the pharmacist to collect the powerful palliative drugs he needed. Watching the pharmacist count the analgesic pills into little brown plastic bottles, Yosra told herself if she was going to be made to act as a nurse, the least she deserved was to help herself to some of the drugs, if only to make the time pass a little quicker.

The day after Suleiman arrived back home, a doctor called from the hospital with his test results. Yosra took the call and, as expected, the news was not good. His lung cancer was advanced, his diabetes acute. The cardiologist said he could have another heart attack at any time.

'And finally, Miss,' said the doctor, 'he has a lot of nodules on a very fatty liver.'

'What does that mean?' asked Yosra.

The doctor paused for a second, before continuing in a more serious tone. 'Miss, may I ask you a question? Respectfully, I mean.'

'Yes . . . of course,' stammered Yosra, knowing the news could hardly be worse than what she had already heard.

'How much alcohol does your father drink?'

'He doesn't drink,' said Yosra. 'He's a Muslim.'

'Well, his liver is showing clear signs of alcoholic cirrhosis. From the test results I would say he was a drinker. And I mean a heavy drinker.'

Yosra paused as she took this in. She thought of her father, just back from hospital, lying in the next room. She could hear the television through the wall and smell the odour of his lingering sickness. Could he really have been drinking all this time, she wondered. Did her mother know? Did anyone know?

'Thank you, Doctor,' she said colourlessly, betraying no emotion. 'Is there anything else?'

Emerald Square is Cairo's newest and swankiest shopping mall. Spread over a whole city block it features a plethora of international brands such as Mango, Virgin, Guess and Starbucks. There is office space, a food court, a medical centre and three adjacent international hotels, all linked by mirrored escalators and decorated in a cartoonish mishmash, part Old Kingdom temple and part medieval mosque. Within two years of its opening in 2004 Emerald Square had received more than twenty-seven million visitors.

Sadly, although Emerald Square is big news locally, turnover and profits for the companies that invest there are not so good. By international standards Cairo remains a retail backwater and every time a new mall opens up an old one closes down, a gloomy reflection of the state of the economy. Only a tiny fraction of Egypt's overwhelmingly youthful population have enough money to shop there.

The owner of the store in Emerald Square where Roda's friend and upstairs neighbour Amira was working was called Ahmed Mustafa. Amira had never actually met Mr Ahmed, but he had a reputation as a wealthy party apparatchik with close links to the Mubarak regime and the National Democratic Party.

The NDP was created under Sadat in a democratic experiment after decades of one-party rule and it remains the political means by which the regime clings to power. Its role is to maintain the status quo, either by doing one thing and then negating it with something else, or more often by doing nothing at all. Its members are rich businessmen united by wealth and a hunger for power. They thrive on inertia and have little in common ideologically, although this is not really a problem as important policy decisions come directly from the president. Resounding victories in rigged elections allow the regime to claim a popular mandate of sorts and the NDP curries favour and distributes rewards through a vast patronage network like that which exists in Saudi Arabia – except in Saudi Arabia power ripples outward in concentric circles from each prince. In Egypt there is only one pharaoh.

Mr Ahmed had made his fortune buying and selling textiles in the provincial capital of Minya, some 250 kilometres south of Cairo. Minya had been one of the great centres of Egypt's cotton trade, but in recent times its fortunes, along with the cotton trade, had tumbled. In the mid-1990s Minya became notorious as the centre of armed Islamic resistance to the Egyptian government and to this day the police still patrol its crumbling colonial-era streets in armoured personnel carriers. Mr Ahmed had many stores and his textile empire extended to several towns and cities besides Cairo.

When Amira started as brand manager she found life at the store not quite as she had expected. The clothes they were selling were the hippest brand in town and aimed exclusively at the young and rich, but the staff stood in stony silence, there was no music and the window display consisted of nothing but several awkwardly posed half-dressed plastic mannequins. By way of comparison, on a quick tour of the other clothes stores in the mall Amira found pop music blasting, engaging staff and glossy photographs on the walls. In the windows beautifully posed dummies oozed sexual longing. Compared to the rest, there was no doubt hers looked decidedly forlorn.

'What's up?' Amira asked the boy working the till. 'Why no music?'

'Mr Ahmed won't allow music in the stores,' he replied formally, standing to attention.

'Why not?'

'Because it's blasphemous,' replied the assistant, avoiding Amira's gaze.

'What about the radio?' asked Amira.

'The only thing Mr Ahmed will allow to be broadcast in his stores is the Holy Koran,' replied the boy curtly.

Amira paused. It was her first day at work. Looking the boy in the eye, she tried to gauge what he thought about these instructions. He stood unblinking and statue-still, revealing nothing. 'Well, I guess you had better stick it on then,' Amira said finally.

With the Koran playing over the store's speakers, customers could have been forgiven for thinking that the manager had recently died. It was certainly an incongruous mix, young women trying on clothes and parading around to the sound of the Holy Book. Asking around among the staff, Amira discovered that the arrangements in the shop were the consequence of Mr Ahmed's highly personal Islamic retail vision. A strict conservative Muslim, he had forbidden not only music and advertising in his stores but any conversation between male and female staff or between members of staff and customers of the opposite sex. Security cameras had been installed around the premises, positioned not to combat shoplifting but to make sure these rules were obeyed.

Mr Ahmed's niece, a prim veiled girl named Shams, was the store manager and rigorously enforced her uncle's principles. Mr Ahmed, Shams explained, led by example. He never spoke to any of the women who worked in his stores, nor would he ever touch any of the women's garments on sale in his clothing empire, although he did monitor each season's range personally to make sure that nothing too tight or revealing was stocked.

Amira was at a loss as to what she should do. As brand manager the brand image was her personal responsibility and she felt a strong obligation to keep the original edgy American vision alive. But at the same time she was wary of crossing Mr Ahmed's niece or doing anything that might upset the boss himself, especially since she had never even met him. Technically brand manager outranked store manager, but Shams had spent two years working at another of Mr Ahmed's stores prior to coming to Emerald Square and Amira certainly did not want to ruffle anyone's feathers on her first day.

Eventually Amira decided to list on paper all the things she would like to see changed in the store. When she was finished, she toyed with the idea of sending her ideas on a postcard to the brand headquarters in America but did not know the address and doubted whether they would listen to the word of their regional brand manager over an important distributor like Mr Ahmed. So she resolved to try her best to obey the rules that Mr Ahmed had laid down, for the time being at least, while at the same time quietly sounding out what the other staff members thought and whether anyone would prefer a more relaxed working environment. It was hard to know what anyone in the store thought: no one was keen to speak up either for or against Mr Ahmed's rules. If change was going to happen, it was clear that it would have to be Amira who brought it about.

'How come Arabs know all about American stars like Brad Pitt and Jennifer Aniston, but Americans don't know anything about Amr Diab or Ahmed Zeki?' Roda asked thoughtfully. She was watching the television over my shoulder. I could see the pictures on the screen reflected in her dark eyes.

'I don't know,' I replied vaguely, distracted by her long eyelashes and the way her black hair touched against her collarbone as she turned her head.

'We're playing cards, remember,' said Amira sharply.

'But not many Egyptians speak English and we all know who Brad Pitt is,' continued Roda, studiously ignoring her friend's tetchiness.

'Marketing maybe?' I ventured.

'If it's marketing why don't they market Amr Diab in England? You don't need to speak Arabic to listen to music,' reasoned Roda.

'I think Arab music can be a bit difficult for Westerners to enjoy because they are not really used to it.' I could tell my explanation did not satisfy the girls.

'I think it is a real pity that no one in the West hears about Arab stars,' said Reem. 'Westerners don't know anything about us, do they?'

Roda switched channels. On Al Jazeera news of yet another suicide bombing in Baghdad was unfolding in all its gory detail.

'I like Al Jazeera because it is more biased than Al Arabiya,' said Reem.

'I didn't think you were interested in the news,' I said. 'Why is Al Jazeera biased?'

'Biased against Egypt, I mean,' she continued. 'They really lay into the Egyptian government, and that makes me so happy. I am fed up with this regime. I wish America had invaded Egypt instead. The Iraqis were so lucky.'

'What are you talking about?' exclaimed Roda angrily. 'Look at that!' she shouted, gesticulating as the screen where the camera was panning around the smouldering remains of what had once been a busy market. 'The poor Iraqis are all dying because of the stupid invasion.'

'At least they are free,' retorted Reem, prompting her sister to roll her eyes wearily. 'If only the Americans had come to Cairo instead. I think I might write a letter to President Bush, telling him please come and invade.'

Sixteen

After our date at the Opera House Roda and I began to go out together more frequently to concerts, galleries and restaurants. No longer did we see one another only over the card table, but out and about all over town. Like most Egyptians Roda's busy social calendar stretched far beyond the little world of Zamalek bars that I had come to learn about with Jerome, and moving around town with a native Cairene I found the lid lifted on a sprawling city that until then I had thought I knew quite well.

Much of the city remained off-limits, not because of any threat to Roda's reputation but because men on the streets of the capital sexually harass women at any time of the day or night. Parts of town I had visited alone I found Roda could never go to without a chaperone – even the veil offered no protection. What seemed most strange to me was not that parts of the city were unsafe, but that according to prevailing national logic sexual harassment is the fault of women since their very presence is regarded as constituting a provocation to men, the real victims, whose self-control melts like ice cream when exposed to a woman.

But as long as we went to the right kind of places nobody harassed us and no one seemed particularly to care that an Arab girl was going out with a Westerner. Centuries of tourism have accustomed Egyptians to visitors from all over the world and generally people assumed we were both foreigners. If Roda did reveal herself as an Egyptian, people sometimes mistook her for my tour guide, on several occasions even trying to enlist her help to sell me papyrus and other tourist paraphernalia. In such a conservative society however we both knew that we could not date one another indefinitely. In the Arab world the concept of girlfriends and boyfriends, rather like the notion of homosexuality, is not understood the way it is in the West. Women are essentially viewed as either married, virgins or prostitutes.

Since neither of us had had such a relationship before, as we became closer we agreed just to keep moving forward together without asking ourselves too many questions in the simple hope that sooner or later things would become clearer.

Visiting Roda to play cards so often in the little apartment in Istanbul Street, I had started to recognise the people living in the neighbourhood, and they were beginning to get to know me. The block backed on to the walled garden of a villa belonging to a celebrated belly dancer and was owned by a kindly man in his seventies who had spent the rent raised over his lifetime on a large farm outside Cairo. The farm was where he had chosen to live out the twilight years of his life as a stroke had left him partially paralysed and most of his days were spent in bed. After his death the day-to-day management of the block and its tenants passed to his wife, who was known universally as Tant Enayat.

Tant Enayat was a sour-faced old shrew, never seen without her black headscarf and large old-fashioned spectacles. A nosy gossip, she had a strong vested interest in seeing the leaseholders move out but because of Egypt's antiquated socialist housing laws, Tant Enayat (on behalf of her late husband) was not free to sell or raise the rents as long as the leaseholders kept paying whatever sum had been agreed upon many years ago when the original deal had been signed. Tant Enayat pursued every possible eviction opportunity with alacrity and adopted a policy of making life as unpleasant as possible for all her tenants in the hope that they might leave.

The tenants, on the other hand, perfectly content with the system of rent control, were determined to hang on to their apartments by any available means. Each was doing everything in their power to transfer the leasehold to their children or grandchildren in the hope that their property might stay in the family for another generation at least. It was an inherently fractious situation, the result of which was that Tant Enayat was feared and hated in equal measure by everyone who lived in the block. Most days she could be found lurking on the stairwell or prowling the streets nearby, fishing for gossip to use as ammunition in her ongoing struggle to oust her tenants. Nobody dared abuse her to her face, but behind her back her name was dirt.

The other residents of the block, like all the inhabitants of the apartments in Istanbul Street, were drawn from the same relatively affluent class as Roda and her friends. Many of the leaseholders rented out their apartments to Gulf Arabs over the summer, particularly if they went away for a prolonged spell to Beirut or the north coast but before they left they had to strike a deal with Tant Enayat, who always took a generous cut of the rent.

On the top floor a Saudi family had rented the largest apartment in the building as a semi-permanent holiday home. I never saw the Saudi father, but the smells and sounds emanating from the apartment suggested that the mother and her three plump daughters passed their days cooking and watching television with the volume turned up high. All four wore the full-face niqab, elaborately embroidered with sequins and jewels, often with rather frisky leggings and heels poking out from under their burkas. They had a large white new-model four-by-four parked outside and several times each week went on shopping trips with their Egyptian driver to Itihad Street, returning at night laden with bags of designer shopping.

In the third-floor apartment lived the only child of a former Egyptian diplomat to Korea. He had lived with his parents until their deaths in quick succession a few years previously, since when he had been alone apart from a constant stream of single men who could be seen entering and leaving his apartment by day or night. He was friendly with the residents although he had a habit of startling his neighbours by appearing on the landing wearing nothing but a sarong. No one criticised the young man's behaviour in public except Tant Enayat, who was smarting from the fact that the young man's mother's last act on earth had been to transfer the apartment lease into her son's name.

In the other apartment on the third floor an old man with white hair and a sad, weathered face lived alone. Each day he walked to the coffee shop around the corner from the square at the end of the street to read *Al Ahram* and smoke cigarettes. The old man wore a three-piece suit whatever the weather, although he had long since retired. His son was a well-known actor who often appeared on television, but his other four children had all died.

On the second floor, next to Reem and Amina but facing the back of the block, lived a widow, Tant Mimi, and her chubby daughter, a librarian named Abeer. Abeer had married one of her cousins, a man called Mahmoud. Only after the marriage, when Mahmoud moved in, did Abeer discover that her husband was an aggressive alcoholic who drank over twenty cans of beer a day. Since Mahmoud refused to work or contribute anything towards the bills, the family lived off the little inheritance Abeer had been left by her father. Her husband spent his days drinking and whoring, returning home each evening to fight with his wife and mother-in-law. Their screaming was clearly audible at all hours through the plaster wall dividing their apartment from the hallway and throughout most of the public areas of the block.

Next door to Roda lived a Palestinian man in his fifties with dyed black hair who owned a car rental business. His two sons were studying in France, so he lived alone with his wife of thirty years. He had another wife, formerly his secretary, who lived across town. They had married some ten years earlier and now she lived a cosseted life in a penthouse apartment with panoramic views of the Muwazafeen Shooting Club. His first wife had never forgiven him for this and the couple had frequent noisy arguments, typically ending up with him standing in the street outside for hours chain-smoking.

On the ground floor, next to the doorman's hovel under the stairs, lived a boy suffering from Down's Syndrome and his reclusive mother. An elder daughter had moved out recently after getting married. His mother always dressed in black, rarely left the house and had an obsessive-compulsive disorder that made her feet and hands look a powdery white from excessive washing.

As far as the girls were concerned, the heart of Istanbul Street was Faisal's Hairdresser and Salon, where women from across the neighbourhood went to have their hair done and their moustaches and eyebrows removed, an important and regular ritual for any self-respecting Egyptian woman. The hairdresser was in the same building as the Very Special Islamic Kindergarten, and next to that was a gentlemen's barber where I would sometimes stop for a shave. The barber, a burly Nubian called Kamal, had a boxer's build and a broken nose. His young son worked with him, heating flannels, sweeping the floor and making tea for the men waiting. Legally, he probably should have been in school. Opposite Kamal's were a couple of cheap clothes stores, and by night their glaring window displays illuminated much of the street. Every day except Friday a toothless old widow could be found sitting on the pavement outside the shops, selling vegetables and eggs out of a broken cardboard box.

There had been a second kindergarten in Istanbul Street, but its lease had been taken over by a pair of rather austere tailors specialising in clothes for men and women. The tailors were deeply pious as was evident from their bushy beards and the large callused *zabeebas* on their foreheads and they barely spoke to anyone, including their customers. They sewed in silence to endless recitations of the Koran, leaving their veiled secretary to handle pick-ups and drop-offs with a frosty politeness. Unveiled women and foreigners were treated cattily. The other Istanbul Street residents jokingly referred to them as 'al-Qaeda' and rumour had it that they were a contact point for people wishing to travel to Iraq to fight.

Next door to the tailors and opposite Roda's block was the street's largest and noisiest family, headed by Fouad, a cheerful and totally illiterate doorman. Fouad lived in a crumbling corrugated-iron shack built into the underside of one of the apartment blocks. In his early thirties, he looked ten years older and had more children than one could count. The whole family shared an uncomfortable-looking skin infection. Fouad had come to Cairo with his brother from Upper Egypt five years earlier to find work. His brother had moved on to Saudi Arabia and now worked as a handyman in a hotel in Mecca. Fouad settled in Istanbul Street, where he had lived ever since. He still missed the country life and liked to chat about how the fruit and vegetables in Cairo were not like those he used to eat back in his village. His wife spent her days cooking and publicly henpecked him with a severity bordering on sadism.

Like the other doormen in the street, Fouad eked out a living parking and cleaning cars and running errands for the residents of his block. He collected a monthly stipend from each apart-ment, plus occasional tips for daily tasks like locking the front door at night and delivering newspapers. Despite his crippling poverty Fouad was a cheerful soul, who enjoyed playing games with his children, racing them up and down the street through the parked cars.

For the inhabitants of rural Egypt becoming a doorman in Muwazafeen is a considerable achievement, and several of Fouad's younger unmarried cousins had been drawn to Istanbul Street by his trailblazing success. They parked cars for a living and spent most of their time smoking cigarettes and eyeing up passing girls from the shade of the trees.

Late at night at the weekend Fouad's cousins would sometimes take a car they were supposed to be parking for a spin down Itihad Street. In an effort to prevent this happening to them, savvy local residents sometimes tipped car parkers from a neighbouring street to sleep in their vehicles at weekends.

Car parking is a lucrative racket in crowded wealthy suburbs like Muwazafeen, and gangs of men and boys fiercely protect their territory. Rather than hunt for a space yourself – along with the 1.3 million other cars registered in Cairo plus all the unregistered – you can just throw your keys to a parker. It is an illegal unregistered practice run on trust, but also a vital service and can often save you a parking fine.

The doorman in Roda's block was called Hanafi and his humble house under the stairs was split in two by the corridor leading from the hall to a travel agency at the back of the building. Prior to coming to Istanbul Street Hanafi had worked as a desk clerk at a village police station in the Delta, noting down the particulars of criminals after they had been arrested. Hanafi was short and dark and looked uneasy wearing anything other than a *galabiyah*, but his gruff manner and red pinprick eyes belied a kind and honest nature and a wry sense of humour. Unlike most of the other working-class men in the street Hanafi was literate and neither drank, nor smoked cigarettes or hashish. He was a man of firm religious principle, who was never too proud to recycle anything anyone in the street threw away, whether unwanted food or an old pair of shoes. Everything it seemed could either be used or sold. The only commodity he had no use for was empty liquor bottles, which he refused to handle on religious grounds, despite their value and the fact that he was desperately poor, with a baby and a pregnant wife.

Sometimes Hanafi would get annoyed with Fouad's loafing around and the two of them would fight, which would make for an ugly scene. Screaming earthy oaths, each with a bawling child under one arm, they would face off in the street. All their friends and relatives would quickly become involved, the wives would join in, the dogs would start barking and cousins would have to restrain them. After a confrontation everyone in the street was uneasy for days and did what they could to help the two make up. Nobody wanted a disgruntled doorman because they depended on them for so many crucial little everyday things. While fighting strangers or street gangs was acceptable, conflict between neighbours risked starting a vicious circle of bad feeling, where hostilities could boil over again and again until both sides felt honour had been satisfied.

Hanafi had a wife named Sana, who must have been in her early twenties. She also came from Upper Egypt and was pretty and demure with cool, languid eyes. She never spoke to men, including me, but wore her headscarf loosely set back. Most days she could be found sitting on the step outside the block, peeling garlic by the kilo into a bucket or sewing clothes for pennies. Sometimes she would earn some extra money cooking and cleaning for Tant Enayat. Her little boy could always be found close by, shoeless and playing with his sad-looking collection of broken toys.

Most of the week the street was alive with activity no matter what hour of the day or night it was. At least once every twenty-four hours the gasman passed, banging a hammer against the heavy blue metal canisters that looked like milk churns slung over the back wheel of his bicycle, making his steering dangerously wobbly. Every now and then someone needing a refill would lean out of a window and call out. He would unhitch a full can off the back – at least they hoped it was full – and exchange it for the empty one in return for a small fee. Since almost all the apartments in Istanbul Street had piped gas, it was usually only the doormen's wives that listened for his call.

Other salesmen would pass by, peddling water or fruit or baskets or any number of other household commodities. Some used handcarts or wheelbarrows, others donkey-drawn carts. Rag-and-bone men trundled by with their sons by their sides noisily calling out for junk. Often they already had an old fridge or a broken chest of drawers in the back, which they were carting off for recycling in another part of the metropolis. As long as anyone in the street could remember a veiled woman had passed by each morning selling eggs from a wicker basket balanced on her head. A widow dressed all in black, as she passed she always called out the same strange phrase: 'The eggs are peasants, the eggs are peasants.'

The neighbourhood rubbish accumulated steadily throughout the week on the widest part of the pavement opposite the church in an unplanned dump. The smelly sprawl grew larger and more fly-infested until it became both restaurant and play area for the street's wildlife. Mice, cockroaches and weasels scurried in and out of it; stray cats and dogs lounged in it and ate it. It was a harmonious coexistence until the municipal street cleaners arrived once each week after midnight and ruined the party by clearing up the reeking pile with their bare hands.

Sometimes, if a doorman forgot to lock up at night, stray cats and dogs would come into an apartment building to sniff around and rummage in bin bags for the remains of yesterday's food. Some people also kept domestic pets although there was no place to walk them, which meant they either shat in the house or in the street where the children played. In summer all the blocks suffered periodic invasions of ants, cockroaches, lizards and mosquitoes.

In addition to the indigenous wildlife one of Hassan's more entrepreneurial cousins had brought a herd of horses with him from the countryside, which he kept in a makeshift stable under a nearby flyover. During the day he rented them out by the hour to Arab tourists, who galloped them recklessly up and down Istanbul Street and into Itihad Street, causing widespread pandemonium among the traffic. Not only was this dangerous, especially for the horses, it was also illegal, and sporadically the local police would give chase on foot, sending horsemen galloping in all directions and jumping over parked cars like a scene from a cowboy film.

Every Sunday and on Friday mornings a lengthy traffic jam materialised in Istanbul Street as Muwazafeen's Copts flocked to the church for mass. Technically traffic was one-way, but on Coptic holy days like Christmas and major saints' days this was widely flouted. Most weeks there was also either a funeral or a wedding, which brought alternately solemn mourners and flower-covered hearses or joyous crowds vigorously beeping car horns. The rest of the weekend was when the street was at its quietest, since most of the residents would head out of town when they had the chance. Only the doormen and the car parkers would be left behind, dozing with the cats on the warm bonnets of cars or playing dominoes in the shade of the trees lining the verge.

Seventeen

By way of friendly reciprocation for all the hospitality Roda had shown me at her apartment, I invited her several times to visit me in Elephant and Castle. She made a number of polite excuses that I took as an implied refusal. In my naivety I did not understand that for Roda just setting foot in my flat meant putting her reputation on the line. If word spread on to the Muwazafeen grapevine that she had been visiting a foreigner's home alone it could have serious consequences for her. As a foreigner and a man gossip never reached my ears, but for Roda our affair was a deadly serious business. Egyptian men expect their brides to be not only virgins but above suspicion in every possible respect. Being seen with me could permanently mar her chances of getting married.

It was taken for granted that we told no one about our card games, but in close-knit Cairo society, where everybody makes it their business to know everyone else's business, it was only a matter of time before rumours began circulating. Everyone in the neighbourhood recognised me by now and they knew too that I was not married, that I spoke Arabic and that I had a number of Egyptian friends.

Only after several months of pestering would she finally agree to visit me at home. The day she was coming, a quarter of an hour before she was due to arrive she called me on the telephone.

'Look, I'm on my way, but when I get there don't speak to me in Arabic. OK?' she said nervously.

'Why not?' I asked.

'I don't want the doorman to know I am Egyptian.'

'OK . . .' I said, pondering the merits of this plan. 'I think I know what you are worried about. But if you are not Egyptian, what else might you be?'

'Anything else, just not Egyptian. Maybe I'm English, or Indian or Pakistani or something. I could be, right?'

'I guess so . . .' It was true: with her almond-brown skin she might have been any number of nationalities. But somehow I did not think this was going to fool my doorman. 'No Arabic then,' I agreed.

Roda was hoping she might be able to creep past my doorman's lair next to the stairs without being noticed. It was going to be tough. Not only was my doorman uncommonly nosy, he was also an indefatigable sycophant who came running the moment guests arrived on the chance he might be able to earn a tip. I had been warned that he may also have had more sinister motives: rumour had it that Zamalek doormen working in blocks where foreigners lived were paid by the local police to keep an eye on them.

On this occasion the sound of Roda's car door closing was all it took to trigger the doorman's fear that he might be missing out on some baksheesh. Barely had she crept through the door of the lobby when he came scurrying out of his hole, tripping and stumbling over his *galabiyah* in a headlong rush to hold the door open for the foreigner's guest. With a grandiloquent flourish he placed his hand on his heart and greeted Roda warmly in Arabic through stained brown teeth. She nodded and walked past him, feigning total incomprehension, on her way to the polished wooden double doors to the lift. Startled by her abruptness but no stranger to rejection, he persevered.

'Who have you come to see?' he asked helpfully. Roda pressed the call button and looked at the ceiling, her ears burning. In her panic she had forgotten that even if she was not supposed to understand the doorman, she should still have been able to see and hear him. 'Which floor, madam?' the doorman continued resolutely, becoming ever more curious. Roda said nothing, waiting in painful silence as the lift descended. He opened the door and with the faintest of acknowledgements she stepped in.

That evening after Roda had gone I overheard the doorman and one of the car parkers standing outside, speculating about whether the foreigner's girlfriend was an Egyptian. 'I might have an ear of mud and another of dough, but I am not stupid!' I heard the doorman cackle. 'Of course she is an Egyptian! What do you think they are doing together, her and that foreigner?'

'Women are like watermelons,' the parker replied with a dirty chuckle. 'Even if no one has opened them up yet you can bet someone has had their fingers all over them.'

Since Yosra could find no way around her strict curfew, Reem or Amira stood in as Noha's partner in the card circle. In Yosra's absence the girls debated who exactly was responsible for putting the evil eye on their friend. Eventually a consensus was reached that it most probably had been her secretary at work, who had become jealous since Yosra had been given her own office to work in.

'Hey, Reem, what's up with Boutros?' I asked the next time she came round to play. 'Did the priest tell him he was going to hell?'

'I think so,' she replied, her long brown hair swaying as she laughed. 'Actually it was worse than that: the priest told his mother *she* would! He saw the first priest and the guy tried to talk him out of converting and of course it didn't work. So he saw the second priest and he tried and the same thing happened. But then afterwards the priest telephoned Boutros's mother and filled her head with all kinds of crazy paranoid shit and now she is really freaked out.'

'I can't believe it,' said Roda. 'They just want to get married for God's sake. Why does religion always have to make problems between people?'

'What did the priest tell her?' I asked Reem.

'Well, you know she is a really sincere convinced Christian? The priest told her that though it was up to Boutros whether he wanted to convert to Islam or not, if he did convert then there was no doubt he would go straight to hell, and so might she because she was his mother and she hadn't stopped him. When she heard that she totally flipped out.'

'So now it's his mother's problem!' exclaimed Roda.

'And he also told her,' Reem continued, 'that if Boutros did become a Muslim, then the Muslim Brotherhood would come banging on her door at all hours of the day and night to check that Boutros was praying five times a day and not drinking alcohol – and woe betide him if he was caught breaking the rules.'

'Is that true?' I asked.

'Of course not! I'm sure the Brotherhood would be thrilled if he converted.'

'Does his mother know you?' I asked.

'Of course. She knows me well,' replied Reem.

'And does she like you?' I asked, trying to make some sense of this situation.

'She quite likes me. Or at least she did. I think that now she believes I am like this big bewitching influence on her precious only son and that I am going to drag him down to the bottom of hell.'

'I am sure she would have preferred Boutros to marry a nice Christian girl,' added her sister.

Just as in Palestine, where the international community believed Fatah's analysis that Hamas could never breach a glass ceiling of about 30 per cent popular support, many people think that political Islamism in Egypt has no real constituency. But if there were free and fair elections tomorrow the Muslim Brotherhood would probably win outright, or at least form the largest minority. In 2005, in spite of the regime rigging the elections and rounding up hundreds of its supporters, the Brotherhood's candidates won a fifth of the seats available in parliament and formed the largest opposition bloc.

If the Brothers did come to control Egypt one day, they would prove an uncertain friend to the West. America certainly finds their kind of Islamism too strong to stomach. But in the Middle East, like Hamas, its ideological twin, the Brotherhood has acquired a reputation for austerity and justice, gaining much of its popularity by providing welfare assistance to the poor. For many it has all the answers: Islam really is the solution.

Technically the Brotherhood is still an illegal organisation and relations with the regime remain tense. Under the infamous emergency laws thousands of its members have passed through Egyptian jails over the years. Many are still there; many more have been tortured. It is admirable of the Brotherhood to stick to peaceful democratic methods to bring about political change, especially when the government blatantly rigs all the elections and routinely arrests its members. One might wonder why the Brotherhood, which can effortlessly raise thousands of demonstrators at short notice, does not attempt a revolution. But the Brotherhood is not a monolithic movement and its leadership is not confident that if push came to shove all its members would actually stand up and fight. Like a group of angry men locked in a cell together, all straining at the door, if they finally get out they might turn on each other and the movement would splinter. If the Brothers do one day come to rule Egypt, all we can hope is that whoever comes out on top does not believe that Egyptian society needs to be burnt to the ground before it can be rebuilt.

★

While our *tarneeb* sessions continued three or four nights each week, Yosra was still at home, looking after her father. By day her brother allowed her to leave the house only to commute the short distance to her grim basement office and back. There the temperature was soaring and the heat brought an infestation of cockroaches.

Usually Yosra would only see two or three clients each day. Some days not even a single one would drop by. Since it only took a few minutes for her to rattle off the same patter to each of them, most of her time was given over to watching the clock and sleeping on the ratty sofa in the dingy back room.

It had only taken one visit to the Sheikh to convince Yosra that for the past seven years an amorous and jealous jinn had been conspiring to ruin her love life. Probably it had made love to her hundreds maybe even thousands of times. Only this, she believed, could explain why her luck with men had always been so bad.

Had Yosra not been using so many drugs each day, her life might have seemed even more depressing, but the sedatives and painkillers lifted from her father's prescriptions blurred each day into the next. Without windows at work, often she was not even sure if it was day or night. Life unfolded in a dreamlike cycle of sleeping and waking, broken only by the somnambulant drive home to eat robotically at the dinner table in silence, before sleeping again, waking, then returning to the office to lie comatose on the sofa. In her mind she endlessly turned over what the doctor had said about her father's drinking; she thought of her failed engagement years ago and of Khaled the orthodontist, who had never called her back.

When Amira heard that Mr Ahmed had gone on holiday to Monte Carlo, she decided the moment had come to put her plan into action. On Shams's day off she summoned the staff together for a till meeting a few minutes before opening time and explained that from now on there would be some new rules in the shop. As brand manager, she had decided that they would play music on the radio. No longer were the staff forbidden to speak to customers of the opposite sex; in fact from now on they were positively encouraged to do so. At the end of the meeting Amira distributed some full-length, glossy advertising posters to be hung in the windows. No one questioned Amira about the new rules and no one asked any questions. The staff simply accepted the changes, as people do when the wind changes direction in a totalitarian state.

The next day Shams returned to work to discover that the coup had taken place. Quietly she asked Amira if they could speak in her office, a windowless room at the back of the store piled high with cardboard boxes and clothes wrapped in plastic. It was so crowded it was barely possible to close the door and neither of them had anywhere to sit except on boxes of next season's button-fly jeans.

'Mr Ahmed is going to be furious when he finds out that you have deliberately disobeyed his rules.'

'Good for him,' said Amira coolly, facing her rival down. 'As brand manager I think I know what is best for the brand.'

'Mr Ahmed gave me clear instructions as to how he wanted the store run in his absence and it was not . . .' she struggled for the words '. . . like this!'

'I will report to Mr Ahmed when he gets back,' replied Amira nonchalantly. 'Until then all you need to do is what I say and let me worry about what Mr Ahmed thinks when he gets back.'

'You have disobeyed his express orders. You have turned off the Koran and replaced it with . . . rubbish!' Shams slapped her palms against her face.

'You think just because you are a Muslim you have to play the Koran everywhere you go? This is a clothes store!'

'There is never a wrong time to play the Koran,' replied Shams.

'You think God is happy that women are checking their butts in the mirror with the Holy Book in the background like it's Nile FM?' replied Amira.

The two glared at each other like pharaohs' cats over the unwrapped boxes of fashion apparel.

'Wait till my uncle gets back and then we will see what happens!' whispered Shams menacingly and turned on her heel to disappear through the door.

Whether or not it was sacrilegious to play the Koran in the shop racked the workforce for several days afterwards. The staff were divided, but most agreed that if it was what Mr Ahmed wanted it was the best thing to do. An online fatwa from an authoritative cleric was found to bolster this point of view. Nobody actually spoke out in support of Amira's position: that it was irreverent for women to try on clothes to the sound of the Koran and that pop music was not only more fun, it was also more suitable.

Eighteen

When Yosra woke one Thursday evening she did not know how long she had been sleeping or where she was. Sitting up on the sofa, she looked around her. Slowly she realised that she was still at work, in the office, on her own. Pulling her hair into a ponytail she wiped the sleep from her eyes and checked the alarm clock next to her pillow. It was already evening and time to go home for the weekend.

She had managed to lose a week with drugs, which was just fine as far as she was concerned, but now it was the weekend, which she was not looking forward to since at home she would not be allowed to sleep all day. Her brother would be there and she would be expected to clean, cook and look after her father. Irritated by the prospect of facing her family, Yosra cursed as she gathered up her handbag and keys. Outside, the sun had already set. Removing her sunglasses, she tried to remember what had happened that day or even her drive to work that morning. She found she could summon up no memory at all. It took her a while to find where she had parked her car.

Groping groggily for her keys in the bottom of her bag, Yosra yawned, almost ready to go back to sleep. Unsteadily she opened the driver's door, climbed inside and threw her bag in the back. There was a bad smell in the car like something rotting. Involuntarily she pressed her hand to her nose in disgust and her skin turned clammy as a wave of nausea swept over her. Thinking perhaps she had trodden in some shit she checked her shoes, twisting in the car seat to inspect each foot. Something, Yosra thought hazily, must have died in the car. She wound down the car window, one hand still pinching her nose, and slowly reversed out of her parking space, concentrating hard so as not to retch.

Only recently woken, Yosra thought at first she must be imagining the wriggling in the footwell. The sedatives lingered in her system and it took her the best part of a minute to realise that what she was feeling around her feet was not just the movement of the car. A moment later, when an evil-looking weasel caked with black dirt from the street jumped nimbly onto her lap, she realised that there was a wild animal in her car.

Yosra let out a piercing scream. Startled, the weasel squeaked and dug its cruel curved claws through her jeans into the flesh of her thigh. Writhing with pain and fear, she knocked the weasel out of her lap with her hand, sending it bouncing onto the passenger seat, where it leapt once again back onto her lap exposing a row of teeth like tiny fishhooks. Throwing open the car door, Yosra continued screaming until she ran out of breath. The weasel, as boneless and bouncy as a rubber band, sprang out of the car and belted off down the filth-strewn gutter between the parked cars and the dusty pavement before disappearing through a gap in a fence.

A stream of prayers came from Yosra's lips as she looked down at the holes in her trousers that the verminous creature had made. Touching where she had been scratched she realised that what had happened had not been a dream. Then, in spite of the anaesthesia that had gripped her soul all week, she began to cry. Fumbling for her handbag on the back seat, she reached inside for her scent and a bottle of her father's pills. Shakily she counted several pills out into the palm of her hand. Throwing her head back she swallowed them down in one gulp without water and immediately felt a little better. Liberally squirting the scent around the car to mask the terrible smell, she set off for Roda's house, still retching but eager to share with her news about the awful thing that had just happened.

'It probably got in through the aspirator,' said Roda.

'Wow, someone put the evil eye on you real bad,' added Noha seriously.

'I can't believe it. I just can't believe it,' said Yosra, still looking shell-shocked as she cradled her tea and puffed nervously on a cigarette. 'It was the most disgusting thing that ever happened to me in my entire life. I swear to God, I thought I was going to die.'

'Are you going to have a rabies shot?' I asked as gently as I could.

'You think I need one?' replied Yosra anxiously.

Roda and I looked at each other. 'I think you probably do,' I said.

Yosra looked grim-faced. 'Doesn't that mean twenty shots in the stomach?' she muttered, turning visibly whiter.

'Not any more,' said Roda. 'Just four or five big fat ones in your arm and your butt.'

'Oh God,' Yosra muttered miserably. 'I had to take three Valium on the spot just to get over the shock. And my car still stinks like something died. Afterwards I found this half-eaten something in my boot – I think it was a rat – and there was shit everywhere and old bits of food . . .'

'It sounds like it had been living in your car for days,' said Roda.

'That is so gross,' interjected Noha.

'Where is your car now?' I asked.

'It's being valeted by the doorman. I asked him to call me when it was done and it's been two hours already. I called my brother and I don't have to go home until it's done.'

Although we all felt sorry about what had happened to Yosra, we were pleased to see that she looked so animated. The shock

seemed to have jump-started her out of her funk. As the pills
finally kicked in inside her head, she began to get over the shock
of her encounter and the conversation turned to the other topic
uppermost on Yosra's mind, her father's drinking.

'Roda, I swear to God, I don't know what to make of what
the doctor said to me. As long as I can remember my father has
prayed; he's done the haj and the umrah; he has always been so
conservative. Do you think there could have been some kind of
mistake at the hospital?'

'I doubt it,' said Roda, scratching her chin. 'Have you asked
your mum?'

'Are you crazy? I couldn't tell her what the doctor said. It was
a big enough shock for me. It would be the end of her. But I did
ask her if she thought he had ever drunk alcohol.'

'And what did she say?' asked Roda.

'She said she knew my father had some wild friends back in
the 1960s, but she did not think he had ever touched alcohol in
his life. She said she used to eavesdrop on conversations he had
with his friends and she found out that he used to smoke hashish
and before they got married he had dated many other women.
I know one of his close friends was an opium addict, but he's
dead now. Mum said she has never had the confidence to ask
Father if he had taken opium too.'

'Did she say how many women he had been with?' asked Roda.

'Quite a few, I think. Before they get married men go with a
lot of women. I can't see why he should be any different.'

Yosra hands were shaking and her face was grey. She had huge
bags under each eye and looked like she had not slept in a week.
We all knew that Yosra was liberally abusing her father's medica-
tion and the girls' faces showed their concern that her drug use
was spiralling out of control.

'Yosra, why don't you come and meet this new guy I heard
about from a friend at work?' suggested Roda cheerfully. She had
long since decided that what her friend needed more than

anything to shake her out of her depression was a boyfriend. Whenever Roda was out and about, at work or at family occasions, she always kept an eye open for bachelors of the right age and class to introduce to Yosra.

'He is single and they say he is looking to get married. He sounds like a nice guy. I think you might like him.'

'OK,' said Yosra tentatively. 'But I am still grounded; I don't think my family will let me go.'

'Why don't you tell your mum that you need an evening off so you can meet a suitor? She wants you to get married, doesn't she?'

'It's my brother. By day he works in the prison. By night it's like he's working in another prison. He listens to all my phone calls. He checks my mobile all the time. He makes a special point to check what calls I make and receive, and if he finds any unexplained numbers he calls them back and tells them never to call me again. If the phone rings when he is there, he makes me answer it in front of him.'

'What a dick,' said Noha.

'But you call me sometimes,' observed Roda.

'That's because I have labelled all my friends in my phone with the names of work colleagues.'

'Very clever of you to stay one step ahead,' I remarked.

'Unfortunately it's too clever for me too. Roda's number is listed under the name of my boss so I keep calling him by mistake when I am stoned. It's very confusing.'

'Why don't you ask your mother today?' persisted Roda. 'When is your brother next going away?'

'Next month, in Ramadan, I think they're sending him to a prison out of town somewhere. Maybe we can meet then?'

'That's perfect!' said Roda brightly, pleased at her little victory. 'I think you will like him. He's the cousin of someone I met at the salon. I think his name is Tamer. He's in his thirties and half Russian.'

Nineteen

Each time Roda came to visit me in Elephant and Castle, she tried the same technique as on the first occasion, passing through the lobby as quickly as she could, head down, mouth closed, hoping the doorman would not notice her come in. More often than not he came slithering out of his den next to the garage relishing the challenge of trying to make her speak Arabic and so betray herself as an Egyptian. If he failed to appear, we still never lingered in the corridors for long. Walls had ears in Elephant and Castle.

Usually his efforts to make her talk came under the pretext of a few helpful directions while holding the door open. The trap set, he would lean in close, an expectant smile on his lips, scrutinising Roda's face for any indication that she understood what he was saying. Sometimes on her way out of the building one of the car parkers would casually call out some useful instructions in Arabic to see if Roda understood. 'Your car is parked around the corner,' they would shout without pointing. It became a game, each man trying to be the one to shame her first. Roda was remarkably resilient and never let a word or the slightest sign of understanding slip out. Like all Egyptian women, pressured to maintain a pristine public image at all times, she had become an accomplished actor.

It seemed to me that our lame attempt at concealment was

never going to work, but Roda was determined to stay the course. She had to do what she could to protect her reputation. Over the weeks, as Roda paid more visits to Elephant and Castle, she stayed later and later but never overnight. We always took care to avoid any public displays of affection, and whatever the doorman and his friends thought about our blooming relationship in private, their desire to stay on the right side of me meant that they were happy to at least act like they could keep a secret. When Roda was not around, the doorman took to tipping me a knowing wink, dirty finger pressed against his tobacco-stained lips, as if to say, 'Your secret is safe with me.'

After weeks of furtive coming and going between Istanbul Street and Elephant and Castle Ramadan arrived and with it a distinct change in the rhythm of daily life. During Ramadan days start late and pass slowly. Evenings are family time, which most of my Egyptian friends spent having breakfast with their relatives as soon as prayers had started on television. Ramadan is calculated on a lunar calendar and so each night prayers came a few minutes earlier.

As a non-Muslim I did not fast, but because by day most Egyptians do and most restaurants and *shisha* bars except tourist havens are closed, there was not much respite. The fast would be broken with a glass of water or juice, followed by a mound of home-cooked food – chicken, lamb or beef and heaps of rice. Then, when everyone was bloated and semi-comatose on the sofa in front of the television, boxes of sweets and pastries stuffed with dates and powdered with icing sugar would be passed around. By the time the feast was over, it was normally necessary to sleep for an hour or two. Upon waking everyone would shower and dress as if it were morning, before heading out to meet friends. At night the city came alive. The streets were thronged with families eating and shopping; pop music blasted from cars trapped in midnight traffic jams. Every table in the coffee shops was occupied with people smoking *shishas* or playing backgammon. The shops, brightly decked in festive colours, stayed open into the small hours.

As the month progressed, finding opportunities to meet became gradually harder. Never try to date a Muslim woman during Ramadan. You can't get a drink. The nightclubs, bars and restaurants you would normally take her to are all closed. Most people you meet during the day are thoroughly grumpy because they are hungry or gasping for a cigarette or a glass of water. You can be sure she will have innumerable family commitments throughout the month that will impinge on your plans – distant relatives dropping by for breakfast or a midnight lunch, or family across town to visit. Even La Bodega, that staple expat watering hole, refused to serve alcohol at all during daylight hours and by night to anyone the waiters judged might be Egyptian and therefore possibly a Muslim.

Although there is little concept of private life at any time of year in Egypt, during Ramadan family, friends and neighbours seem to think that they have a special licence to interfere with how people behave. From the doorman downstairs to the sheikh on television Ramadan is when self-righteous men everywhere dole out religious advice and check up on others to make sure they have observed their fast and prayed five times a day.

The Egyptian Ramadan regime is not as strict as in some Arab countries like Saudi Arabia or Kuwait, where public non-observance can get you arrested, but the fact that the fast in Cairo is not legally enforced makes its almost universal observance all the more remarkable. Even the most wheezing and irascible taxi driver will give up cigarettes for the month – at least until the daylight dwindles so that the imam can no longer differentiate between a white and a black thread and the call for the evening prayer rings out.

One morning a few days after Ramadan began I was sitting at my desk in Elephant and Castle writing. I was doing my best to fast but was finding it hard: visions of fast food dripping with sauce kept drifting through my mind. I heard a knock on the door. Opening it, I found a severe-looking Egyptian lady carrying a clipboard and wearing a business suit standing on my doorstep. An unassuming servant girl wearing a white veil and industrial rubber gloves accompanied her. The girl could not have been more than eighteen years old and was carrying a large plastic jerrycan.

Brandishing a laminated ID card in my face, the lady explained that she was from the Ministry of Health and Population and had been sent to disinfect my block. All she needed, she said, was to be let inside so she could pour some disinfectant down my sink and into the drains, and once that was completed, two hundred Egyptian pounds. This was not, she added quickly, voluntary. She had a job to do: she had been sent from the government, and if I would just help her do it she would collect the money and be on her way. The girl said nothing. I eyed the pair suspiciously. I was wary of scams as I had been swindled before. The woman certainly looked like the type that might be sent by the government and had an ID card that declared she had been. Two hundred pounds sounded a lot, but it did not strike me as particularly likely for someone to have made up such an improbable story. Besides, I thought, she could never have made it into the building without passing my doorman. I knew from Roda's experience that he was a streetwise old rogue who would be unlikely to let strangers come to my door without genuine business.

'OK,' I said warily. 'The girl can come in and do the disinfecting or whatever it is she has to do. But you have to wait here.'

This being a satisfactory arrangement, without a word the servant girl scurried inside. I closed the door gently in the lady official's face before following the girl into the kitchen, keeping a close eye on her to make sure she did not steal anything. Unscrewing the cap from the jerrycan, she carefully poured a shot of steaming viscous liquid down my kitchen sink, taking great care not to let any of what appeared to be a highly corrosive substance splash or spill on her.

The outsized rubber gloves she was wearing were so cumbersome she found it difficult to screw the lid back on again, but unsure what dangerous liquid she was carrying, I resisted the urge to help her. Once she had finished in the kitchen she asked to be directed to every sink in the apartment, where she carefully repeated the same procedure.

When she had finished treating my drains, I escorted her back to the front door, taking care not to touch her steaming jerrycan, where the official in the suit was still waiting. She quickly filled out a large bill for me on her clipboard, which she presented with a flourish. I paid in cash and went back to my work.

A few minutes later there was another knock on my door. It was Roda, who for once had managed to slip unseen past my doorman. 'You'll never guess what happened to me just before you showed up,' I said, before quickly explaining the whole strange story.

When Roda heard that I had handed over two hundred Egyptian pounds in cash to a woman on my doorstep who said she was from the government, she exploded. 'You stupid idiot!' she cried. 'Would you do that in England?'

'I suppose not,' I conceded, feeling rather ashamed of myself and beginning to think I might have been duped. 'But this would not happen in England,' I muttered angrily.

'When did this happen?' Roda asked.

'Just a few minutes ago,' I said. 'Just before you arrived.'

'She's probably still in the building. Come on. We are going to get your money back.'

Bursting out of the apartment, we ran up and down the stairs looking for the two fraudsters. We quickly spotted them, two floors down, lugging the heavy can down the stairs on their way to the front door.

'Wait a minute! You stop right there!' shouted Roda over the banister down the lift shaft. 'Don't try to escape. We know your game!'

The pair looked up at us, ditched the jerrycan and fled. They would have escaped had it not been for the doorman, disturbed by the rumpus, emerging blearily from his hole like a monster from the deep and cornering them at the foot of the stairs.

'Stop, thief! They robbed him!' said Roda, running down the stairs after them.

'Quick, quick let's go!' shouted the woman with the clipboard.

'What's all this then?' said the doorman, standing squarely in their path. 'You two just wait a minute!'

'They came to this man's apartment saying they were from the Ministry of Health,' Roda blurted. 'They tricked him into paying money because he is a foreigner and he did not understand. You should have stopped them! Why did you let them into the building in the first place? You should have been able to tell they were up to no good!'

The doorman eyed the two felons menacingly. They had gone as white as the girl's veil. Then turning his attention back to Roda, the expression on his face turned to a grin of deep satisfaction.

'So you are Egyptian. I knew you were all along.'

Twenty

Yosra managed to escape when her brother was sent to work in a prison deep in the desert. It was her first piece of luck in weeks. Before he left Hassan gave their mother strict instructions, but without him Yosra knew that her life would be much easier. Salma didn't have the heart to punish her daughter and Yosra's father spent most of the day asleep in bed. Her curfew effectively lifted, we began to see more of Yosra once again over the card table in Istanbul Street.

'You have got to be kidding,' exclaimed Roda. 'He makes you do what?'

'I have to lie on the floor for three hours, without a mattress or anything, not even moving or blinking,' said Yosra matter-of-factly. 'Just concentrating, with these two speakers playing the Koran on the floor right next to my head.'

She was looking even worse than the day she had come round after being attacked by the weasel. Her puffy eyes and sickly pallor took us aback. Weeks of self-medication were writ large across her face.

'Isn't that a bit boring?' asked Noha.

'And bad for your ears?' added Amira.

'Of course it's boring, but it's the only way to get rid of the jinn,' replied Yosra.

For weeks Yosra had been making regular trips to the Sheikh.

The sessions had been getting longer, the remedies steadily more bizarre, but there was still no sign of a resolution to her love problems.

'I honestly can't believe you have been taken in by all this rubbish,' snorted Roda.

Yosra looked hurt.

'Look, I am not saying that there are no such thing as jinn,' Roda began in a more measured tone. 'Maybe there are. Only God knows. But what evidence do you have that anything he says is really true?'

'You just have to believe, I guess,' said Yosra doubtfully. 'It only works if you believe it. But I promise you I definitely felt something warm touching me when I was lying there, like fingertips all over my body.'

'They were probably his, the dirty old man.' Amira chuckled. 'You're lucky your mother was there or he would have had you.'

'Has the treatment been working?' I asked.

'It's not like everything has been going perfectly,' admitted Yosra despondently. 'The office boy took away the sofa so I don't have anywhere to sleep at work.'

'What's that funny smell?' asked Noha, leaning in close to Yosra's head and wrinkling her nose.

'That would be me.' Yosra blushed. 'The Sheikh told me to cover my whole body in musk oil each night before I sleep.'

The girls looked at each other open-mouthed.

'He what?' said Amira.

'It's a real pain,' Yosra continued. 'It means I have to wake up an hour early every day to scrub it off or else I smell like a ferret.'

'Gross!' blurted out Noha. Realising she had hurt Yosra's feelings, she added quickly, 'I just feel so sorry for you – I mean finding out that a jinn has been following you and stuff . . .'

'Urgh,' said Yosra disgustedly, making a face. 'It makes me feel physically sick. I can't believe that this small black goblin has been having sex with me as I sleep.'

'How do you know he's small?' asked Noha curiously.

'Because when he makes love to me in my dreams, his face only comes up to the bottom of my breasts,' replied Yosra glumly.

The next time Roda came round to my apartment she found a note under the windscreen wiper of her car when she left. 'Whore!' it read. 'Have you no shame, even during Ramadan?' It was harmless, just words, but it made for an unpleasant surprise.

We thought at first it could have been the doorman or one of the car parkers, but they were all illiterate and probably not foolish enough to risk their jobs with a stunt like that. The author was to remain a mystery. Roda nevertheless decided it would be better if she did not come round to my house for a while. I, on the other hand, never stopped visiting Istanbul Street to play cards. I had been so many times that I knew the route through Muwazafeen like the back of my hand. Most days the traffic was so congested I could have walked from Elephant and Castle to Muwazafeen from car to car without putting a foot on the ground.

Each evening I hailed a black and white cab from the street outside my house and heard a new, sad saga from a different taxi driver – about the war in Iraq, about the rent he had to pay for his taxi, about his dream of going to America or about a million other things that were weighing on his mind as he sat smoking in traffic jams. How the traffic was that day was always a major topic of conversation because Egyptians discuss traffic like British people talk about the weather, the forecast forever changing.

Every day I would field the same friendly enquiries: 'How long have you been in Cairo?', 'Are you married?' and inevitably, 'Are you a Muslim?' Only occasionally did we sit in sweaty silence, the air conditioning broken, petrol fumes slowly filling the cab, listening to the Koran or an old cassette of Om Kalthoum on a crackly car stereo. Sometimes the journey would be enlivened by an adventure, either because the driver was a country bumpkin who got us lost or because the cab broke down or we had a small accident. Bumps happened all the time, but Egyptian taxis are like dodgems: covered in dents and scratches, but rarely moving fast enough to build up enough speed to really hurt someone. On several occasions I noticed the road passing under my feet through holes in the floor and more than once I had to get out and push.

No matter how cordial the conversation, the journey inevitably ended with a tussle over the fare. Although all Cairo cabs have meters, they were calibrated when petrol was laughably cheap and any taxi driver today who relied on them to calculate his fares would swiftly go out of business. This meant the price always had to be negotiated upon arrival, which frequently led to a heated exchange ending with a slammed door.

The worst days to travel were when a funeral was taking place in Muwazafeen's central place of worship, the Mustafa Mahmoud mosque. For the death of an important man, his family would have the authorities cordon off several major roads for parking and mourners. The disruption this would cause gridlocked the whole suburb in one mass of cursing travellers made up of everyone who had not been invited to the funeral.

Since so many of my Egyptian friends had family commitments during Ramadan, the card circle was rarely complete. So to keep myself occupied I called Dwayne, knowing that his family were too dysfunctional to entertain much, but when I did his mother gave me some surprising news. He had gone to Iraq.

His mother said that he had been desperately looking for a job and had been to at least a dozen interviews without success. Finally he applied for a vacancy passed on to him by an old school friend working for an international accountancy firm. Coming from telesales he thought he stood little chance of getting a job at such a prestigious company with so many highly skilled applicants, but at the end of the interview he was told that there was just one more question which would decide whether he would be hired or not. That question was simple: would he go to Iraq?

'Yes,' Dwayne said without a second's doubt. Although they had not even discussed pay, Dwayne was ready to leave at once. Taken aback by his enthusiasm, the interviewer asked him to take some time to think about it, underlining that it was dangerous work. He even said that in Dwayne's shoes he would not go and he certainly would never advise anybody else to go. Three weeks later Dwayne was in Baghdad.

His mother told me tearfully how she had tried to stop him. She said he kept telling her he knew it was dangerous but was sure it was the right decision. The last time she spoke to him before he left was on the telephone when he was on his way to the airport. She lost her temper, screamed at him and told him not to be so stupid, but he hung up on her.

Ramadan passed slowly. I received occasional invitations – Roda and Noha invited me to several breakfasts in Istanbul Street – but most of the time Roda and her family were busy elsewhere in the city seeing relatives. But, going out or staying in, the daily focus of the holy month was the same for me as it was for millions of others across the Arab world: the evening television schedule. I spent hours just watching television, stuffing myself with syrupy sweets and flicking from channel to channel. The flagship shows were soap operas, scheduled to run back to back all night long, starting shortly after breakfast, just when the audience was feeling its fattest and most sluggish.

When not watching Egyptian, Syrian and Lebanese soaps, I flicked through the dozen or so Arab satellite TV channels given over to round-the-clock music videos. Several more stations offered music videos at least some of the time, but the exact number on offer varied, as despite their enormous popularity none of these channels is self-financing and there is a constant cycle of start-ups and bankruptcies. I quickly learnt to tell the gyrating singers apart, as they morphed sultrily from doe-eyed virgin to nymphomaniac in each video. Once upon a time it was Christian Arab women, often Lebanese, who embraced Western music video culture. Today Muslims are doing it too and their fame reverberates through the Arab world. While Algerian and Moroccan singers have lucrative careers in Europe and France in particular, stars from the Nile and the Lebanon score in the Levant and the Gulf.

Singers like Ruby, Elissa and the smouldering Nancy Ajram, all household names in Cairo, have done more to bring about a sexual revolution in the Arab world than the combined efforts of scores of liberal male intellectuals throughout the twentieth century. The undisputed megastar of Egyptian pop, Amr Diab is a local version of Ricky Martin. His melodies are sentimental and romantic and owe more to Spanish music than they do to Arab traditions, but there is no denying his hits are catchy, albeit so overplayed that after barely a week in Egypt they conjure up images of Mobinil, the nation's ubiquitous mobile phone provider, and Pepsi, for both of which he has made jingles.

As music channels lose money they are underwritten by mobile phone companies and music producers, who make their money back from ringtones, from amorous viewers who pay to send anonymous text messages scrolling across the screen or by selling CDs and tickets for live shows. As conservative critics have been quick to point out, music videos are really little more than advertisements for media and telecommunications companies. Not all videos are sexual: occasionally there are tributes to someone who has died, such as assassinated Lebanese Prime Minister Rafiq Hariri. Other videos champion a cause such as the plight of the Palestinians or the Iraqis, while others are overtly Islamic.

That said, combining sex and advertising is nothing new. Egyptians have been enjoying the two together since at least the 1930s, when prostitution was still legal in Cairo and Amun cigarettes featured a picture of a topless woman on the packet. Music videos are just the latest incarnation of an age-old phenomenon and the perfect antidote to the other most popular stations on Egyptian television – the rolling news channels with their graphic scenes of death and destruction.

In recent years text messaging has spread like wildfire across the Muslim world because it is cheap, because Arabs are talkative and because relatively few people have access to the Internet. In 2003 a Malaysian court ruled that under sharia law a man may divorce his wife via text messaging as long as the message is clear. A strange new hybrid language has emerged for texts, a kind of pidgin Arabic written in English script, but with symbols and numbers representing certain letters not found on the English keyboard.

The Egyptian state, which exercises control over all the media, does not approve of pop music of any kind. State newspapers refer to music videos simply as 'porno clips' and in official venues and on national television and radio music is restricted to classic hits from thirty or forty years ago. Music from porno clips plays in taxis, private cars and *shisha* cafés.

One difference from Western music videos is that in the Arab world poverty is too close to be portrayed. Videos tend to depict simple romantic fantasies blissfully detached from the real world. A scantily dressed singer has a secret rendezvous in a luxury hotel with a handsome Western man in a tuxedo. A light-skinned woman in European clothes fawns over a blue-eyed man in a new-model convertible. Usually the action takes place on the streets of a picturesque European city, but if it is shot in Cairo it will often be in a palatial villa surrounded by a wall high enough to keep ordinary Egyptians out.

The glorious exception to all this schlock is *shaabi* music, a kind of raucous amateurish pop music that is proudly Egyptian, drawn from the working class and originating from singers performing at street parties and weddings. *Shaabi* singers typically have no formal music training but a chirpy ragamuffin humour.

The undisputed king of *shaabi* pop is the flamboyant, self-proclaimed illiterate Shaaban Abdel Rahim, or as his fans know him, Shaabola. Shaabola can neither play a musical instrument nor sing and before he stumbled on fame – whether this happened by accident or design is still not clear – he was a professional ironer. With a large gold watch on each wrist, glazed piggy eyes and a slicked-back mullet, Shaabola is reminiscent of Elvis in his Las Vegas years, but with more leering.

Shaabola's songs are aimed at the man in the street and tackle topical issues like Nile pollution, the war on terror and taxes. His hallucinogenic straight-to-video music clips typically show him dancing shambolically in front of a projector screen in a louche suit. An avowed dope smoker, Shaabola is loathed by the intelligentsia but has a massive following on the street and is a regular guest on television talk shows. He has also made forays into acting, playing sleazy underworld characters not unlike himself. Although he likes to play the fool, Shaabola is a shrewd political operator whose repertoire includes songs tactfully supportive of the Mubarak regime. By listing the government's 'achievements' in his songs, like bringing mobile phones and satellite dishes to Egypt, he has managed to preserve his liberty and promote his career.

Shaabola has proved so successful that one of his songs was even picked up by McDonald's to advertise its McFalafel sandwich, the Middle East's answer to the Big Mac. McDonald's dropped the song after just a few weeks, according to Shaabola because of pressure from pro-Israeli lobbies in America: one of his biggest hits of recent years was called 'I hate Israel'. When Shaabola was pressed on why he had licensed his song to the American fast food outlet in the first place he pleaded ignorance, claiming that since he was illiterate he could not read the contract and had no idea to whom his song had been licensed, an excuse which immediately cleared him of any wrongdoing in the eyes of the great Egyptian public.

Twenty-one

'You look great,' Roda said for the umpteenth time as she stroked Yosra's dyed and heavily back-combed bouffant. 'Your hair looks really lovely.'

We were in Roda's apartment preparing for Yosra's big date. Yosra had omitted to tell her family that she was on a date because she was not sure what her brother would say if he knew Roda had arranged it. Her family had once been fond of Roda, but after word reached them that she was dating a foreigner none of them wanted Yosra to have anything more to do with her.

'Thanks,' said Yosra grimly. She was sitting on the sofa, her face glazed, slowly chewing the skin from her bottom lip. The television blared in front of her, but her mind was somewhere else, her gaze fixed somewhere in the middle distance. She was not nervous. Her brain was too anaesthetised for that and besides she had had countless dates like this before and knew exactly what to expect – disappointment.

Customarily on an Egyptian blind date the girl arrives accompanied by a chaperone whose role is to act as both interlocutor and confidante. Typically the chaperone will be a girlfriend or a female family member. Ideally she will already know the man in question and perhaps even have had a hand in setting up the date in the first place so as better to lubricate the wheels of the first awkward encounter. The chaperone's presence also serves to

sanction the meeting officially, insuring against improper con-
duct and preventing any observers jumping to the mistaken
conclusion that some kind of illicit affair is taking place. In this
case Roda was to be the chaperone even though she had never
met Tamer before. I had invited myself along too because I was
nosy and wanted to check whether the Sheikh's spells had had
any effect. Bringing a foreigner along on a first date is definitely
not standard protocol and I hoped it was not going to be too
much of a shock for Tamer.

Roda, Yosra, Noha and I knew almost nothing about the man
Yosra was about to meet, so as we prepared to leave the conver-
sation turned to the girl who had mentioned his name as a
potential suitor in the first place. Her name was Heidi and she was
a girl Roda had met at the hairdresser. Heidi, Roda informed us,
was having her own problems getting married. She was an
Egyptian Protestant searching for the same, which meant she was
looking for a partner from within a tiny subset of the Christian
minority. Heidi's parents were struggling to find her a husband
from a pitifully small pool of suitors. An arranged marriage was
the best she could hope for as the chances of meeting a Protestant
without her parents' intervention were slim to none.

'I just really hope he's tall,' said Yosra. 'For me that is the most
important thing. And, please God, not a lawyer.'

'What's wrong with a lawyer?' A lawyer sounded rather good
to me.

'Only very few English-speaking lawyers make money here.
Most do not do very well,' Roda interrupted. 'There are not
enough jobs so most of them end up either unemployed or
working for the government. It's not a career people aspire to.'

Roda's phone rang. It was Tamer, saying he had just arrived at
the *shisha* bar where the date was scheduled to take place. He
wanted to know if Yosra had arrived there yet.

'What shall I say?' said Roda in a coarse whisper, cupping her
hand over the receiver.

'Tell him we are on our way,' said Yosra, blowing a languid smoke ring.

'Aren't we going to be late?' I asked. 'Didn't you arrange to meet at eight?' The clock on the wall already said 8.30 and we were still sitting in the apartment.

'Stop being so English,' said Yosra. 'You need to get on Egyptian time. If you say eight you mean nine. Besides I don't see why I have to rush for this guy.'

Perhaps as a defence against disappointment, Yosra would convince herself that she did not care about the guy she was about to meet. Bitter experience had taught her what she was looking for, and what she wasn't. Yosra claimed she could tell within the first ten seconds if the date was going somewhere or not. One of her favourite tricks to winnow out the unsuitable was to announce that the reason that she was still unmarried at thirty-three was because she hated children. If the guy agreed, he was struck off at once.

'He says he's parking his car,' said Roda, still with her hand over the mouthpiece.

'Good sign,' mouthed Yosra to me. 'He's got a car. Try to look at his keys to check what kind it is.'

I wondered fleetingly how Tamer was feeling at that moment. Did he have butterflies in his stomach about the girl he was about to meet? Maybe he was hoping that tonight would be the night to bring him true love. Perhaps he was gay and going along only because his family had told him to.

'Bad news,' announced Roda solemnly as she hung up.

'What?' snapped Yosra, expecting the worst.

'He's got a terrible accent.'

This was sure to be a significant strike against him in Yosra's eyes. Egypt is a highly stratified society and someone's accent and vocabulary say a great deal about their background and class. The minute an Egyptian opens his mouth it places him somewhere in the city's complex social hierarchy.

'Come on, let's go,' said Roda.

'I guess we'd better,' said Yosra gloomily.

We walked down the chipped marble stairs and out into the dusty street. Crimson fingers ran across the darkening sky, dramatically silhouetting the washing lines and satellite dishes on the rooftops. A warm wind was whipping up as it did every evening.

'Hanafi!' shouted Roda into the darkness. 'Hanafi!'

There was a jingling as Roda's doorman came loping out of the building next door holding a battered shoebox full of car keys. Fishing around in the box, he handed Roda her key.

'Hanafi, I want you to take the car to the garage tomorrow morning and have them take a look at the gearbox again,' Roda commanded. 'They were supposed to have repaired it and it's still making funny noises.'

'Yes, Doctor,' grunted Hanafi. 'Anything else?'

'That's all,' replied Roda.

'Good evening,' he said, respectfully.

Roda unlocked the door of the car and the three of us climbed inside.

'I saw this documentary about Osama bin Laden on CNN the other day,' said Yosra. 'It was called *In the Footsteps of the Martyrs* or something and he was trekking through the mountains in Afghanistan and stuff. What he went through, I mean it's amazing, especially when you think he could have just lived a life of luxury in Saudi Arabia instead.'

'You didn't know all that already?' I asked.

'Well, I knew who he was of course, but they never show any documentaries about him on Egyptian TV so this was the first time I actually learnt something new about him.'

'And did it change what you think about him?'

'Sure it did,' said Yosra. 'I used to hate the guy and now I think he's amazing. They really made him look great.'

'Shall I put some music on?' asked Roda. 'How about Dalida?'

'Good idea,' agreed Yosra.

As Roda fumbled with the car stereo the muezzin's sonorous call started up, ringing out simultaneously from the radio and from the minarets of more than four thousand mosques across the city. Thanks to modern technology the prayer call, the *azan*, is now broadcast via the radio, television, Internet and all Cairo's mosques simultaneously, five times a day. Synchronisation was intended as a measure to prevent noise pollution: the Ministry of Religious Endowments wanted to end the drawn-out cacophony that had existed when each mosque began prayers according to its own clock. It was a controversial decision that angered many Cairenes. Attempts to regulate religion have traditionally been greeted suspiciously and many suspected that synchronisation was in fact part of a nefarious anti-Islamic plot, most probably hatched in Washington, to control the information disseminated at prayer time. At times I found the *azan* almost threatening, as if prayer itself has become infused with militancy, but that evening each drawn-out syllable shimmered and settled like a fine silver shroud stretching from mosque to mosque across the city.

'What are you waiting for?' I asked Roda, whose hand was still hovering over the stereo. 'Where's the music?'

'Wait a second. I can't put a CD on until the call to prayer has finished. It's *haram* to switch it off halfway through.'

Haram is Arabic for both 'forbidden' and 'sacred' and the root of the English word harem. When the call to prayer ended, Roda flicked on the CD and Dalida struck up. A one-time Miss Egypt, Dalida fled the country in the 1950s and spent the next thirty years singing about how much she missed the place, selling more than seventy-five million records in the process. Roda and Yosra knew all the words to the tragic Jewess's patriotic hits and they joined in with gusto.

'Which one do you think is his car?' asked Yosra, breaking off as we drew close to the *shisha* bar. A sea of hundreds of cars double- and even triple-parked stretched as far as the eye could see.

'And how could I possibly know that?' said Roda, pulling up the handbrake with a jerk. Quickly the local car parkers descended on us, emerging from the darkness like zombies, rapping on the car windows and demanding we hand over our keys.

'We don't have to deal with this,' said Roda with a groan, stepping on the gas and taking us down a sidestreet.

'How did you know about this alley?' I asked.

'I used to know two sisters who lived near here. We were never best friends but we went out together a lot.'

'What happened?' I asked, sensing something more, unspoken.

'They got involved with this extreme religious group and it became hard for us to stay friends. We used to go to the hairdresser together and do our eyebrows and manicure, but now they are veiled and they won't even wear scent or make-up because they think it's *haram*. They never leave the house so I don't see them any more,' Roda shrugged. 'Too bad.'

Twenty-two

Over more than ten years Yosra had been on hundreds of blind dates with all manner of men. She always sat in the same hotel *shisha* bar. Sometimes she sat facing the window; sometimes she sat facing the door. None of her dates had led anywhere. Nothing had ever worked out.

Perhaps because of my presence at the table this time, the date was agony at first. Tamer, aged about thirty-four, was a pallid, balding engineer and cripplingly shy. In retrospect he deserved more credit than I gave him at the time for keeping so cool. Having some strange Western guy turn up on your blind date must be an uncomfortable surprise.

'He's my fiancé,' explained Roda, gesturing confidently at me. 'And I know your cousin Heidi. My name is Roda.'

Yosra was rubbing her stomach and grimacing. 'Ow!' She winced. 'I walked into the table and banged my rabies jab.'

Tamer smiled as politely as could be expected and mumbled something that I guessed to be some kind of welcome. I grinned back as unthreateningly as I could and we shook hands. He had the kind of handshake that made you want to go home immediately and take a shower.

'He's got virgin written all over him,' whispered Roda to me in a stage whisper as we sat down. I hoped Tamer did not understand English.

The rules of the Muwazafeen dating game run like this. The guy calls the girl and fixes a time and a place to meet. He selects the venue, usually somewhere trendy like a hip coffee shop or a *shisha* bar, though never somewhere where alcohol is served. She arrives fashionably late accompanied by her chaperone, and the three sit together for an hour or so and chat. Once the girl has a pretty clear idea about whether she wants to see the guy again she concocts a phoney excuse about having to go, before leaving politely with her chaperone. If the guy likes her and wants to see her again, he lets the chaperone know, who passes this on to the girl, who then decides whether she wants to go on a second date.

This means on the first date, as in the West, the girl has the upper hand and the onus is on the man to be assertive, present himself well, talk about what he does for a living and make it clear how much he earns. The girl can expect him to lay out the key facts about himself: whether he owns a car or flat or other object of substantial value, whether he has been married, engaged or imprisoned, and generally outline his credentials as prospective husband material.

On this occasion Tamer was so shy we spent the first ten minutes in total silence, interrupted only once by the waiter coming to take our order. Every so often he turned to Yosra and opened his mouth as if about to speak, but nothing came out, leaving him gawping like a landed fish. His self-confidence ebbing, he jammed the nozzle of his water pipe back in his mouth and sucked heavily to calm his nerves, until he summoned up enough courage for another attempt. Yosra meanwhile sat coolly, saying nothing, her face an unreadable mask. Roda studied the drinks menu intensely.

I felt sorry for Tamer. He had obviously made an effort. His shirt was clean and ironed, his hair brushed sideways over his pate to hide the bald spot. He looked well scrubbed and generally had an air about him of a man who had spent some time looking in the mirror, squeezing his spots and psyching himself up for what was obviously destined to be a nerve-racking evening. As the minutes wore on, the silence became more leaden. After several more abortive attempts to speak Tamer's self-confidence seemed to take leave of him completely and he gave up any effort to talk at all. Sitting quite still in his chair, his eyes bored down into the table in front of him, only occasionally glancing up at mine, panic etched large across his face. I tried my best to offer what assistance I could from the other side of the table, smiling reassuringly and inwardly wishing him well, but it seemed to make no difference. His mind apparently paralysed, he uttered not a single word, until after what seemed like hours of excruciating torment I decided to help out.

'So, Tamer, what is it exactly that you do?' I ventured.

It was as if the air that hung between us had finally cracked and given way.

'I work for the government in the Customs and Excise Department,' blurted out Tamer very fast, as if he had been wanting to say exactly and only this since the moment we had walked in the door but had just not been able to find the words. Yosra's sphinx-like expression did not register this momentous announcement.

'That's sounds interesting,' I said as cheerfully as I could. 'What kind of stuff do people export?'

'Textiles mainly, as well as manufactured products. I work with public vehicles mainly. The parts are imported and assembled in Egypt and then we export them all over the world.'

I was not sure how best to carry on from here but, the conversation started, I felt we could hardly return to silence. Since Tamer was still too nervous to have what might be called a conversation, we continued the question-and-answer session with me asking all the questions.

It emerged that Tamer spoke Russian fluently. His father, an architect, had been studying in the Soviet Union in the late 1960s when he had met his Russian mother. I thought this was interesting so asked him more until Roda kicked my shin hard under the table. I flinched and abruptly shut up. 'You are not supposed to be the one getting to know this guy,' said her face as she glared at me. But, the ice now broken, at least Tamer could start telling Yosra a little about himself, as he was supposed to, while Roda and I made hushed small talk on the other side of the table. And then fortunately the conversation was saved by a topic that animated everyone: ID cards. All Egyptians had something to say about this because the system was in the process of being changed, producing widespread chaos.

Under the new set-up, every Egyptian citizen was required to hand over their old paper ID card, which they had been happily using for years, so it could be replaced by a new kind of laminated plastic ID with a photograph. What this meant in practice was that every citizen was obliged to present in short order a large amount of personal documentation, including their birth certificate, passport (if they had one), letters from current and previous employers, driving licence, tax information, signed affidavits from academic institutions and other miscellaneous documents at a number of crowded, smelly public offices where they would get ignored, frustrated, angry, sweaty, groped and finally sent away until they eventually found the correct person to bribe.

Getting their new ID filled everyone with dread, but like all bureaucratic procedures was as grimly inevitable as death itself. State ID is a requirement simply to set foot in a government building or on a university campus, which meant that absolutely everyone had to comply. By comparison so few Egyptians pay income tax – only about 300,000 people nationwide – the government recently began running radio advertisements asking them to pay up for the good of the nation.

Rescued by bureaucracy, our conversation staggered forward like a gassed rioter. When the hour was up, Roda tipped Yosra the wink so she knew it was time to spin the prearranged story about sick relatives, which I knew to be also my cue to leave. Saying our goodbyes to Tamer, who generously insisted on paying the bill, we thanked him and left. Grateful the whole awkward episode was over, we breathed a communal sigh of relief as we walked back to the car, careful not to disturb a pack of mangy dogs sniffing around some burst garbage sacks in the street outside the *shisha* café.

'How dare she?' raged Roda as soon as we got into the car, confident that we were now safely out of earshot. 'How dare Heidi not show up?'

Heidi had promised to come on the date too. Since she was the one who had got the two parties together, it was extremely bad form for her not to show up without any explanation. She had not even called.

Then we drove back to the apartment, Dalida still on the stereo, dissecting as we went every second of the date from when we walked through the door to the moment we said goodbye. The overall verdict was borderline positive. Sure, Tamer had been a bit shy, but Yosra had been on enough dates to know that shyness was usually only skin deep. She was more concerned by his height: Tamer had not stood up once during the evening so none of us knew how tall he was.

'How do I know if I want to see him again if I don't know how tall he is? He's a virgin for sure,' she added.

'He looks like it,' I conceded.

'He can't be a virgin. He's Russian,' countered Roda.

'You know, that's the most attractive thing about him,' said Yosra. 'That he's Russian. It means he might be a bit more liberal than Egyptian men.'

The last thing Yosra wanted was to marry a guy like her brother. But marriage was still a long way off. All that could be done now was to wait and see if Tamer asked Heidi to organise another date. Only time would tell if the mystic Sheikh had uncovered the root of Yosra's dating problems.

Twenty-three

Doing business in Egypt during Ramadan is a bit like trying to do business in France during August. Office life crawls along like the last week of the summer term. Calls go unanswered; no work is done. If by chance you manage to catch someone in the office for the few brief hours they are there, usually they just wish you a happy Ramadan and laughingly tell you to call back next month.

Strenuous communal efforts at temperance prompt the entire national workforce to knock off at two o'clock in the afternoon with the intention of returning to bed to grab a few hours' sleep before breakfast. Unfortunately, since everyone leaves the office at the same time, bed usually remains a hazy mirage at the end of a long and extremely bad-tempered traffic jam snaking through the city. Drivers sit in a testy silence broken only by the buzz of flies, the interminable recitation of the Koran on the radio and the drumming of a hundred million tetchy tobacco-stained fingers on car doors.

Roda and I were stuck in just such a traffic jam one afternoon in Ramadan. It was October, but the sun was beating down so hard that the heat coming off the road made the white sails of the feluccas in the distance shimmer on the green Nile rolling gently along beneath us. We were in a taxi on the Sixth of October bridge, a river crossing so long and important that if the Israeli air force ever needed to reduce the great country of Egypt to her knees with a single bomb, besides the Aswan High Dam this would probably be the best place to drop it.

We were not going anywhere in particular, just savouring some private time together, since Roda no longer felt comfortable coming to Elephant and Castle and neither of us wanted to run into the neighbours at Istanbul Street. We were almost certainly the only people in that long line of hot cars perfectly content to be there that day and we could scarcely have picked a more picturesque spot.

Engrossed in one another's company, we chatted on the back seat, enjoying for once the feeling of being alone. Except of course we were not alone: from the corner of my eye I could see our driver keeping a beady eye on Roda in his rear-view mirror, scowling from time to time as we laughed, doubtless worried we were getting up to something sinful in the back of his cab during Ramadan. Every now and then he muttered an oath under his breath, like a medieval monk confronted by the sight of a naked woman. The white foreigner and the Egyptian woman having a civilised conversation in the back of his cab were making him visibly edgy.

I was complaining about the tribulations of dating in Ramadan while cunningly preparing, I hoped, the ground for my next move: a trip for a few days to Lebanon. A friend of mine living in Beirut was travelling to America and had generously offered me her apartment while she was away. With its Mediterranean climate and melting-pot society, Beirut seemed like the perfect antidote to the crush and conservatism of Cairo. An Arab Gretna Green, in Beirut lovers are free to kiss, canoodle, hold hands. Romance flourishes in Lebanon because history and geography have combined to make it the most liberal Arab country. When you have been through a bloody civil war you come to understand that there are more important things in life than bothering lovers holding hands in the street. The chance to take a break there was too good to miss.

I knew it was going to be difficult to sell to Roda. Most Egyptian women cannot just up and travel abroad with a foreign guy whenever they like; they at least need a chaperone, ideally a closely related male one. If word got out Roda was alone abroad with a foreigner, a non-Muslim too, it would spell trouble upon her return. Though fortunately Roda did not have the kind of male relatives who would throw acid on her face for defiling family honour, it would naturally be assumed that we had absconded to have sex and the consequences could be serious.

'So how about we get out of town, go somewhere no one knows us?'

'Like where?' said Roda.

'Well . . . how about Beirut?'

She smiled and her smile turned into a laugh. 'I can't go to Beirut with you, but thanks for asking,' she replied, touching my cheek tenderly.

I was not surprised or hurt that I had been rebuffed. What I was asking was difficult and likely to require some persistence, and I could always ask again later. But in the meantime it seemed our conversation was too intimate for the delicate sensibilities of our driver.

The taxi, which had been barely moving anyway, lurched to a halt.

'You can't do that in here,' snapped our driver, a stubbly middle-aged man with a Saddam Hussein moustache and a shirt covered in engine grease. 'I won't have indecency in my cab.'

Roda and I looked at each other in bemusement. 'This is a respectable taxi. I don't need your kind in here. You can get out right here.'

Now maybe because I am a Westerner I have some sympathy with taxi drivers in Cairo. I have chatted to a fair few and know that they work long hours for next to nothing. Many times I have found myself talking to a driver who has turned out to be a highly qualified professional – a university professor or an aircraft engineer – moonlighting because he cannot make ends meet with his day job. And then there is the frustration of sitting in hot smelly traffic jams all day, telling indifferent strangers about your family problems.

As an Egyptian woman Roda had a less compassionate view of taxi drivers. For her taxis spelt harassment, being flashed and getting ripped off. Besides, Cairo is a class-ridden society where people are expected to know their place, and nobody has to listen to personal remarks from a cab driver.

'What did you say?' asked Roda.

'You can peddle your seedy trade in the street and anywhere else you like, but not in the back of my cab, not in Ramadan, no thank you.'

'Why don't you mind your own business?' I suggested.

'Don't tell me to mind my own business. This is my cab and I say what goes!' he shouted back, gesticulating angrily in the mirror at me.

'You are a small-minded, nosy old man,' screamed Roda, 'who should know better than to harass people in his cab. Why don't you mind your own business? We don't care what you think,' she continued angrily.

'It's my cab and I'll say what goes on in it. No perverts!'

'We haven't done anything wrong,' I replied.

'You're the pervert,' Roda added quickly.

'Your kind make me sick!' spat the driver, waving a grubby finger in the air. 'God protect me from your depravity! This is a respectable taxi. Get out!'

'Come on . . .' said Roda turning to me. 'Let's leave this arsehole.' We opened the door and stepped out into the sunshine on the bridge. 'Which way?' I said, shielding my eyes from the glare and scanning the traffic, which stretched bumper to bumper in either direction as far as the eye could see.

I slammed the door as hard as I could; it shut with a tinny click. '*Kusumak ya ibn al-mitnaka*,' I muttered through the open window at the driver, a colloquial phrase that translates approximately as, 'Your mother's pussy from a fucked mother.'

Now in English, at least in British English, although admittedly this sounds rude there are worse things you can say to someone than insult their mother. It is a strange fact in Nordic countries that the rudest insults you can hurl at someone pertain to the devil. But it is an interesting comment on Mediterranean society that insulting someone's mother is just about as low as you can go, particularly if you are speaking to a man.

There are many ways you can insult someone's mother around the world. You can call her a prostitute. You can say she has a moustache. In Spain you can threaten to shit in her breast milk. In China you can call someone's mother a turtle, and the Russians, justifiably proud of their robust approach to profanity, call swearing the mother language. When it was suggested that the reason French star striker Zinédine Zidane had headbutted Marco 'Matrix' Materazzi during the World Cup was because the Italian defender had called his mother a prostitute and a terrorist – a complicated combination – the French understood at once. 'Of course he did,' they muttered into their croissants. 'Who would have done anything less?' For his part, the Matrix later admitted that he had insulted Zidane, but denied he would ever say something so offensive.

Anthropologists disagree over why mother insults in certain parts of the world remain such a taboo. What is incredibly rude in one language can often sound rather funny in another, just as there are often two different words for the same part of the body, one extremely vulgar and the other quite acceptable. Some scholars attribute sensitivity about mothers to veneration of the Virgin Mary, but that does not explain the power of mother insults in the Muslim world. Freudians might suggest that by hinting someone's mother likes having sex with other men you threaten an unconscious sexual desire. Muslims have their own traditions about mothers and in the sayings of the Hadith one of the Prophet Muhammad's companions asks him, 'Who deserves my good treatment most?'

'Your mother,' replies the Prophet.

'Who next?' asks the man.

'Your mother,' replies the Prophet again.

'Who next?'

'Your mother.'

'Who after that?'

'Your father.'

This can be taken to mean that the mother deserves three times more respect than the father and in Arabic 'mother' can also denote an outstanding example of some sort, as when Saddam Hussein predicted that the Gulf War would be the mother of all battles. Egypt is known throughout Africa and the Middle East as the mother of the world.

Mention the M-word in Egypt without total respect and it is a press-button certainty that trouble is going to ensue because any man with even a shred of self-respect is compelled to respond quickly and often violently. Simply say, 'Your mother . . .' under your breath to an Egyptian man, as if articulating an offensive but only semi-verbalised thought, and fireworks are guaranteed to follow.

All of which explains why, the moment Roda closed the car door, the taxi driver reached for the wrench under his seat and his face blackened in fury. He did not look like a mummy's boy, but after I dropped the mother of all insults I was not going to stick around to find out. 'Time to go!' I shouted as he threw open the car door and began to manoeuvre his belly out from behind the steering wheel.

In the minibus next to us a row of shapeless veiled women pressed what I guessed were their noses against the glass, excited at the prospect of seeing an Egyptian bludgeon a foreigner to death in the street. It was strange, I thought fleetingly as I circled the taxi, keeping it between me and the cabby, that while women are generally treated as second-class citizens, motherhood should be regarded with such veneration. When I so rudely slandered the taxi driver's mother, I did not know even whether the woman was alive or dead, let alone the number of sexual partners she had enjoyed. All we could be sure of was that the woman was no longer a virgin. Maybe she really was a prostitute, which could have been quite an interesting talking point. But as the taxi driver ran after us, still flourishing the wrench about his head, I decided now was not the moment to ask, nor were these details of much importance.

'Run!' I yelled as I legged it passed the static cars, pulling Roda after me. Noticing the taxi was empty, drivers honked frantically. Others waved and cheered as we pushed past their wing mirrors. People got out of their vehicles to intervene or just to look. Looking back we saw the cab driver with his hands on his thighs. Gasping, he cursed and waved his wrench, but because it was Ramadan he had had nothing to eat or drink all day and was never going to be able to catch us.

Twenty-four

Had I not nearly been cudgelled by a taxi driver, had it not been Ramadan, had someone not pinned a spiteful note on her car, Roda might never have agreed to come to Beirut with me and things might have turned out differently. But as the month reached its heady close with the feast of Eid al-Fitr, I came to realise that Cairo was suffocating our relationship as surely as it was suffocating everything that lived under its insalubrious brown fug. The time had come for me to use the one advantage I had over millions of unfortunate Egyptians. It was time for me to leave for a while.

Roda kept me guessing as to whether she was going to come with me until the very last moment. In the airport departure lounge as the gate was closing I was convinced she was not going to show up until she burst through the glass doors waving her green passport and dragging an enormous canvas suitcase. 'Sorry I'm late,' she said breathlessly. 'Half the streets of Muwazafeen were cordoned off because one of the pimps died.'

We were not the first or last couple driven to escape the stifling atmosphere of the region by visiting Lebanon. Youth from across the Arab world, if they have the means, are drawn by Beirut's heady sensuousness and fragile liberalism – a beautiful city atop a political volcano. The precarious sectarian balance, approximately one third each Sunni, Shia and Christian, makes for infernally complicated domestic politics and an unsteady governnmental system that looks set to collapse at any moment. The weakness of Lebanon's national goverment means that actual power lies in the hands of sectarian leaders who constantly renegotiate the historic relationships that bind them as they squabble endlessly over how the country should be run. Nor are the intricacies of Lebanon's politics solely the business of the Lebanese. Foreign powers from the Vatican to Tehran to Washington play their proxies like marionettes with sometimes explosive results.

On holiday, in the affluent parts of Beirut at least, it was easy for us to forget the tensions below the surface. Chic galleries in Christian East Beirut featured erotic art shows; the nightclubs were swimming with gilded youth showing off their skiing suntans and chatting effortlessly in Arabic, French and English. Something of 1960s France lingers alongside the pockmarked buildings of the old Green Line, and with such beautiful women, fine wine, delicious food and world-class hashish, if you avoid its densely populated southern suburbs and bombed-out slums, Beirut remains a sybarite's ideal holiday destination.

The romance of our escape was heightened by a looming political crisis. News in the papers each day suggested the country might soon be torn apart all over again. Little did we know but Hezbollah were adding the finishing touches to an elaborate system of tunnels and fortifications that they were itching to test out on the Israeli war machine, while their opponents were busy hatching plans to eradicate Hezbollah from the south of the country for good. The circling storm makes the pleasures of today seem only more precious.

Beirut was the perfect tonic after the claustrophobic conservatism of Cairo. People had seen me come and go at Roda's apartment dozens of times and the pressure of inquisitorial relatives, snooping landladies and interfering doormen was growing too much. In Cairo people often seem to regard it as their social or religious duty to interfere in other people's relationships, usually under the guise of protecting the virtue of a girl. Of course we had neighbours in Beirut too, but they were whisky-slugging Christians who only wanted to regale us with wartime sniper stories and chat about the current wave of political assassinations sweeping the country. Rafiq Hariri, a giant of Lebanese politics, had been assassinated the previous Valentine's Day, shocking even our neighbours, who had long ago become inured to all but the most appalling events. They quickly guessed, but could not have cared less, why we had come to town.

Left to our own devices, we rejoiced in the simple freedoms of walking hand in hand in the street, eating together unremarked in restaurants and kissing in taxis, all things lovers in the West take for granted but which millions of Arabs are systemically denied, and by the time we got back to Cairo we were not just refreshed – we were engaged. We flew back to Cairo via Hatton Garden in London, and one wet weekday morning when the city was hard at work we went shopping for rings. We needed three because we were getting engaged Egyptian style. The man wears his wedding ring on his right hand and the woman wears her engagement and wedding rings also on her right hand. When they marry the rings are slid from the right hand to the left without removing them, by putting the ring fingers together, symbolising an engagement leading seamlessly into a lifetime of marriage.

Clang, clang, clang, clang. I opened my eyes. It was morning in Roda's apartment and the gas man was passing by outside with his cylinders. Fumbling for my glasses I sat up. Roda was already awake and making tea. 'Don't try to take a shower,' she said. 'There's no hot water again. I'm going downstairs to ask the neighbours what's going on.'

'Sure thing,' I said blearily, struggling to my feet. The door of the apartment closed behind her with a click.

Sunlight was streaming through the shutters. I peered down into the street where a cat was sunbathing on a parked car. Friday morning was always the most peaceful time of the week in Istanbul Street. The doorman's wife sat on the kerb watching her ragged child play in the clouds of pollen and dust. Beirut seemed a world away, a movie I watched last year. Cairo is so encompassing that when you are there all other realities seem to fade away. I thought of Hatton Garden and it seemed surreal that at that very moment crowds of London commuters were heading to work in the rain. It felt impossible that the two places could exist at the same time.

As I buttoned my shirt a memory flashed into my head of being woken in the middle of the night by the neighbours fighting. Mahmoud, Abeer's alcoholic husband, had come home drunk in the early morning and urinated over his mother-in-law. She had woken us up screaming, 'You pissed on me! You pissed on me, you animal!' Then Abeer woke up too and Mahmoud beat her and the screaming got louder until he threw open the shutters on the balcony and shouted drunken obscenities into the street. 'My wife is a whore! I swear on the hair of my mother-in-law's pussy, my wife fucks men in the street all day and all night!' I rubbed my eyes against the glare and wondered what had happened to Roda.

Outside the front door someone was clumping slowly up the stairs with an awkward lopsided gait. It sounded like they were lugging something heavy, and every few steps they paused to wheeze like a pirate captain with emphysema. Silently I stirred my tea, straining to recognise who it was. A hacking cough gave her away: Tant Enayat, the sour-faced wife of the owner of the block. She prowled the block's corridors like the Minotaur, tackling anything in her path. If the residents heard her coming they would cower inside their apartments until the monster had passed.

I winced as I heard Roda's footsteps jogging lightly up the stairs, knowing any second she would reach the landing and

come face to beady face with the looming square spectacles of
Tant Enayat. She was the last person either of us wished to have
interrogating us about our private life. If she discovered we were
engaged doubtless she would want to know whether we were
planning to stay in the apartment after we were married or move
out, allowing her to get her grasping hands upon it.

Roda's footsteps stopped abruptly at the top of the stairs.

'Good morning.' She sounded surprised.

'Hello, my girl,' Tant Enayat rasped. 'How's your family? All
well, God willing?'

'Thanks be to God, they're all fine,' replied Roda, recovering
herself.

'Thanks be to God,' muttered Tant Enayat. 'Oh look! You're
wearing a ring. Are you engaged?'

'Yes,' replied Roda. 'To a British man.'

'Well, heavens above! Whatever next? To a British man, no less!
Well I never . . .'

There was an awkward pause. I stood with my cup hovering
halfway between the table and my mouth, willing Roda to slip
away.

'Well, I better be off . . .' began Roda, but she was forcefully
interrupted.

'So he's converted, has he?' demanded Tant Enayat bluntly. No
congratulations, no kind words. Just straight to the point.

'Yes, actually,' replied Roda quickly. 'He's a Muslim now.'

'Oh that is wonderful. Praise be to God,' said the landlady with
genuine conviction, before adding in a stage whisper that echoed
around the landing, 'But is he a Muslim in his heart or is it just
empty words?'

'Only God can know what is in a man's heart,' replied Roda
diplomatically.

'Yes, yes . . . of course,' agreed Tant Enayat sounding a little
disappointed. 'So what happened to all the Egyptian men? Are
they all used up?'

'No, there are still plenty left,' Roda replied, squeezing out a painfully insincere laugh.

'And what does he do for a living?' the landlady continued like a whip on a horse's back.

'He's a journalist,' replied Roda.

'A journalist, eh? So has he bought you somewhere nice to live for when you get married?' Aha, I thought. I knew that was coming.

'No, we are planning to stay right here in Istanbul Street,' replied Roda. 'We won't be moving anywhere.'

The landlady hawked and coughed, then said throatily, 'Listen to me closely, my girl. One of my other tenants married a Christian. He told her he had converted to Islam too. He said he prayed all the prayers and studied the Koran and went to the mosque, and then one day you know what happened? She followed him out of the house and found out that he was secretly going to church every Sunday.'

She hissed the last line of this terrible tale as if she was pronouncing the climactic lines of the curse of Tutankhamun.

'Can you imagine? The shame! Of course the whole street soon found out. So these are not empty words. You had better watch out in case something like that happens to you.'

There was a silence and I wondered momentarily whether perhaps Roda had been petrified by Tant Enayat's basilisk gaze.

'Thank you for the advice,' Roda said after a pause.

'Some people just can't stop themselves talking about these things,' the landlady cackled menacingly, 'but don't worry about me. I won't tell a soul. We all know what a good family you three girls come from and no one in Istanbul Street would like to see you ruined.'

Maybe it was because of the mystic Sheikh; perhaps it would have happened anyway. God knows Yosra had had more than her fair share of dead ends, false starts and let-downs. But while

Roda and I were in Lebanon a man materialised in Yosra's life. His name was Jihad and despite his pot belly, sheepish smile and lopsided spectacles, it seemed that finally everything might be about to come right for Yosra.

Jihad was a mousy man, softly spoken and shy. Unusually for a pharmacist he spoke no English but he owned a chain of five shops, a rare and admirable achievement since most would-be entrepreneurs in Egypt are squashed early on in their careers beneath the twin megaliths of bureaucracy and corruption. The best-laid plans usually grind to a halt under the weight of all the backhanders and 'insurance' payments necessary to establish a new business.

Yosra and Jihad had first come to know one another five years earlier during their final year at college. He was one of the very few men Yosra had met neither through family nor friends. After graduation he married the top student from their year, a veiled girl called Manar, who Yosra had always found rather intimidating. By chance, a year later Manar and Jihad had moved into an apartment just a few doors down from Yosra's house in Muwazafeen.

Seeing Yosra come and go in the street outside their block, Jihad often used to wave her a friendly hello. Their friendship never developed much further than that, but Yosra liked to watch the couple from a distance as their lives progressed. It was not long before Manar had a child and soon after a second and then a third. The couple seemed happy and busy, a picture of satisfied family life.

And then one day Manar walked out. She had won an academic scholarship to a university in America to further her pharmaceutical studies and had secretly made up her mind to go. Jihad only discovered she was leaving the day before she went, when he accidentally uncovered the paperwork his wife had been preparing while looking for his socks in her bedroom closet. There were visa forms from the American embassy as well as letters of invitation and other documents embossed with the stamp of the faculty of pharmacy at the University of Oregon.

Confronted, Manar admitted that she was leaving to start a new life in America. She told him the opportunity meant more to her than life in Cairo with her family. All the application forms had already been completed and she had enrolled herself at college for the coming academic year. The news came as a terrible shock to Jihad and he tried everything in his power to dissuade her. In desperation he offered her an instant divorce with a generous settlement including the car, an apartment and one of his five pharmacies in Muwazafeen. She left for the States the next day. They divorced on the way to the airport.

Unexpectedly left on his own, Jihad quickly discovered that he was not able to run things without a woman's help. Manar had cooked and cleaned for him, shopped for the house and looked after the children as well as helped run the pharmacies. At a loss what to do next, Jihad did what any man would do in such a situation: he invited his mother to move in. When Yosra's mother Salma heard over *tarneeb* what had happened, she was horrified. When she told Yosra the whole story the pair agreed that for Manar to leave her children to further her studies in America was an act against nature itself.

Twenty-five

It was a lazy hot weekend, our first in Cairo since returning from Beirut. Yosra, Roda and I were sitting in Roda's car drinking fresh watermelon juice and smoking apple *shishas*. Roda and Yosra were exchanging news in detail, as they always did when they had not seen each other for more than a day or two. Roda was telling her friend about our engagement plans; Yosra was telling us about the exciting new romance she had stumbled into with Jihad.

'So, the next time I saw him in the street, I went up to him and said how sorry I was to hear that Manar had left,' explained Yosra animatedly. She looked so much happier and healthier than when we had last seen her, before leaving for Lebanon. Her skin had cleared and lost much of its grey pallor, and the large puffy circles around her eyes had faded.

'And what did he say?'

'He invited me to have a juice at Emotions Café because he said he wanted to talk to me about his problems.'

'You went on a date with him?' said Roda, eyebrows arched in disbelief. 'Yosra, I can't believe this!'

'No, it was not a date,' said Yosra bashfully. 'We were just talking about his problems. Like old friends do.'

Roda shot me an incredulous look. 'How come I never heard about this guy before?' she asked suspiciously.

'Because he was married,' said Yosra innocently. 'And you know I don't see married men.'

'So did you see him again after that?' asked Roda.

'We've seen each other a couple of times, but we talk every night on the telephone. When my brother is away and his kids are in bed he calls me on my mobile and we chat. He's told me all about his marriage and what a horrible bitch his wife was. He said if he ever saw her again, he would murder her.'

'Hardly a surprise,' I interjected grimly, puffing on my *shisha*. 'If I was him I would want to murder her too.'

'You know the thing is,' continued Yosra, ignoring me, 'it's been so interesting hearing him tell me how they met in college and about his marriage and everything, because I feel like I already know his story but from the outside. Only now I am hearing it from him. Of course I feel sorry for Jihad and I could never understand or forgive what Manar has done to him, but at the same time I feel like, now she has given him up, it's like some kind of balance has been restored, like maybe now it's my turn. Do you know what I mean?'

'What are his kids like?' asked Roda, thinking ahead.

'They are real brats but his mother looks after them. And, you know, he says that all the time he was married to Manar he often used to think that he should have got to know me in college instead of her.'

Roda looked distrustful. 'That's what he told you, is it?'

'Uh-huh.' Yosra nodded, exhaling *shisha* smoke.

'What is it you like most about Jihad?' I asked.

Yosra pondered for a moment. She looked so happy talking about him, happier than at any time I could remember. 'Well, I guess it's his honesty and the fact that I have known him such a long time that we can be such close friends now. And also because he gave me this . . .'

From her pocket she pulled a turquoise talisman. It was a three-fingered Hand of Fatima, to ward off the evil eye, on a thin silver chain.

'Just what you need,' commented Roda.

'I'm going to hang it from the rear-view mirror of my car to stop any more weasels breaking in,' said Yosra smiling.

The waiter, walking from car to car outside the café, interrupted us with fresh tobacco heads and a brazier of hot coal to refresh the *shisha*. Removing the plastic mouthpiece from the end of my pipe, he took several short, sharp puffs to start the smoke circulating before replacing the mouthpiece and handing the pipe back to me. We sat smoking for a minute, lost in our thoughts. Only the gurgle of bubbling water and the soft rattle of coals on tinfoil broke the silence. The sweet smoke of apple tobacco rose into the air.

'You realise now you are getting married you have to convert,' Yosra said to me.

'Do I?' I asked innocently.

Roda and I had talked about this but the idea still seemed preposterous and somehow unreal. I was more concerned with the practical logistics of the wedding like finding a venue and an affordable hotel for all my friends and family to stay in when they flew over. We would have to get married in Cairo since there was no way all Roda's friends and relatives were going to be able to secure UK visas in time for a wedding. Since becoming engaged I felt as though all my old concerns had been swept away and replaced by new ones I had never thought of before. I was hoping that if I just ignored it long enough the question of conversion might simply disappear. But as time passed, far from disappearing the question seemed to loom ever larger.

A long blue plume of smoke like a dragon's tongue uncoiled out of my nose as a dozen questions unfurled inside my mind. Did I really have to convert? How did you do it? Would I have to get circumcised? Could I then have four wives? Would it, as the Brotherhood promised, be the solution to all my problems? Doubt was beginning to creep in. Perhaps I was foolish trying to bridge the gap between East and West. Maybe further down the road we would encounter some kind of cultural roadblock. Perhaps clashing civilisations would prove irreconcilable. Having grown up in the Middle East, I knew that Arab–Western relationships sometimes foundered over matters like a woman's personal freedom or the raising of daughters. Many Muslim men believe that a girl's education is only of secondary importance. Western women are sometimes surprised to find out how much more limited a woman's personal freedom is in the Arab world.

But such problems only arise if the man is an Arab and the woman a Westerner. In our case the man was the Westerner and Roda and her sisters were already very liberated women who drove, worked and were much more educated than me. She was not about to find out that I secretly believed all women should be veiled and only allowed to leave the house with their husband's permission.

'Conversion is a must,' said Yosra emphatically. 'Muslim women can't marry Christian men. The Koran clearly forbids it. It's *haram*.'

'What about the other way round?' I asked. 'What about if a Muslim man wants to marry a Christian woman?'

'Of course that's *halal*. It's permitted,' she affirmed. 'But that's totally different. Muslim men can marry Christians – and Jewish women too – on condition that their children are brought up Muslim.'

It hardly seemed fair that I had to convert when plenty of Muslim women have married Christian men without anyone changing their religion. During the Ottoman era sultans' daughters were regularly packed off to marry Catholic potentates to forge convenient alliances. Dynastic strategic reasons always trumped religious differences.

'What happens if I don't convert?'

Both girls let out a long sigh. 'Then it's illegal. You have to,' Roda said. 'It's not possible if you don't.'

'If you don't convert when you are married you will have to leave Egypt and never come back,' explained Yosra. 'If you do come back both your lives will be in danger.'

'You have to convert,' stated Roda emphatically, before adding more quietly, 'if you want to get married.'

'And what religion will your kids be?' asked Yosra.

'Whatever religion they want.' I could see from the look on her face she thought I was being facetious.

'You have to have Muslim children,' said Yosra. 'That's a must. One of the main responsibilities of a Muslim couple is to make sure they have Muslim children.'

'How can anyone make sure what religion their children will be?' I replied. 'I was brought up a Catholic and now it looks like I'm about to become a Muslim. You can say what you like to kids but you can never be sure they are going to follow your faith.'

'Well it has to say "Muslim" on their birth certificate,' stated Yosra bureaucratically.

'If you don't convert and we marry and have children, officially they would not have a religion entered on their birth certificate, which means they would not be entitled to an identity card, and without an identity card effectively you don't exist,' explained Roda.

'You can't access social services, apply for a passport, enrol in school, use a public hospital, get vaccinated . . .' Yosra counted the impossibilities off on her fingers as she spoke.

'I doubt even a private school would enrol them,' Roda added. 'In short, the whole thing would be out of the question.'

The two girls stared expectantly at me, waiting for what I had to say next.

'I guess I need to convert then,' I mumbled.

Twenty-six

Over the summer, while Mr Ahmed was in Monte Carlo, Amira tightened her grip on the store in Emerald Square. Boldly abandoning the old rules, she pushed on with her plans to implement more contemporary ideas. Each month she had large, sometimes provocative glossy posters printed showing boys and girls together wearing the brand's clothes and displayed them in the windows. She played loud pop music over the store speakers and encouraged the male and female staff to actively engage with customers whenever they saw fit. Amira knew she was taking a risk. When she went to a company launch party at the Sheraton Hotel in Dokki to celebrate the opening of a new store, she was the only woman not wearing either a headscarf or veil. In the back of her mind she was aware that every change she made was going to have to be accounted for when Mr Ahmed returned.

In the meantime her coup was bringing in good results. Sales shot up; profits tripled; staff volunteered for more overtime and the number of days lost to illness dropped sharply. Amira's confidence grew and soon the store was one of the most popular in the mall. The only objections came from Shams, Mr Ahmed's niece, who, though largely muted by Amira's commercial success, still offered symbolic displays of resistance, by 'forgetting' to put up posters or change the CD. Magnanimous in victory Amira

tried to make up with her rival, but Shams had been so humili-
ated her pride forbade it. She preferred instead to bide her time
until her uncle returned, when she clearly thought scores would
be settled and honour satisfied.

Eventually news arrived at the store that Mr Ahmed would be
returning at the end of the month. As the day drew near, the staff
were noticeably quieter and a general sense of foreboding
descended on the store. Each day when she arrived at work a
cold knot of fear tightened in Amira's heart, although she never
gave the slightest indication how anxious she was, continuing
with her marketing as if there was nothing in the world bother-
ing her.

Not long after the end of Ramadan Amira arrived at the store
after a weekend away to find that the landscape had shifted like
desert sand. There was no music playing and the posters had all
disappeared from the windows. The staff greeted her in subdued
tones, avoiding her gaze and offering only monosyllabic answers
to her questions. At the morning meeting Amira ran through her
notes as she always did, noting the sales figures and listing the
main tasks and objectives for the day, but she could tell some-
thing had changed.

'And at one o'clock I want Shams to pick up the catalogue
from the printers,' said Amira authoritatively as she ticked off her
checklist. 'Are there any questions?'

The staff sat still and silent; the atmosphere was funereal.

'Adel, you can go with her.'

'That won't be necessary, Adel,' interjected Shams.

'And why is that?' replied Amira, still feigning normality.

'Because Mr Ahmed has given me instructions to fire you.
And that is just what I am doing.' Narrowing her eyes Shams
stood up and pointed at her rival. 'Goodbye, Amira. You're fired!'
she said spitefully.

And that was the end of Amira's job at Emerald Square.

★

'I can't believe it,' said Nadia, jaw slack, a look of total incomprehension on her face. 'I just can't believe they did that to you.'

The day the news broke of Amira's dismissal, Nadia and her baby daughter moved back into the little apartment in Istanbul Street. Her husband had beaten her up again and she did not know when she was going to be able to go back.

'It's incredible, isn't it?' replied Amira, resigned now to what had happened. She had dropped by to tell us. Without a job to go to she had all the time in the world to see friends. She looked as tired and faded as the checked sofa she sat on.

'My programme was working so well too,' she added despondently. 'But Shams told Mr Ahmed everything. She even gave him the CCTV tapes, which showed what had been going on – the music playing and the staff talking to the customers and stuff. I did not have a leg to stand on. Apparently I had contravened the most basic Islamic ideals and there was no place for me at Ahmed Mustafa and Sons . . .'

'Life is like a cucumber,' said Nadia wisely. The girls nodded.

'What is that supposed to mean?' I was bemused.

'Half the time it's in your mouth, the rest of the time it's in your arse,' replied Rime with a grin.

We sat in silence for a moment contemplating the misfortunes of the day. Amira stirred her mint tea pensively.

'So now what?' Roda asked.

'I don't really know . . .' Amira said. 'Looking for another job, I guess.'

'And what about Reem? What's her news?'

'Oh my God, you mean you have not heard what happened?' said Amira, suddenly animated.

'No!' exclaimed Roda and Nadia in unison, sensing a juicy morsel of news. 'Tell us, tell us!'

'She had to flee at two o'clock in the morning because Boutros's Christian friends found out that he was marrying a Muslim.'

'Oh my God!' said Roda.

'If they catch her they will tear her apart!' added Nadia a touch melodramatically,

'What happened?' enquired Roda, wide-eyed.

'Well, the priest told Boutros's mother that if her son converted she would go straight to hell for all eternity.'

'OK . . .' We all nodded.

'And he also said that if Boutros converted then the Muslim Brotherhood would come banging on her door to check he was praying and being a proper Muslim.'

'Is that true?' I asked.

'No, of course it's not true. He was just trying to frighten her so she would stop Boutros converting,' replied Amira. 'But the stupid woman believed him and flew into a total panic. So she calls all Boutros's friends and tells them that her son is going to convert to Islam and that they have to stop him at all costs. So right away Boutros's friends – who are all meatheads by the way – call him at work and tell him to cancel the marriage and forget about converting, otherwise they cannot guarantee the safety of his fiancée.'

'What does that mean?' asked Nadia naively.

'It means they are going to do her in, you dummy,' Roda told her sister impatiently.

'Oh my God!' said Nadia, slapping her face in horror. 'Poor Reem!'

'As soon as Boutros heard what his mother had done, he called Reem and told her she was in danger and that she had better get out of the apartment as fast as she could. She packed and left three days ago, totally terrified.'

'Where is she now?' I asked.

'I swore on my mother's life I wouldn't say,' Amira replied darkly, before adding in the same breath, 'but she's in Jeddah Street staying with Sherine Rifaat.'

'Is she still going to marry Boutros?' asked Roda.

'Reem told me that the conversion and the wedding are both still definitely on,' Amira confirmed.

Amira's tale of what had happened to her sister sent a frisson of fear through me. As a Westerner, I found it unfathomable that Boutros's friends could be so inflamed by religion they would threaten his fiancée. But I still had not grasped how passionately feelings run over the issue of conversion. The little inkling I had of what a sensitive topic conversion can be came from an aborted newspaper feature I had embarked upon soon after I first started playing *tarneeb* with Roda and her friends. One of the girls told me of a Muslim girlfriend of hers who wanted to become a Christian. Thinking this might make an interesting feature I contacted the woman by telephone and spoke to her about her reasons for wanting to leave Islam, but it was not long before I ran into a brick wall.

The woman worked at a secure private psychiatric hospital on the edge of Cairo. It was more like a five-star hotel than a hospital and was crammed full of wealthy Arab wives and errant sons admitted anonymously and against their will by their families in the Gulf to protect family honour. Most of the inmates did not have major psychiatric problems, but many had a history of drug use, alcoholism or promiscuous sex. Patients' families paid handsomely for their relatives to be confined at the hospital but treatment was rudimentary and drugs and alcohol rife, smuggled in by the staff to sell on the lucrative hospital black market.

The woman told me that she had been struggling with her faith for many years. She had reached the conclusion that she would like to convert to Christianity because Islam, she said, was too controlling. If her husband discovered her thoughts or found out what she was planning she was afraid of what might happen to her. She said she knew she was guilty of apostasy and thought he might take it upon himself to kill her. I tried to set up a meeting with her to find out what she was going to do next, but after several weeks of broken engagements she backed out. Soon after, she broke off contact with me for good and I never found out what happened.

Keen to pursue the story, I had got in touch with some American Christian missionaries working in Cairo via the Internet. Their website boasted that they worked undercover converting Egyptian Muslim women to Christianity. Although proselytising is both dangerous and officially prohibited in Egypt, many American churches undertake this kind of missionary work. As soon as I told them I was a journalist they refused to answer any of my calls or emails.

A specific penalty for apostasy is not given in the Koran, but it is not uncommon to meet Muslims who believe it should be punishable by death. In 1995, after a row with an orthodox cleric at Al-Azhar over interpretation of the Koran, one liberal Islamic theologian was labelled an apostate and forced to flee to the Netherlands. The professor had devoted his whole life to studying Islam, but so unacceptable was his exegesis the authorities at Al-Azhar ruled that he could no longer be deemed a Muslim. In violation of both his basic human rights and the Egyptian constitution, a Cairo court annulled his marriage, ruling it impermissible that a non-Muslim man remain married to a Muslim woman. In exile, the professor was divorced against his will.

Amira's story of what was happening to her sister seemed just as alarming since it was happening right there, under my nose in Istanbul Street. The prospect of conversion was beginning to make me feel uncomfortable. At least, I reflected, my friends were not about to lynch my fiancée.

It was not that I had any particular problem with Islam; I would have had just as much difficulty declaring myself a Hindu. Becoming a Muslim seemed perhaps marginally less daunting, since historically speaking at least I could take comfort in the fact that I was almost certainly part Muslim anyway. Most Europeans who research back more than a few hundred years into their families find they have Muslim ancestors, because at its peak Islam extended across a large swathe of southern Europe. During the reconquest many thousands of Europeans were forced to convert from Islam to Catholicism on pain of death.

Even the British royal family has extensive Muslim ancestry. No fewer than five of Queen Elizabeth II's ancestral lines can be traced back to the Prophet Muhammad. The Queen is descended from the kings of Portugal, Pamplona and Navarre, all of whom could trace their lineage to the Prophet, while Princes William and Harry can also claim an Islamic pedigree via their mother from the Andalusian Queen Isabella I of Castile. When Queen Elizabeth visited Morocco in 1980 the Moroccan media pointed out that the Prophet might actually be her forty-first great-grandfather, although this has never been conclusively proven and merits further investigation.

Being obliged to convert in order to marry sits oddly with the Egyptian constitution, which stipulates the equality of 'all citizens before the law without distinction of race, origin, language, religion or creed'. It also runs contrary to the International Covenant on Civil and Political Rights, which is part of Egyptian domestic law. But this was academic as far as my predicament was concerned. In modern Egypt, as I was growing to understand, a conservative interpretation of Islam reigns. Although I might like to think my faith was nobody's business but mine, this was a distinctly Western outlook, untenable in the Arab world. If a hundred conversations with taxi drivers had taught me nothing else, I had learnt that people in Egypt care a great deal what religion you are and no one considers it a private concern. Many Egyptian Muslims regard it as their personal responsibility to check that other Muslims are observant, not least because it might be jeopardising their own afterlife if they do not.

Twenty-seven

Like a glittering coin at the bottom of a deep blue lake, a shimmering silver moon hung in the sky over Cairo. I was zooming along the highway in a cab on my way back from Heliopolis. In front of me the road uncoiled for miles, snaking on concrete stilts past rooftops and mosques, giving me a grandstand view of the heart of the heaving Arab metropolis.

Ancient Egyptians believed that the night was when the sun god made his way through the underworld, steered by the sky and the moon. I was being steered through the night by a large hirsute taxi driver with an ugly brown *zabeeba* on his forehead. As he drove the cabby was animatedly telling me a story about his time in the army when he had been punished by being put in a tiny cell, standing room only, to peel a mound of potatoes higher than he was. Each time he took his hands off the wheel to show me just how high the potato pile had been, the car swerved alarmingly.

'Then they slam the door behind you and lock you in,' he shouted, clapping his hands together like a jailer before grasping the wheel again. 'You have to peel your way out, one potato at a time, posting each one through the letter box in the cell door.' He posted his cigarette butt through the taxi's broken window, like an imaginary prison potato, into the whistling slipstream. It splintered into sparks and disappeared into the night.

'How long does it take to peel your way out?' I asked politely.

'All day, maybe more.' He coughed emphysemically. 'And by the time you are finished, you are knee deep in potato peelings.' He laughed like a great broken drain.

The taxi driver had the happy-go-lucky demeanour of a true believer, a man who had total faith that when he went to bed each night, should the house fall down on his head while he slept he would find himself being directed straight to heaven. Looking out the window I wondered whether if I was a Muslim I would find myself fluttering up towards heaven with the taxi driver when I died, eternally grateful to Roda that I was not destined to spend forever simmering away in hell with all my infidel friends and relatives.

If the Koran really is the revealed word of God, I thought, it seemed a great pity that He omitted any mention of basic science or mathematics. Rather than pages and pages of social rules, just a few simple equations dealing with gravity and relativity and perhaps a hint that germs spread diseases and the pace of human development would have been incalculably improved. Even if Islam was the one true religion, it was divided and subdivided into so many sects and denominations that choosing the right one and observing its rules sufficiently thoroughly to get myself into heaven seemed unlikely. Heaven must contain only a tiny fraction of the total number of human beings who ever graced the earth. Like a game-show contestant given one last chance to reconsider which shell concealed the holiday in paradise, I had the uncomfortable feeling that, whatever I did, I was going to lose.

Nobody at head office had thought it necessary to let Yosra know that the reason her furniture was being removed was because the company management had decided to turn her office into its new boardroom. So when the removal men showed up, as usual she was asleep at her desk. They took away everything except her table and uncomfortable wooden chair and the next day came back and demolished the cupboard where she hid the pillow and blanket that she had brought from home.

With nowhere to sleep, to pass the time Yosra borrowed some pornographic English language novels from Roda to read while chain-smoking at her desk. Most afternoons Jihad dropped by to chat about his problems and if Yosra had no clients the two of them would make out on her desk. Frustratingly, although Jihad lived just a few doors down from Yosra's apartment in the same street, it was out of the question for the couple to meet there. The door-man and neighbours all knew Yosra's face well and if she dared so much as set foot in the building word would spread at once.

Two weeks had now passed since Yosra had started seeing Jihad and Roda was growing concerned that the relationship was not progressing as it should. She was protective of her friend and searching for a sign that Jihad was serious and willing to commit.

'So is he going to marry you?' asked Roda bluntly, sitting beside me on the dirty floor of Yosra's office. I flipped idly through Yosra's books.

'Jihad says he is not able to make any critical decisions for six months because he is so psychologically traumatised at the moment,' said Yosra, filing her nails behind her desk.

'What about you? Why do you have to wait for him to be ready to make up his mind?' asked Roda suspiciously, shifting uncomfortably on the grimy lino.

'We decided not to make any long-term life plans right now,' replied Yosra. 'We don't want to rush into anything too fast,' she added with the blasé demeanour of a woman who had weathered a dozen relationships in the past.

'Long-term what?' said Roda, rolling her eyes.

'We're just enjoying fooling around right now, having fun. What's wrong with that?' Yosra added coolly.

'Where do you think you are? Holland?' snapped Roda. 'Get a grip of yourself, for God's sake.'

Her sharp words punctured Yosra's paper-thin façade. She sat upright in her seat and tetchily lit a cigarette. 'Look, Roda, I have my needs as a woman, I mean my sexual needs, and I have a right to satisfy them. And Jihad is a very sexual creature,' she said smokily.

'Really?' I asked, amazed. 'Do you have a lot of sex?'

'Just dry sex,' replied Yosra coyly. Dry sex preserved the woman's virginity. 'You know . . . just fooling around.'

'Yosra, sex is not the most important thing in a relationship,' explained Roda tersely. 'It's more important to find someone you can face over the breakfast table every morning for the rest of your life.'

'Not with Jihad,' said Yosra knowingly. 'Sex is the most important thing in our relationship and it's all we need to be happy. You obviously don't understand Jihad like I do.'

Roda rolled her eyes and sighed. 'I think you have been reading too much porno.'

'That reminds me,' said Yosra turning to me. 'What is a *ménage à trois*?'

Twenty-eight

Faisal's Hairdresser and Salon in Istanbul Street was a meeting place for women from across Muwazafeen. All kinds of services were on offer: haircuts, henna dying, hair extensions, pedicures, manicures and, most popular of all, various methods of hair removal. Friday night was when it was at its fullest, crammed with women smoking, chatting and socialising. The only men allowed in the place were the two hairdressers who worked in the non-veiled section. The veiled section was strictly women-only.

Hair removal is a practice that dates back to the time of the pharaohs. Women in Egypt have been using the same methods to depilate themselves for thousands of years. *Fatlah* is one effective traditional method, but like most is rather painful. Cotton thread is twisted through the index and middle fingers of each hand then moved like scissors up and down close to the skin to trap and remove unwanted facial hair. *Halawa* is another popular method, an infernally sticky gunk made from sugar, water and a few drops of lemon. First rolled into a ball, it is then squished onto the skin before ripped away to remove the hair at the root like waxing.

The head hairdresser in the salon was a man in his early thirties called Salama. Salama's chief foe was Girgis, the elderly Coptic hairdresser he worked alongside. Rake thin with tufty white hair, Girgis was a widower grandfather, aged about sixty-five. He was almost toothless, with tattoos that bore witness to his religion and his glory days, the kind you acquire in prison inscribed with a hot needle and a broken biro, Jesus on his left arm, a cross on his right. Next to the cross was a barely legible date – 1971 – the year he had had it done.

While Salama was a conservative who believed strongly that women ought to cover up, Girgis was a boozer who enjoyed flirting with the female clientele. 'O sweet Jesus!' he would say with a wicked twinkle in his eye. 'Don't you dare lose weight or put any on! You are just perfect the way you are!'

Salama nor Girgis never missed an opportunity to perpetuate the well-established vendetta between them. Since Girgis was always outnumbered, he normally came off worst in their frequent confrontations, and after a savage public humiliation he would retreat into a back room to tend to his damaged pride. But he would never stay down for long, bounding back out again when an opportunity presented itself for a strike back against Salama or against any other Muslim who got in his way, according to the prevailing sectarian logic in the salon. 'Don't feel sorry for Salama,' he would say with a chuckle, 'if the Koran is the truth, then he's going straight to hell. It's sinful for a Muslim man to touch a woman's hair.'

Salama never denied this charge, but maintained that his was a necessary sacrifice as only a man could make a woman truly look beautiful.

Since both hairdressers cited a divine source for their belief, each regarded his own faith as immutably superior. Compromise was out of reach.

One Friday night Istanbul Street was snarled up with cars dropping off customers at Faisal's when a sleek black Mercedes drew up outside Roda's block. Clearly in a rush, the driver parked her car haphazardly, obstructing the road. Hanafi shouted at her to move it, but apparently unused to being told what to do by a doorman, the woman ignored him, but she had not even made it inside the door of the salon when Hanafi clipped the door of her Mercedes with someone else's car he was trying to park. Predictably the woman went crazy and started screaming obscenities the whole street could hear, and that was what woke me up. Hanafi, well used to life on the streets, shouted back just as coarsely.

The shouting and swearing escalated until the whole street was involved, either egging the pair on or trying to cool them down. Then foolishly the women used the M-word, in this case calling Hanafi's mother a lioness, a serious insult in Egypt, and that was when things really got ugly. Had she been a man Hanafi would probably have belted her, but he was reluctant to hit a woman, especially an apparently rich and well-connected one in a public place, because he knew it might land him in jail. The police would have sided with the woman and doubtless she assumed she could say what she liked for exactly that reason. Although women are sometimes beaten at home and even in police stations in Cairo, it is shameful for a man to attack a woman in public, and if he had even his own friends and family would have intervened. But by making the elementary mistake of picking a fight on Hanafi's territory, where the people around were nearly all either his blood relatives or close friends, the woman had both put the doorman in an advantageous position and also made it necessary for him not to lose face.

Sana, Hanafi's young wife, was slim and pretty, but when Hanafi instructed her to 'get that bitch' she hauled the unfortunate woman out of her Mercedes and threw her on to the street with a boxer's zeal. To the delight of the gathered crowd, the pair rolled over and over in the street, spitting catty insults, pummelling one other, tearing each other's clothes and pulling hair. The rich woman fought back, but she was no match for the doorman's petite wife. By the time the police arrived, she had been beaten and scratched black and blue.

Saved by the police, through her sobs the woman told how

she was on her way to have her hair done when Sana had attacked and robbed her of a necklace worth several hundred pounds, a mendacious, vindictive allegation designed to land Hanafi in as much trouble as possible. She was hoping that, due to their obvious difference in social status, the police would believe her story rather than Sana's. The crowd laughed at her and heckled her claims.

Hanafi knew how to handle the situation. Before becoming a doorman he had worked as a clerk in a village police station where he had learnt all he needed to know about the law, in particular how to extricate yourself from legal entanglements when you do not have much money. Everyone in Cairo has their own way of surviving and Hanafi knew more than his fair share of traffic cops and desk clerks. When he heard what the woman claimed his wife had stolen, he immediately filed a counter-claim for the theft of one necklace plus matching earrings from his wife worth several thousand pounds.

The next morning I found Hanafi standing outside the block in the sunshine, his hands on his hips and a broad smile on his face, admiring the cars parked outside like a proud farmer surveying a bumper crop of prize-winning vegetables.

'Peace be upon you,' I greeted him.

'And peace be upon you too,' he replied cheerily.

'What happened last night?' I asked.

By registering a competing claim, Hanafi said that sooner or later, rather than take the whole ugly affair to court, which would take months or even years, the police would simply drop the whole case. If it ever did come up for review it would be handled by the police in the station nearby, where he knew enough people to wriggle out of any serious trouble. Besides, he told me, he was making a bigger claim and had more witnesses.

'You should have seen her go,' he said beaming, gesturing proudly at his wife sitting shyly on the step behind him. 'She really beat that rich bitch. That's what happens if you pick a fight in someone else's patch. She got taught a lesson she is never going to forget.' Sana smiled unconvincingly. One of her eyes was bruised purple and she had bloody scratch marks on her cheek.

'How are you feeling?' I asked her.

Saying nothing, she held her veil up to her mouth to hide her face.

In an attempt to establish whether Jihad was serious about marriage and to give Roda an opportunity to cast an inspecting eye over her new lover, Yosra arranged for the four of us to go on a double date the following weekend to a swimming pool at one of Cairo's five-star hotels. Jihad had no clue that our rendezvous had been set up to give the two women an opportunity to examine him thoroughly and resolve important lingering questions about his intentions and character before his relationship with Yosra proceeded any further.

More than anything else, Yosra wanted to ascertain how much freedom Jihad would give her if she were to marry him. She needed to know that she would be able to come and go when she liked, smoke cigarettes without being punished and choose her own clothes. Above all, she wanted to be sure she was not going to be forced to wear a headscarf.

The date started badly. Jihad got lost on the way to the hotel, so Yosra asked a man selling watermelons for directions. Jihad took this as a serious insult to his masculinity and scolded her harshly for causing him to lose face in front of a stranger. By the time we arrived at the hotel, a frosty silence prevailed.

The outdoor swimming pool was crowded with Arab and European tourists and their screaming children. Although it was now autumn, the weather was still baking hot and the water lukewarm. We stretched out on the burning sunloungers and ordered drinks, hoping that when prayer time came the crowds might thin out. As we lounged, I watched both girls surreptitiously following Jihad's every move from behind their sunglasses. They winced when he emerged from the changing room in faded floral swimming trunks, holding a towel neatly ironed by his mother. They muttered and tutted into their magazines when they spotted him eyeing up a middle-aged Scandinavian tourist with a carcinogenic suntan under the next-door umbrella.

'I have to go and see the dentist next week,' said Yosra to Roda, breaking a long silence. 'Would you like to come with me?'

'Sure,' replied Roda lazily. 'What day were you thinking?'

'I don't know,' replied Yosra. 'That depends when he is free.'

'He?' interrupted Jihad, looking up from his newspaper. 'The dentist is a man?'

'Yes,' replied Yosra innocently. 'Is there a problem with that?'

'I told you before,' said Jihad grouchily. 'I don't want you seeing any male doctors.'

'He's a dentist,' said Yosra.

'Whatever,' replied Jihad irritably, shaking out his newspaper. 'It's the same thing.'

Roda and Yosra exchanged glances at this remark. It was another ambiguous sign. Earlier, plucked eyebrows had been raised when he mentioned in passing that he thought all women should be veiled, but when I pressed him further Jihad denied that he would impose the headscarf or veil on Yosra if they were to get married.

I felt sorry for Jihad. He cut a sorry sight struggling out of the pool, a sad middle-aged man suddenly thrown back into the game late in the day. He had not seen his divorce coming until it was too late. Now, as he tried to recover from what had clearly been a hammer blow, he seemed to be hoping that Yosra would fill the gap his wife had left. The two made an awkward couple, flirting like teenagers as they lolled by the edge of the pool. Part of me wondered whether perhaps there might be another reason why Jihad's wife had left him. He always seemed hearty with me, drinking beer and cracking jokes, but as I had come to learn, public and private behaviour in Egypt are often two very different things. Maybe his wife would see a more conservative face than the one he showed a foreigner beside the pool.

When Jihad went to the bathroom Roda and Yosra seized the opportunity to consult and update each other on how they thought the date was going. 'No more male dentists or doctors,' whispered Roda, eyes wide. 'Are you kidding? You'll need his permission to leave the house next! And he'll definitely make you get veiled.'

Yosra looked pained. 'He said I wouldn't have to.'

'He's lying, I can tell,' Roda said breezily with a wave of her hand.

'His sister is not veiled and she seems to have a pretty free lifestyle,' replied Yosra thoughtfully.

'But his ex-wife was veiled,' retorted Roda. 'Look, Yosra, men like this go from being spoilt sons to over-protective husbands the minute they get married. They turn into arseholes. You already have a problem with your brother. Marry this guy and you have another one.'

'What do you think?' said Yosra, turning to me. 'Do you think I can handle his rules?'

'I think marrying him might be putting yourself in a trap,' I said warily. 'It's hard to know for sure, but what Roda says is true. He's clearly looking for someone just like his wife and who knows what rules he might impose on you once you got married.'

Yosra looked crestfallen. She was clearly fond of Jihad and had been hoping for more positive feedback. Although she complained about being told what to do, I could see that actually she secretly quite enjoyed the unfamiliar feeling of being ordered around by a man who was attracted to her.

'If it turns out badly then I guess I can just find myself a boyfriend and have an affair,' said Yosra with a smile, making light of our remarks. 'You just think he's conservative because you are a Westerner and Westerners don't care what their wives do. It's different for an Arab man. He's just being protective.'

'Maybe,' I conceded doubtfully. 'I guess you have handled your brother all your life, so you can probably handle him.'

'I have not handled my brother, at least not well. We fight all the time and I lie to him every day about where I go and what I do.'

'Well, can't you see that you might get in that situation again?'

'Who fights with their brother all the time?' asked Jihad. He had returned unnoticed.

'Jumanah does,' lied Yosra with effortless ease. 'Jumanah and her brother. They are always at each other's throats.'

'That's too bad,' said Jihad, smoothing out his towel and sitting back down on his lounger. 'Yosra, would you rub some cream on my back?'

Twenty-nine

On her mother's instructions, Yosra continued to see the mystic each week and every night anointed her whole body with musk oil. As her relationship with Jihad blossomed, her confidence grew and for the first time ever she made important changes to her life on her own initiative. At work she telephoned her boss at head office and insisted he either have her furniture returned or transfer her to a habitable, cockroach-free office. At home she decided the time had come to break some long-overdue news to her unsuspecting mother.

'I am going to smoke a cigarette on the balcony,' she announced brazenly one night when her brother was away.

'Smoke a what?' replied Salma blankly. The words had gone in but her brain had not yet engaged.

'I'm just smoking a cigarette,' repeated Yosra clearly.

'A cigarette?' squawked her mother. 'Like a bitch in the street? What would your brother say!'

'What he does not know won't hurt him,' replied Yosra coolly. 'Oh, and by the way . . . I smoke. Every day. You know those cigarettes Hassan found in Jumanah's bag during Ramadan last year? They weren't Noura's, they were mine.'

Salma's mouth opened and closed mechanically. 'I hope God finds the right husband for you and delivers you from this nonsense,' she stammered finally. The next night she hid Yosra's cigarettes behind a photograph to stop her father finding them.

Each day it seemed increasingly likely that Jihad would ask for Yosra's hand in marriage, and Yosra mulled over all the opinions she had been given as to whether he would prove a good husband. Views varied, although it was universally agreed that since getting a boyfriend Yosra's life had improved drastically. Yosra accepted Jihad was not perfect but the prospect of marriage seemed ever more attractive, until one day Salma received a telephone call that plunged her daughter back into a state of confusion. Khaled, over whom Yosra had pined for several weeks during the summer, suddenly reappeared. His mother informed Salma that Khaled had now recovered from his tennis injury and she would like to know when her 'beautiful daughter' would be available to meet up. A council was immediately convened over a game of *tarneeb* to discuss this turn of events. Roda, Noha, Nadia, Amira, Yosra and I gathered in Istanbul Street to decide what Yosra should do next.

'Fourteen–eight,' said Amira, laying a card on the cluttered coffee table. She winked at Yosra through the cigarette smoke fogging the room. 'We're winning!'

'No cheating!' snapped Roda.

'We're not cheating,' replied Yosra with a smile. 'We don't need to. Your deal,' she said, handing me the pack.

I shuffled and cut the deck.

'Thank God it's the Prophet's birthday tomorrow,' said Yosra. 'I am going to lie in bed all day.'

'I have to get up early to go with my mother to the market,' moaned Amira. 'So there's no need to tell me and make me feel awful.'

'Well, you ate cheesecake in front of me when I was on a diet and made me feel awful,' retorted Yosra.

'Come on and play,' commanded Roda, eager to even the score.

We played the next round in silence, the concentration on everyone's faces palpable. Finally Yosra spoke, more to herself than anyone else. 'God, my life is a mess,' she said flatly. 'A few weeks ago I was desperate for Khaled to call me and now, just when things have got going with Jihad, suddenly he pops up out of the blue.'

'Why don't you just go and meet him?' said Amira. 'It's not like you are married or anything.'

'That's what my mother said,' replied Yosra hesitantly. 'But what about Jihad? I think I am in love with him.'

'You can't marry Jihad,' said Roda. 'He's too conservative.'

'All Egyptian men are conservative,' replied Yosra with a sigh. 'But I don't know . . . It's true he does have three children and they're brats. Maybe I should at least give Khaled another chance . . .' She trailed off and looked down at her cards. 'I know I should feel happy that for the first time there are two men in my life, but I really don't,' she said quietly. 'It's so confusing.'

'It's that stupid mystic you've been seeing who's to blame,' Roda said. 'He's been a catastrophic success.'

There was silence in the room as we contemplated the powers of the mystic.

'It's all the fault of the jinn,' asserted Yosra darkly. 'I can still feel him close by.'

Yosra was torn. There had been so many miserable dates, so many awkward, inadequate suitors dredged up by her family in their search for a husband. For years she had done what had been asked of her, living as other people wished under her brother's controlling gaze. Now, for the first and probably the last time in her life, two men were chasing her, her brother was away in the desert and she was still single.

'Why do you think Khaled got his mother to call?' mused Roda. 'Why didn't he call you himself?'

'I can tell you why,' stated Nadia knowingly. 'He's been chasing some other girl for the last few weeks, but it didn't work out so now he's back.'

We all agreed this analysis had the ring of truth about it.

'You don't think he injured himself playing tennis then?' asked Yosra.

'Forget it!' snorted Nadia.

'What did your mother tell you?' asked Roda.

'She told me to meet Khaled, at least to see how it goes. She would definitely rather I have an arranged marriage with him than marry a man with three kids. Besides, since Khaled and I were never committed, it's no insult to my honour if he has been seeing another girl. He's a man. He can do what he likes.'

'It's so depressing that men can do that and women can't,' interjected Amira. 'Before we were married my husband used to push and push me to make out with him, and when I refused he would get angry and call me names and stuff. But then one day when we saw his sister just sitting in a car with some guy, he went mad and hit the roof. Why did he care about her reputation but not mine?'

'It's double standards,' agreed Roda. 'It drives me mad.'

'It's like whenever a man says something we always have to believe him, like he knows what he is talking about,' continued Amira angrily. 'Faisal's friends are always bragging about all the girls they have slept with and all the sex they have had, like they know everything and have done it a million times.'

'What will you tell Jihad?' I asked Yosra. 'Will you tell him if you go on a date with Khaled?'

'I don't know,' she replied. 'I guess I could.'

'If I was you I would definitely tell him,' said Roda. 'Tell him your mum is making you see a suitor you are not sure about. Put him in the problem with you. That's what my dad always says.'

'And if he knows you are meeting other guys he might get the message that if he wants to propose he had better get on with it,' added Amira.

'Which one are you more attracted to physically? Khaled or Jihad?' I asked.

'Well, I don't really know Khaled. To be honest I can't remember what he looks like. We only met once and that was months ago. And Jihad, well, to be honest, I like his company more than his looks.'

'But you have to be attracted to him physically too,' pressed Amira.

'He's a bit too much like Sisayed,' admitted Yosra.

Sisayed, full name Al Sayyid Ahmed, was a sanctimonious and pompous patriarch from the pages of the novels of Naguib Mahfouz. Prone to belching, he was not even capable of taking off his shoes without the help of his wife.

'Doesn't sound very promising,' commented Roda. 'I hope he can shave by himself.'

'And I usually like taller men,' continued Yosra. 'But I guess I should at least see Khaled one more time. Otherwise I might spend the rest of my life wondering what might have happened.'

Thirty

Yosra's rendezvous with Khaled was arranged for that weekend at the Shooting Club, a sprawling open-air sports and entertainment complex covering several city blocks. On Thursday nights its leafy gardens and walkways are thronged with families, the living, beating heart of bourgeois Muwazafeen. Following the rupture after Yosra and Khaled's first date at the start of the summer, both families knew this would be their final opportunity to pair them off. To prevent wires crossing again and to maximise chances of a successful outcome, the mothers agreed that this time round everyone would be better off if they accompanied their respective children.

Yosra invited Roda and me to tag along too. She was eager for Roda to see Khaled in the flesh so as to be better informed when it came to discussing matters later on. With both mothers present, it was not going to be possible for us to sit at the table, as we had done when Yosra met Tamer, but by telling us exactly where the two families were planning to meet, Yosra hoped we could at least pass by and catch a glimpse.

That weekend was a three-day holiday since the Prophet's birthday fell that Sunday. The club was heaving with Cairo's affluent classes in festive spirit, dressed to mingle, to see and be seen. Crowds milled around enjoying one of the last warm nights of the year. A small group of professional beggars had assembled outside the high club walls to show off their wounds and diseases in the hope of squeezing some charity out of the holidaying families.

Walking through the gate, Roda flashed her membership card at the guard. Nonchalantly I breezed in behind her, but as the only white guy among dozens of Egyptians, I was never going to make it without being spotted. The guard collared me.

'Where is your membership card?' he asked officiously.

'I forgot it,' I mumbled schoolboyishly. 'But I think I am a member.'

'Then you have to go to the main gate and let them check your name on the computer.' He blocked my path. 'Otherwise you can't come in.'

'Surely we can come to some kind of arrangement?' I suggested with a smile, reaching inside my jacket for my wallet. He grinned and a moment later I was inside exchanging jokes with him.

'If anyone stops you inside and asks how you got in, just tell them you dropped your membership card somewhere after you came through the gate. OK?'

'No problem,' I said, vaguely bemused that he was now giving me advice on how to fool his colleagues.

'Otherwise they can give you a hard time.'

'Thanks for the tip,' I said as I wandered off into the mêlée.

Inside the walls of the Shooting Club the night was alive, the atmosphere beneath the decorated trees festive. Men and their wives, wearing headscarves or full-face veils, sipped sugar cane juice and pushed double buggies of toddlers smeared in ice cream. Children pushed past one another to grab a kebab from sweaty-faced chefs in smeared white overalls, carving great grey slices of gristly meat as fast as they could from two rotating pyramids of *shawarma* each as big as a stuck cow. From an upstairs window loud techno music was pumping out of the gym. Thursday was women's day so red exercise mats had been placed against the windows to guard against snoopers and a matron with a face like an aubergine stuffed with rice sat on guard at the door.

Through the crush, beyond a green wire fence a dozen tennis matches were taking place on a strip of bright pink asphalt. On the immaculate croquet lawns it was standing room only for the grim-faced pensioners struggling to concentrate above the hubbub, as they solemnly plonked their balls around. Behind another high wire fence on another pink asphalt court about fifty schoolgirls in headscarves and green and blue uniforms were practising their volleyball skills, bouncing balls off the palms of their hands high into the night sky. As balls skittered and slithered in every direction, the teacher shouted instructions, but the girls were either oblivious or deliberately ignoring her. In an incongruous nod to the fact that the end of summer was approaching, an inflatable snowman as big as a two-storey house stood in one corner of the grounds. With forked-stick arms and a partially erect carrot for a nose, it leered and wobbled over passers-by.

Slowly we made our way towards the nerve centre of the Shooting Club, the clubhouse, with its faux-colonial restaurant and members-only non-alcoholic bar. This is the fashionable epicentre of Muwazafeen on a Thursday night, where retired officers read the newspapers beneath stuffed animal heads while well-to-do families air-kiss and parade their sons and daughters about for everyone to admire. Somewhere inside, Yosra and Khaled were embarking on their big date.

Outside the clubhouse on the patio a widescreen television was showing two local teams playing the last minutes of extra time in a football match. Several groups of well-coiffed young men sat at the wrought-iron tables with one eye on the match and the other on passing girls. Slipping between the tables, we elbowed our way to the clubhouse door. Inside the rooms smelt of smoke and leather, and the air was cooled by big wooden ceiling fans turning slowly high above our heads. Well-worn leather sofas and comfortable armchairs stood in groups, occupied by elderly gentlemen in suits reading the newspapers motionlessly, like exhibits in a wax museum.

Roda and I were moving cautiously now as we knew that Yosra and her suitor were somewhere close and we did not want to stumble on them unannounced. Going from room to room, we stayed close to the walls, scanning the crowd for Yosra's familiar profile. Every girl seemed to look like her; every woman seemed to resemble her mother. Suddenly Roda spotted them: Salma, Yosra, Khaled and his parents were sitting in one of the rooms off the main entrance hall just beyond a set of open sliding glass doors. The five were gathered around a coffee table, talking and laughing. At least Khaled's parents and Salma were laughing. Yosra, who was facing the door, looked decidedly glum. Her hair was styled in a large Farrah Fawcett bouffant and through her heavy make-up her face shone with the dark glassiness of too many benzos.

Khaled's elderly father looked distinguished in a dark suit with white hair and moustaches. His mother was wearing a houndstooth jacket with a large gold brooch. Frustratingly, Khaled himself had his back to us and all we could see of him was the back of his head with its shock of silver hair. Creeping to the glass doors, I strained to hear their voices over the noise all around. The spot they had found was almost private, enclosed on three sides by the back of the conservatory. Inching our heads around the doorframe, like snipers peering over a parapet, we tried to catch a glimpse of Khaled.

'We can't see him,' I whispered.

'I know,' Roda whispered back. 'But his hair is really white.'

'He looks about sixty!'

'He's forty-three,' clarified Roda. 'Look, no drinks. They've only just sat down.'

'I am going to try to crawl in so I can see his face better,' I said, gritting my teeth.

'Don't – they'll see you.'

'I have to. I want to hear what they are saying.'

Getting down on my knees, I crept around the doorpost, half crawling half sliding, like a man tunnelling his way out of prison, heading for the back of the sofa where I could hear Khaled's parents boasting loudly about their holiday house in Agami. Behind me, Roda waited in fearful silence, aware that at any minute they might turn and see me.

Barely had I made it a metre into the room when Yosra looked up and spotted me. Her jaw dropped in horror and for a moment I thought she was going to scream out loud. But clamping her mouth tight shut like a trap, her face smoothed over and she adopted once again her usual sphinx-like expression, registering nothing but gently anaesthetised boredom.

Quickly, I slithered back behind the doorframe.

'Did she see you?' whispered Roda urgently.

'Yosra saw me. But what about the others?' I asked urgently.

'I don't think so,' said Roda. 'Did you see Khaled's face?'

'Not very well.'

'Her mum is going to kill me.'

'Her mum didn't see you,' I said. 'Besides, if she finds out you can just say you were passing by when you spotted them by accident.'

'And decided to spy on them by crawling around on the floor?'

Since to go into the room was out of the question, Roda and I decided to remain in the hall outside, just out of sight. Straining our ears, we could make out some snippets of conversation.

'Of course, Khaled has been making great headway in orthodontics,' his mother bragged. 'His surgery is one of the finest in Heliopolis.'

I could just make out Khaled's face reflected in the glass top of the coffee table. He looked too old for his mother to be representing him like this.

'Yes, yes . . . mmm . . .' Salma cooed politely. 'Well, Yosra has had so many suitors from Heliopolis, but this time her father insisted on someone from Muwazafeen. The best people are all from Muwazafeen, wouldn't you agree?'

Then Yosra began talking in a low voice and we could not make out what she was saying.

'I'm embarrassed standing here,' said Roda. 'We can't just hang around eavesdropping. People are going to wonder what we are up to. Security will catch us and you don't even have a membership card.'

I did look a bit suspicious, crouched down by the door with Roda kneeling beside me. All around us people were walking back and forth, enjoying the atmosphere. Behind me a very old man with skin like paper was sitting at a table with his mouth open and his eyes closed, looking for all the world as if he had already died. Next to him, his Suzanne Mubarak-clone wife – enormous blue hair and a Botoxed expression of vague surprise – was watching me intently with piercing black eyes. Her long painted fingernails curled tightly around her cup of tea as she stared, as motionless and unblinking as the stuffed animal heads peering down at us from the club walls.

'You're right,' I said, dusting myself off and standing up. 'People are beginning to notice. We should go or someone is going to catch us and then there will be a scene.'

'We can hear what happens from Yosra later,' agreed Roda.

An hour later Yosra telephoned us at home.

'I'm in the bathroom at the club,' she hissed. 'Where are you?'

'We left because we couldn't hear anything and we were going to get caught. How's it going?'

'It's going OK, but I thought I was hallucinating when I saw you guys creeping round the door. Thank God no one else saw you.'

'Thank God,' agreed Roda. 'How's Khaled?'

'He's all right. Well . . . he's a bit dull. Listen, I have been quizzing him about his ex-wife. He did not tell me her family name but he mentioned that she lives above Emotions Café. That's very close to me.'

'That's great news,' said Roda. 'Maybe we can find out why they split up. They don't have any kids, do they?'

'No kids,' confirmed Yosra.

'Thanks be to God,' said Roda. 'Stay with it. Just listen carefully so you remember everything he says and then we can talk tomorrow.'

There was a long pause. Then, 'I don't like arranged marriages,' Yosra declared sullenly.

'Did you tell him that?'

'Yeah.'

'How did that go down?'

'Not very well. And I told him that he had ruined everything between us because he disappeared for months.'

'I see,' said Roda. 'Was he upset?'

'He said it's not his fault and that his mother interferes in his private life.'

'You knew that anyway, didn't you?'

'Yeah, I guess so. Look, I have to go.'

'Take care, we're all with you!'

'OK, will do.'

'Call us again when you get a chance!'

The next evening after work Yosra came round to Istanbul Street to fill us in on the details. Roda, Nadia and Noha had gathered to hear the story. Sparking up a cigarette, Yosra sat down on the sofa and recounted what had happened after Roda and I left.

'Well, basically, he's nice, and he has manners and money, but he's a bit of a bore. Last time we met he was so much better.'

'Did you ask him why he had not called you?' asked Roda.

'You bet I did. I scolded him for it. After what he did to me I felt uneasy about meeting him and I told him that. Of course he didn't know what to say. Then I asked him why his mother was always involved in everything he did and why it was always her who called my house and not him. I mean he's forty-three for God's sake and I am thirty-three!'

'What did he say to that?' Nadia pressed her.

'He said that once he had got into trouble when he was younger because he had called some girl at home and her father had answered and he had got mad, shouting, "Who are you to call my daughter at home? You are not her fiancé; you are not her husband, don't call again." And from then on his mother has always done the calling.'

'How long did you sit with his parents at the club?' asked Roda.

'We only sat with them for a few minutes. That was when I saw you country whores spying on us! You nearly made me laugh out loud in front of his mother. But then afterwards we went outside on the terrace, just Khaled and me, and we talked for two hours.'

'Two hours!' Roda nodded enthusiastically. 'That's great! And did the mothers like each other?'

'Who cares what the mothers thought about each other?' snapped Yosra. 'We are the ones who are going to be living together for the rest of our lives if we get married.'

'What did you talk about?' asked Noha.

'The tenants in the building he owns and some of their problems.'

'God, how boring,' said Noha.

'At least he's trying to share his problems with you,' said Roda optimistically.

'Do you think you could marry him?' persisted Noha.

Yosra looked uncertain. In spite of her lengthy private chat with Khaled, she still had some unresolved questions. 'I don't know,' she said. 'I've got a funny feeling something is not quite right. I mean, how is it that such an eligible bachelor is still dating in his forties?'

'Good question,' said Roda.

'Yeah, why is he still single?' wondered Noha.

We looked at each other. Yosra had been on enough dates to know when something was amiss.

'Why don't you get in touch with his ex-wife?' suggested Roda. 'We can ask her. Didn't you say she lives around here?'

Although Khaled had given no more details about his ex-wife than her first name and the name of the café over which she lived, it took just a couple of phone calls to piece together the missing information. Her name was May, and although she had since remarried and moved she lived with her new husband in her parents' family apartment just a few minutes drive away from Yosra's house.

When Yosra told her mother that she had uncovered Khaled's ex-wife's address, the pair agreed that it would be foolish to miss an opportunity to shed some light on his background. Doubtless his ex-wife had a story to tell about why they had divorced. She might even be able to explain why Khaled was single at forty-three.

So the next morning Yosra paid May's family apartment a visit. Hassan, fresh back from the desert, insisted on accompanying her. He was adamant that his sister was not going to knock on strangers' doors on her own. Before they left he even ran his own background check on Khaled through the police computer to see whether there was any record of him having been in trouble with the law. He was sorely disappointed to come up empty-handed.

Since Yosra's visit was strictly on women's business Hassan agreed to wait in the car in the street outside while his sister climbed the stairs up to May's family apartment. An elderly woman opened the door.

'Hello,' said Yosra brightly with a smile. 'We have not met before but my name is Yosra. I was wondering if May was at home, please.'

The woman gestured for her to come in. 'Welcome, welcome. I am May's mother. I will call her for you.' Turning inside the tastefully decorated apartment she called, ' May, your friend Yosra is here.'

'I'm not her friend,' explained Yosra. 'I've never met May before, but I think maybe you can help me. I was considering marrying her ex-husband Khaled and I thought perhaps you could advise me.'

'Khaled?' the mother replied, raising her eyebrows. 'How is he now? Did he find the right doctor? Is he better?'

Yosra looked at her blankly. 'I don't know what you mean.'

'Ah, my child, come inside and sit down.'

Over mint tea and dates Yosra explained everything to May and her mother. She told how she had first met Khaled earlier in the summer through her mother's contacts and how after their first encounter he had mysteriously never called back. Then she explained how a few days ago his mother had unexpectedly been back in touch and about the second, more elaborate date during which the families had sat together at the Shooting Club. She said that soon she must reach a decision on whether she wanted to marry Khaled and she did not know what to do.

May and her mother listened politely to Yosra's story before they began to speak. First May told how, like Yosra, she had met Khaled through her mother several years ago and how she too had been struck at once by Khaled's gentle character and good business prospects. A marriage had been arranged a few weeks later, but not long after she discovered that Khaled had a serious problem. 'He was totally and utterly impotent. Nothing was possible. Zero. We tried to resolve it, but there was nothing anyone could do. The marriage lasted less than a year.'

'Nothing worked!' cried May's mother, throwing up her hands. 'Can you imagine? We took him to the finest doctors in Bab el Luk and Tahrir Square. They tried everything but in the end they all said the same thing: only God could grant him an erection. My daughter left his house the same way she came in,' said May's mother with a look of disgust. 'A virgin!'

Yosra's worst fears had been confirmed: the reason Khaled was unmarried in his forties was because he was an impotent mummy's boy. As bad as a womaniser or an alcoholic, to marry him would be a catastrophe, the girls agreed.

Which left Jihad. With hindsight and given Yosra's predilection for pharmaceuticals, it should always have been clear that faced with a choice she would choose to marry a man who owned a chain of pharmacies. But while Yosra had been discovering that Khaled was not the man she had thought he was, Jihad had been on a rendezvous of his own which was about to throw Yosra's plans into confusion all over again.

In the West it is highly unusual for a divorced couple to remarry, but in Islam there is a deeply human understanding that when emotions have abated, with the timely intervention of a friend or relative they can sometimes be made to realise that they moved in haste. There is even provision for this in Islamic law provided you do not do it too often. If you divorce the same woman three times, on the third occasion she is legally required to marry and divorce another man before she can marry you again, a ruling which has provided a rich seam of plots for Arab soap opera writers: a man divorces his wife in a moment of anger for the third time only to realise that before he can get her back he must wait until she has married, slept with and divorced someone else – and he has to help her do it.

So when Jihad met up with his ex-wife – who had come back from America to visit her children – the two managed to patch up their differences with the help of her parents and got married again. When Yosra found out, she was devastated. From no suitors to two suitors, she was now back where she had begun. There was nothing to be done except reflect on how it had all gone wrong and how things might have turned out differently.

On her last visit to the mystic Sheikh he placed his thin hands upon Yosra's head and once again recited words from the Koran. 'Now you are free,' he then announced in a booming voice that echoed around the garage, 'to resume your ordinary life unhindered by the mischievous influence of the spirit world. Go forward.'

Yosra's mother was overjoyed that her daughter was free of the jinn that had possessed her for seven long years. Finally, she said, the time had come for Yosra to find a husband. But as they thanked the Sheikh for all his kindness and left, Yosra felt nothing but sadness. At thirty-three, broken-hearted and still a virgin, she knew that it was probably too late. The jinn had possessed her through her springtime, ruining her engagement and every relationship she had ever had. Her chance of happiness had passed by like a midsummer night's dream.

Thirty-one

Yosra's leaving party was at the Grand Café, a popular coffee shop and *shisha* bar aboard a boat moored on the Nile. With nothing left for her in Cairo, she had spent her savings on a black market visa from Dwayne's father and bought a plane ticket to Dubai to start a new life. It was a daunting step and the decision had not been reached easily. Yosra had never set foot outside Egypt or as much as spent more than a night or two away from her parents' apartment. Her father was sick and she would be leaving her mother and brother to care for him. Roda and Noha had done all they could to encourage Yosra, pushing her to go, believing only by leaving Cairo could she escape her miserable job, her suffocating family, the drugs and everything else that was bringing her down. Abroad she could start again, in a new country with more prospects and opportunities.

Rather than resign her position at the health insurance firm, Yosra managed to arrange a year's unpaid leave. This is a curious feature of Egyptian employment. If you do not hand in your resignation and are diligent about renewing your leave annually it is possible to take unpaid absence for many years and still find your position available upon return, often with a promotion and a pay rise for long service.

We sat out on wicker sofas on the deck of the boat, which was low and close to the gently flowing Nile. The black water looked like the dark soupy leaves of the Egyptian national dish, *molokheya*. The sun was setting over Giza and out on the open water feluccas were still cruising around as serenely as swans, their lateen sails garishly embroidered with Pepsi and Coca-Cola logos billowing in the evening breeze.

Around us the café was filling up fast with Cairo's gilded youth and wealthy Arab tourists. Young men and women were greeting one another in American-accented English before settling down on the sofas to suck on water pipes and toy with their designer mobiles. All around us young Arabs were flirting and chatting by text message or via Bluetooth connections, and as the sun went down in a blazing orange ball loud Gulf Arab pop music, more percussive than Egyptian pop, struck up over the speakers.

My mind was far away. I had decided that someday very soon I was going to become a Muslim. Watching the crescent moon rise in the night sky, I reflected on what this would mean for my life – and after my death. Under my breath I repeated the *shahada*, powerful words of faith and devotion that once spoken irreversibly confirm your acceptance of Islam. '*Ashhadu an la ilaha illallah wa ashhadu anna muhammadan rosulallah,*' I said quietly, taking care not to stumble over the words. 'I witness there is no God but God and I witness that Muhammad is the Prophet of God.' This simple phrase represents the first and most important step to becoming a Muslim. Saying it is one of the Five Pillars of Islam and the basic creed upon which all other convictions are built. They are the first words newborn babies in the Islamic world hear and the first words a child learns to recite. They come as second nature to practising Muslims but to the uninitiated can be a bit of a tongue-twister.

'When you become a Muslim, what Islamic name are you going to choose?' asked Noha, sucking on her *shisha*. 'I didn't mean to interrupt but I overheard you practising.'

It is customary when someone becomes a Muslim for them to choose a new name to reflect their fresh start. Typically converts take names with heavy Islamic overtones to reflect their new-found faith. Cat Stevens became Yusuf Islam; Cassius Clay became Muhammad Ali.

'That's a good question which I've been mulling over for several days,' I replied. 'How about Hosni?'

'Sounds like a penis,' countered Noha.

'What about Amr?' Reem offered. 'That's a good name for a guy.'

'He can't be called that,' snapped Roda.

'Why not? Amr is a nice name.'

'I once had a boyfriend called Amr,' she said briskly. 'So forget it.'

'Saddam Hussein?' I suggested. No one found this very funny. 'How about Sami?' I liked Sami as it could be both a Christian and a Muslim name. When I lived in Yemen Sami was what I was called since no one could get their tongue around Hugh.

'Not bad,' said Yosra. 'But you have to have another one. You can't just be called Sami.'

'Sami, Sami, Sami,' sang Noha in time with the music.

All Yosra's close friends had come to bid her farewell and the coffee shop was humming. Over mocktails and *shishas* they shrieked with laughter as they played with their mobiles, downloading love messages, gossip and pornography from other people sitting around them. Switching on the Bluetooth on my mobile I found fifty people in the immediate vicinity exchanging data files.

Prior to the arrival of Bluetooth, Arab youth met by writing down their telephone numbers on pieces of paper and handing them to strangers in the street or tucking them under someone's windscreen wiper. This was the easiest way to bypass highly sexually segregated social gatherings and flirt with attractive strangers. Modern technology has superseded this system, and within just a few minutes not only had I made some new friends, I had also been sent footage of a man having his head chopped off in Iraq, some prostitutes being beaten up in a Cairo police station and some remarkably graphic footage of what looked like pop sensation Nancy Ajram having her arsehole waxed in a Lebanese beauty salon filmed by wobbly mobile phone through a hole in the blinds.

As the coffee shop filled up, the atmosphere grew more festive. The music was pumping louder and a crowd of young Arabs decked out in sunglasses and designer club wear began to accumulate at the front door. They strained impatiently against the bouncer's rope, pushing to be allowed inside to dance away the unseasonably warm evening. Only at our table was the mood sombre. Yosra's friends were agreed that a new start in Dubai was just what she needed but they were all sad to see her go.

'Have you bought your ticket?' asked Roda, sipping a juice.

'Yesterday,' replied Yosra glumly.

'And your passport?' asked Noha.

'I collected it this afternoon from the Mogamma.'

'What are you going to do when you get off the plane?'

'My cousin is collecting me.'

'Where are you going to stay?'

'At his house, with his wife and two kids.'

Yosra stared out over the Nile, chewing her lip absent-mindedly. On the Corniche a working-class wedding was taking place and the sound of the horns and drums and the cries of joy carried loudly across the water.

'God willing, you will have a fresh start in Dubai,' Reem said earnestly.

'God willing,' replied Yosra apprehensively. 'I am going to miss you guys a lot.'

'It's the best thing to do,' said Roda. 'Better than staying and rotting here.'

'You have to get out of this town,' said Noha. 'There's no future for anyone in Cairo. Look for the possibilities beyond the horizon.'

'My brother told me I should stay,' mumbled Yosra, turning to look into our faces. 'I think he might be right.'

'Why does he think you should stay?' asked Roda cautiously.

'He says it's shameful to leave when Father is sick. He says it is an aberration for an unmarried woman to leave her family to start a new life on her own in another country.'

Since their father had fallen ill and Hassan had become the man of the house Yosra had believed strongly that it was her duty to obey his commands and his words were weighing heavily on her.

'I should not be going. A daughter's duty is to stay and look after the family,' said Yosra bitterly. 'My brother knows what is best for me.'

'That is rubbish,' retorted Roda angrily. 'Hassan is a transparent hypocrite who has never shown the slightest inclination to look after your father. All your life he has let you shoulder family responsibilities while he gets on with his career and whatever else he likes.'

'He's a man. It's different for him. His career is important to him,' replied Yosra, struggling to hold back the tears. 'What if my father dies when I am in Dubai? I would never be able to forgive myself.'

'You have to start living for yourself,' urged Roda.

'If I go now, in a year or two I know I will realise that my brother was right. He always is. I know by stopping me he is really trying to help me. He knows sometimes I make the wrong decision.'

'You are not making the wrong decision,' Roda said emphatically.

Yosra looked downcast. 'What if the plane crashes? What if I die on the way?'

'Don't be ridiculous. You are more likely to die crossing Itihad Street. Look, this is the greatest opportunity of your life. This is your chance to start again. Would you rather stay here and suffer as you have for the last few years?'

'I guess not.' Yosra shrugged. 'But my brother said it was *haram* to leave my family.'

'For God's sake, forget your brother. He is the most self-serving person I know. Next time he quotes the Koran at you, tell him from me that the future is God's will and that he should know better than to try to control it.'

'All right, I will do that,' said Yosra, managing to crack a smile at her friend's irresistible enthusiasm.

Then the DJ put on the hit of the summer, the Islamic mix of 'My Umma' by the British-Azeri singer Sami Yusuf, and everyone went wild, leaping up on their chairs and tables, dancing and clapping along. The café exploded in a frenzy of cheering and shouting, while the waiters and management dashed around like farmyard hens, pleading with the customers to get down from the furniture because this was a no-dancing coffee shop. In a moment our table had jumped up and we were dancing too. My last memory of Yosra was her belly-dancing joyously on her chair, singing at the top of her voice as she clapped along to the music and surrounded by all her friends.

Two days after Yosra left, Dwayne arrived back from Baghdad and we threw a party at Roda's flat to celebrate. He regaled us with his experiences starting with how he had been shot at the day he arrived as he drove into Baghdad from the airport. For the last three months, Dwayne told us, he had been living in a gilded cage, a villa with a gym, a library and maids, where he was forbidden to set foot outside. The villa was in Baghdad's red zone – the area beyond the relative security of the government green zone – and British and South African former special forces soldiers managed their security and every move. Inside the fortified compound Dwayne worked alongside a mix of staff from across the Arab world – Saudis, Jordanians, Palestinians, Egyptians, Algerians – all living on top of one another in a paranoid, pressurised if somewhat pampered environment. To stop them becoming too divorced from real life in Baghdad their guards posted photographs of the deaths and abductions outside on a central noticeboard. Nobody ever spoke of politics or the future: it was divisive and far too depressing.

I could scarcely believe that the boy I remembered as an amiable pothead was now investigating cases of fraud in multi-million-dollar construction contracts commissioned by the American military. He had never even expected to get the job in the first place. The experience had transformed both Dwayne's perspective on life and his personal prospects. He was well paid in Iraq even by Western standards, and locked up inside the villa twenty-four hours a day Dwayne had not had the opportunity to spend his salary. By the time he arrived back in Cairo he was vastly better off: in three months he had earned enough to put down a substantial payment on a villa in a new luxury development in Sixth of October City and also to fulfil a lifelong dream. With the money left over he had produced his very own porno clip, which he was planning to sell to one of the many twenty-four-hour Arab music channels.

In the short time since I had last seen him Dwayne had become more confident, focused and career-minded. He had only come back to Cairo because the job was deemed so stressful the company sent everyone on compulsory paid leave every six weeks. He could hardly wait to get back to Iraq to earn more money.

Before he left, Dwayne was planning to clear up some unfinished business that had been weighing on his mind throughout his stint in Iraq. Six months ago his girlfriend's father had laughed in his face when he said that he would be financially independent in two years. Now Dwayne's dream would come true and he called up the girl's father and told him gleefully just what had happened since he had turned Dwayne down.

Thirty-two

The sun beat down on the traffic jam as we edged our way through the dusty streets towards Al-Azhar. It was the day of my conversion and by way of moral support I had enlisted Hanafi, the doorman at Roda's block, to drive me there. I had no particular need for company; I just wanted to have someone with me on my journey that day.

'That old-model Mercedes,' said Hanafi, jabbing his finger against the dusty windscreen, 'we call that a "crocodile". And that new kind there, that's the "duck's butt".' Although he was never going to be rich enough to afford one himself, Hanafi had parked thousands of cars and over the years had built up an encyclopedic knowledge and an abiding interest in everything concerning the automobile industry. He was explaining to me how cars in Cairo have different names, depending on their make or year they were made.

Hanafi had just been recounting the details of his unforeseen adventure the previous evening. He had been sitting outside the block in Istanbul Street at midnight smoking a *shisha* when a car pulled up and some men got out. Pulling him from his chair they bundled him into the back seat and drove him out to the slums. It turned out they were relatives of the woman his wife had beaten up and out in the darkness they roughed him up. In case he was in any doubt as to who was responsible the thugs then took him to the apartment belonging to the girl's mother, where he was made to apologise for his wife's actions in front of her whole family. Given what sounded like a traumatising experience, he was surprisingly buoyant that morning. Nothing seemed to be bothering him at all.

'You're lucky they did not beat you more badly,' I observed as we sat in the traffic jam.

'Thanks be to God, God is merciful,' he replied, smiling. He had not shaved for several days, his eyes were red and his face was scarred and blackened; his teeth were brown and he smelt bad. 'After I explained to the girl's mother what her daughter did to my wife, she understood what happened and we made peace and then I left.'

'I guess you're just lucky.'

'See that Mitsubishi Lancer?' Hanafi said, ignoring me. 'That's the 1992 model and we call it Safeya el Amary. She's a beautiful actress with eyes just like those headlights.'

The road to Al-Azhar winds through the Islamic quarter past the medieval market of Khan al Khalili. The great souk's zigzag streets and canvas-covered alleys teem with traders and tourists and are a world away from the wide boulevards of Muwazafeen. The market has survived largely unchanged for centuries and its little shops and passages provide the backdrop to the novels of Naguib Mahfouz.

Not far from the souk, Al-Azhar mosque was the pre-eminent centre of learning at the heart of Fatimid Cairo. Its university is the second oldest in the world (the first was founded in Morocco) and in days gone by it drew scholars from across the known world. Today the university is splintered into campuses across Egypt and divided into strictly segregated faculties for men and women. Al-Azhar still likes to think of itself as the stronghold of Islamic learning, Koranic studies and particularly Sunni jurisprudence, although when the doors first opened in AD 975 the Shiite Fatimids presided over how the university was run.

Besides celebrated writers and poets, Al-Azhar can also count among its alumni the founders of Gama'a al-Islamiyya, Hamas, the Black Hand and the Muslim Brotherhood.

The traffic crept forward under the scorching rays of the midday sun. Hanafi and I sat bathed in sweat despite the air conditioning set on full blast, as clouds of dust swirled in the exhaust fumes all around us. Finally the traffic seized up altogether with no one moving in either direction. In the rear-view mirror a sea of shimmering bonnets and roofs extended as far as the eye could see into the hazy distance. It was gridlock. Frustrated drivers pressed their horns as one until the honking and hooting rose in a deafening crescendo that echoed around downtown Cairo.

'Probably an accident,' I said, shuddering at the memory of the last traffic accident I had seen. Nobody wears seat belts or helmets and road deaths kill far more people than Islamic extremists have ever done. Cars break down all the time; overcrowded buses drive into the Nile; men changing tyres on motorways routinely get squashed; bad weather, speeding, poorly maintained roads and a total disregard for both the law and personal safety make Egypt's roads the most dangerous in Africa.

This is in large part due to the driving test system. You do need a licence to drive, but the practical test in Cairo consists of a short drive a few metres forward then reversing back again. When I took the test there were so many cars waiting in line, after a couple of hours the examiner took pity on us and issued everyone with passes without actually seeing any driving at all. Next I needed to register my pass so I could actually receive a licence. Inevitably this meant paperwork. After an hour standing in the sun passing documents and passport photographs through a chicken-wire grille to a veiled harridan I was sent off for a medical certificate. Fortunately these were thoughtfully provided by a small group of entrepreneurial policeman standing on the next street corner in exchange for a small fee. Finally came a check of my vehicle's roadworthiness, which meant an inspection of the car boot to see whether or not there was a fire extinguisher inside, since a law had recently been passed stipulating that all vehicles needed to be equipped with one. Whether your car had lights, brakes, mirrors or indeed anything besides four wheels and a fire extinguisher was of no importance. If you needed to hire or buy an extinguisher for the exam, the same group of helpful policemen could arrange that too. Alternatively, and for another small fee, it was possible to take the test in the examiner's car, a clapped-out brown Lada from the former Soviet Union with peeling paint and a three-foot gear stick.

After a few minutes of cacophony a traffic policeman appeared at the junction ahead of us. We watched him wave his baton frantically, like the pharaonic creator god Atum rising from the waters of chaos, running back and forth in an attempt to impose some order on the traffic. For a man paid a monthly salary of about ten dollars plus bed and board, he was remarkably conscientious. I shuddered to think of the health consequences of exposure to traffic exhaust all day long. A survey of Egyptian traffic policemen conducted by the faculty of medicine at Cairo's Ain Shams University found that levels of lead and other heavy metal toxins in their blood were all well above average – a dire situation compounded, in this case at least, by the cigarette the officer was smoking. An estimated ten to twenty-five thousand people die each year in Egypt from particulates and lead in the air, and pollution costs kids who grow up in Cairo 4.25 IQ points.

Blowing his whistle and cursing, the policeman did not look like the kind of man who worried about his sperm count or the lead in his bones. He probably slept like a baby, I thought, entrusting his health, like most people in Cairo, to God.

'Hey, professor, what's the problem?' Hanafi shouted at the cop.

'The prime minister is passing by,' he shouted back above the noise of the hooting, trying to steady a massively overloaded truck threateningly revving its engine with his bare hands.

Hanafi rolled up his window to shut out the noise and fumes, and switched off the engine. 'It's Mr Clean,' he said with a wry smile, putting the seat back and curling his filthy feet up under his greasy brown *galabiyah*. To the amusement of Egyptians everywhere, the Egyptian prime minister really is called Mr Clean. Yawning, Hanafi rubbed his eyes, resigning himself to a long wait. 'I really hope we don't make the prime minister late,' he said sarcastically.

'You don't like him?' I asked.

'He's better than the last one,' Hanafi said. 'He was a drunk.'

'How do you know?' I asked.

'The cops in the station told me; they work as bodyguards to all the ministers. I would hate to feel we had made him miss his appointment.'

'Do you think we are going to have to wait a long time?' I asked, checking my watch. 'I need to get to Al-Azhar.'

'Once I slept seven hours in a bus because Mubarak was passing,' replied Hanafi cheerily.

I scanned his face hoping he was joking. He was not. Like his ancient predecessors who had laboured under the Egyptian sun, Hanafi had surrendered to his rulers' egoism long ago. For him, the regime's authority was as incontrovertible a fact as a five-million-tonne pyramid in the desert.

'I don't understand why he has to cordon off all the streets like this just so he can drive home.' I was getting grouchy.

'It's the global war on terrorism,' replied Hanafi, half closing his eyes. 'He thinks he'll be blown up so he has to stop all the traffic so he can drive very fast.'

As extremists killed the last president it is easy to understand why the government should regard assassination as a real threat. Meanwhile the government presents Islamism as an atavistic force of darkness determined to knock Egypt off its trajectory towards modernity and democracy. In reality, the danger of extremism has been inflated as an excuse to rule without consent, trampling democracy and civil liberties wholesale along the way. After decades of political stagnation, with living costs sixteen times higher than thirty years ago and a quarter of the population living below the poverty line, the biggest threat to Egypt's transition to modernity remains the regime itself.

Egypt does have some democratic features, like a critical press and a Supreme Constitutional Court that still clings to independence by its fingertips, and undoubtedly a small number of businessmen have become extremely rich thanks to the regime's economic liberalisation, begun under Sadat and expanded by Mubarak. But economic and political liberalisation are not the same thing and there is as much evidence to suggest that Egypt is becoming more authoritarian as there is to suggest that it is becoming more liberal.

The president has total immunity from criticism and routinely steamrollers the Supreme Court. The number of death sentences and civilians tried in military courts has spiralled and torture is widespread in police stations across the country. It would be unfair to say that local government is up to its knees in corruption, when in fact it is up to its neck at least. Instead of cleaning the rubbish off the streets regularly my local authority liked to spend its money taking out large advertisements in national newspapers congratulating its top brass on their birthdays or sending them good tidings during the Eid. According to the UN, Egypt's development lags behind Libya and Syria, not because it is poorer but because its resources are so unevenly distributed. While some people get a generous slice of the cake, men like Hanafi stay on the breadline.

Intriguingly, the exact make-up of the regime is not clear. No doubt a small number of powerful men dominate all the agencies that constitute the state, but no one seems to know exactly who they are. Even apparently senior ministers and generals can find themselves unexpectedly dispatched to some remote foreign posting when the wheel of fortune turns. As they leave with the state press snapping at their heels, you are left wondering how you could have presumed them to be a pillar of the regime in the first place. Except for the president, history has shown that all other posts are readily interchangeable.

I hoped, as I sat in the traffic jam listening to Hanafi snoring, that someone somewhere was in control. The thought that the Egyptian juggernaut had come unhitched from its moorings altogether and was even now sliding off down the tracks was the only thing more frightening than believing that power was concentrated in the hands of a single man. I imagined President Hosni Mubarak somewhere across town straightening his tie in the mirror while muttering to himself, '*L'etat c'est moi.*' At least, I thought cheerfully, Egypt does not have nuclear weapons yet.

'So why did Mido leave Holland?' asked Hanafi, inspecting his toes. 'He was a big star.'

Mido, aka Ahmed Hossam, is Egypt's star striker and the country's highest-paid footballer. He started his career playing for Zamalek before moving, to great national acclaim, to Ajax in Holland.

'I don't know,' I replied lazily. 'Didn't he play during the World Cup?'

'Ah, that's because he's a true Egyptian,' said Hanafi, brimming with admiration. 'Who does he play for now?'

'Tottenham Hotspur,' I replied.

'Tottenham who? Why doesn't he play for a proper team like Chelsea or Manchester United?'

'I don't know,' I said sleepily, pondering the traffic jam.

'Do you think the royal family in Britain is plotting to overthrow the government one day so they can rule the country?' asked Hanafi.

I was on the point of trying to explain the intricacies of constitutional monarchy to him in Arabic when his mobile rang.

'Wait a minute,' he said, groping around in his pocket. 'I had better take that.' He flipped open the phone. 'One of the pimps is passing by . . . How should I know? Hours, probably . . . I'll let you know. Bye.' He snapped shut his mobile. 'Does this happen in your country?'

I thought about this for a moment. I had seen Jacques Chirac drive by with a motorcade in London once, but I could not recall them cordoning off the whole of central London. Tony Blair whizzing by had never delayed me.

'I don't think so,' I said.

'Ah! That's because you have a system.'

'Wait a minute,' I said as the cars ahead of us started to pull away. 'We're moving!'

Thirty-three

People travel to Al-Azhar from across the world to convert to Islam. The airy public office where I was to do the same was filled with a diverse assortment of international visitors. It was rather like a small-claims court in California where I had once sued my landlord.

Each new arrival waited patiently for their turn to see the sheikh, who sat in the centre of the salon on a Louis Farouk sofa upholstered in garish green with gold braid. It reminded me of the sofa in the family's penthouse when I had first come to Cairo as a teenager to work during my summer holidays. The sheikh looked imperious in his spotless red fez wrapped around with a white cloth. His pebble glasses suggested long hours spent studying arcane religious texts in dusty theological libraries. Sunshine streaming through the ornate Islamic windows dramatically enveloped the sofa, the sheikh and the aspiring convert sitting beside him.

Brandishing the documents that they had brought with them to support their cases, the crowd muttered quietly between each act of conversion as if enjoying a cabaret evening. Although each conversion was basically the same, everyone in the room kept an eye on proceedings in case any helpful tips emerged on how best to conduct oneself when one's turn came around.

The floor of the salon was covered with a lurid carpet decorated with multicoloured Islamic designs. Large green plants sprouting from brass pots stood in each corner and a weathered map of the world, stained with fingerprints and teacup rings, hung on the wall. The map showed Islam's progress around the globe: each country was colour-coded according to the Muslim proportion of its population. The Middle was all a deep red, as were large swathes of Africa and southern Asia. Europe and Australia were a rather unhealthy-looking yellow, while North and South America were chalky white except, I noticed, for Chile, which was the same sallow colour as Europe.

Several framed pictures of the Kaaba on a busy day in Mecca also hung on the walls, beneath which were displayed gold-leaf quotes from the Koran in stylised Arabic script wreathed in what looked like tinsel. The largest wall of the salon was lined with built-in cupboards bursting with stacks of yellowing religious literature and books in English, German and half a dozen other languages. A printed sign in English and Arabic on the back of the door next to the cupboard read, 'The procedure of embracing Islam is free of charge.'

As Hanafi and I entered we each uttered, in a loud head-turning voice, '*Salam aleikum*', to register our arrival in the room. The assembled aspiring converts nodded solemnly and answered back piously as one. The sheikh turned his eyes towards us fleetingly and gave a faint nod.

'I recognise that sheikh from TV,' whispered Hanafi in his thick Upper Egyptian accent. 'He's a big star.'

Looking around for empty seats we found none, so instead stood quietly observing. On the sofa with the sheikh were two blonde middle-aged European women wearing white headscarves delicately edged with gold. He was speaking to them in broken English with the calm self-importance and total confidence normally reserved for leading cardiac surgeons and barristers. The women looked nervous and to my secret relief they stumbled awkwardly over the *shahada*.

The ceremony was remarkably simple. All the aspirant had to do was say the *shahada* in Arabic then repeat a few short verses from the beginning of the Koran after the sheikh, much as you repeat a few ritualistic words after the priest in a Christian marriage ceremony. In fact conversion in Egypt is so simple not all Muslim countries recognise the Al-Azhar process because they believe it to be too fast to provide novitiates with a proper basis in Islam. For me it was a bit of a disappointment: expecting some kind of theological test I had brushed up my obscure Islamic protocol surrounding topics like menstruation and *halal* dieting just in case the sheikh decided to quiz me.

When each ceremony was complete, the sheikh invited the converts to jot down their names and some personal details in a big leather-bound tome, like an old-fashioned guestbook in a country hotel. I wondered who was next and tried to calculate how long I would have to wait for my turn. Although the room was crowded, the sheikh was rattling through the procedure like a marine barber and we quickly realised we would not be waiting long. It was of no consequence that the traffic jam had made us a couple of hours late.

'Would you like to sit down?' growled a voice at my elbow. A hunchbacked gnome of a man with a wispy black beard had appeared next to me and was indicating some empty seats on the far side of the room. Pushing through the seated crowd, he gestured for us to follow. As we did so I noticed that most people seemed to have dressed up for the occasion: the women wore headscarves or full-face veils; the men sported beards, prayer beads and *zabeebas*. Outward signs of devotion were clearly de rigueur and whenever the sheikh said '*ahamdullilah*' or '*in sha Allah*' – which was almost every time he spoke – everyone in the room automatically repeated the words as piously as they could.

'Would you like some tea?' the gnome asked huskily as he seated us beneath the Islamic map of the world. Without waiting for an answer, he hobbled off behind a wooden screen decorated with tinfoil in the corner of the salon and began noisily filling up a kettle.

I looked surreptitiously at the people around. Next to us were three black American women covered from head to toe except for their hands, which were hennaed. They were quietly discussing the life of the Prophet in a deep Southern drawl. Next to them sat a middle-aged European woman wearing a veil and an attractive unveiled blonde girl. They were speaking in French to an Egyptian youth with punky gelled hair who appeared to be the girl's boyfriend. The boy and the woman were earnestly explaining something to the girl, who looked decidedly uneasy. In a corner by one of the pot plants sat three teenagers who looked like Uzbeks dressed in short Muslim Brotherhood pants, skullcaps and *galabiyahs*. They had beards without moustaches and each held a copy of the Koran. Faces turned to the ceiling, their eyes were rolled back in ecstasy and a stream of quiet prayers issued from their lips.

Conversion to Islam can make a big difference to your personal status. In most Arab countries conversion brings about substantial social advantages; in some other states, like China, Russia and Myanmar, Muslims are persecuted and the opposite is the case. In the West most people and governments regard belief as a private affair; you can change your religion on a whim and intermarriage between people of different faiths is an everyday occurrence. In Egypt, however, switching religion is a deadly serious business, particularly for Muslims who want to become Christian. Your faith is considered as fundamental a part of your identity as your date of birth or gender.

Copts, like Reem's boyfriend Boutros, also face serious obstacles converting. A Copt's conversion is only recognised as genuine after months of intensive study and many bureaucratic hurdles have been overcome. Sectarian relations are fragile and irreligious Copts need to be dissuaded from converting simply to make their lives easier. Coptic conversions take place in another part of Al-Azhar, away from the salon where Hanafi and I had come that day.

As we waited, the hunchback hobbled back and forth between his tea-making facilities behind the foil-wrapped screen and the crowd of righteous visitors. Refilling teacups with one hand, he handed out great wads of musty-smelling religious books with the other. Donations were constantly offered and accepted.

'Looks like it won't be long before I am up,' I said, prodding Hanafi. He did not look round; the presence of the celebrity sheikh had stunned him into an awed silence.

Suddenly a loud wailing sound filled the room. Thinking it must be the fire alarm I leapt out of my chair and prepared to evacuate the salon. Everyone in the room leapt up too, including the sheikh in his red fez. 'Let's go!' he shouted.

'Let's go!' echoed the aspiring converts jumping to their feet.

'Prayer time!' boomed the sheikh, clapping his hands.

'Prayers?' I exclaimed, turning to Hanafi, a wave of panic sweeping over me. It was not a fire alarm but the call to prayer, so amplified the words were distorted beyond all recognition.

Wasting no time, everyone began eagerly filing out into the corridor.

'I don't know how to pray,' I whispered to Hanafi in terror. 'I can't go into the mosque with all these people.'

'Just do as I do,' said Hanafi. 'It's easy.'

'Easy? You have got to be kidding. In front of this lot? No way.'

'OK . . .' replied Hanafi, thinking on his feet. 'Why don't we just stay at the back and wait for them to clear off? No one will notice if we stay behind.'

'Good thinking,' I replied. 'Look busy.' We walked briskly around the room as if we were going somewhere. The prayer call was growing more fervent by the second and the salon was rapidly emptying.

There was a tug at my elbow and I found the sheikh's assistant once again at my side. 'Are you coming to pray?' he asked. Although this was a question, I could tell there was only one right answer.

'Well . . . I . . . er . . . I just prayed actually,' I replied awkwardly.

'Just before we arrived,' Hanafi added loyally.

Unimpressed by my pathetic excuse the sheikh's assistant scowled at me. But there was no time to hang around. The mosque was calling and in the blink of an eye he disappeared out of the door. Suddenly Hanafi and I were alone in silence. Then it dawned on me: I had not even converted yet and already I was telling lies to project an image of piety. My God, I thought, I am more Egyptian than I thought.

Hanafi and I inspected the map on the wall and admired the plants until the novitiates started to trickle back from their prayers. I leafed through the heavy leather conversion book, scanning the entries on the tissue-thin paper. Each large page displayed the full name, conversion date, original religion, new Islamic name, nationality, address and signature of every convert next to the sheikh's extravagantly loopy signature. I was struck by how many converts had passed through the doors even in the last month. There was an amazing diversity of nationalities – Indians, Uzbeks, Americans, Brits, French, Chinese, Italians – each with a personal story of what had brought them to Al-Azhar.

Before long the sheikh arrived back, smiling and looking relaxed. Hanafi and I resumed our places and waited for the queue for salvation to restart.

'Some literature, sir?' asked the hunchback with a smile, appearing once again at my elbow. A yellowing stack of poorly bound second-generation photocopies appeared under my nose. I glanced at the top title, 'The Omrah, the Haj and Human Rights in Islam by Dr Muhammad Abdul Wahid Wafy'.

'Thank you very much,' I said politely, taking the book from his hand and proffering some cash.

Satisfied, the hunchback sloped along to the next customer.

'Hey!' whispered Hanafi. 'It says over there, "The procedure of embracing Islam is free of charge."'

'The tip is for the literature,' I whispered back, holding up the book.

'I went to the mosque the other day and the imam told everyone to leave their gold in the collection box when they made their way out. I got up and walked straight out the door. You can't trust anyone these days.'

Suddenly I heard my name called and in a moment I was pushing through the chairs, making my way to the front and taking my place on the couch next to the sheikh. I could feel all eyes upon me as the sheikh asked in heavily accented English if I knew what the Five Pillars of Islam were. Behind his glasses I could barely make out his small cloudy eyes and when I told him I did, he counted them off for me on his fingers. I realised then that this was not an exam I was going to fail.

Then he asked me in a loud voice why I had come that day to convert in the presence of God. When I explained that I wanted to marry a Muslim woman his eyebrows arched a little and he looked perturbed. 'Is that the only reason? Nothing else?'

'Well, I suppose I don't really believe in miracles,' I began, groping around for an alternative explanation. 'I could never understand how wafers could be turned into the body of Christ.'

'Yes, total madness isn't it?' the sheikh interrupted casually, throwing up his hands and distracting my train of thought. 'No other reasons? That's fine then,' he said, quickly moving on. 'Just repeat after me . . .' Then he asked me to repeat some verses from the Koran in Arabic and say the *shahada*, which I managed to produce more or less adequately. 'Congratulations,' said the sheikh briskly. 'You are now a Muslim. Hold on a minute and I will fill out your conversion certificate.' The whole process had taken no more than a few minutes.

As he filled out the certificate the sheikh asked me a few polite questions about myself – where I was from and how long I had been in Cairo. As we talked I entered my details in the book on the table in front of us.

'And what shall your Islamic name be?' asked the sheikh.

'Sami Hussein?' I suggested hesitantly.

'Welcome, Sami Hussein,' declared the sheikh in a loud voice.

As I signed my new name in the book I thought about converts to Islam before me. I thought of Malcolm X, who refused to use a last name because he said they were slave names and John Coltrane, who believed music was the universal language of God. I remembered Cassius Clay, who joined the Nation of Islam aged just twenty-two after beating Sonny Liston in his first title fight, and I thought about a picture book I had had when I was a child about the Christian warrior El Cid, general of the Catholic king of Castile, who switched sides to become a mercenary for the Moors in eleventh-century Andalusia.

The sheikh told me that now I had embraced Islam marriage to a Muslim woman was possible and he reminded me that my children must be Muslim too. As he spoke I could see the deep satisfaction in his face that I had converted and so was somehow more acceptable to him, and that made me sad. The reminder about my unborn children made me suspicious and I wondered fleetingly whether this was why conversion had been so easy.

What I wanted to say to the sheikh was that although like him I was seeking the truth, I doubted those who claimed to have found it. I wanted to ask him why if Islam was a religion of peace the hairdresser in Istanbul Street divided the world into the House of Islam and the House of War and why Yosra had friends who would die to kill American women and children. I wanted to understand why the Koran was full of injunctions to fight and why the pain and suffering awaiting unbelievers is mentioned on almost every page. I wanted to understand why men of apparently perfect faith flew planes into buildings or killed women for staining their family honour.

But people who like to share their religious views with you rarely want you to share yours with them and now did not seem like the right time for conversation. 'I have just one final question,' I stammered as I rose from my chair to leave. The sheikh looked at me imperiously, eyebrows arched above his thick glasses. I cleared my throat, again feeling all eyes in the room upon me. 'Why are there so many Muslims in Chile?'

As we left Al-Azhar, the sheikh's assistant furnished me with a copy of my conversion certificate in triplicate. Outside in the sunny car park Hanafi could barely contain his excitement.

'This is a joyous day,' he said, slapping the roof of the car.

'Did my *shahada* come out all right?' I asked.

'It was all great! Thanks be to God.'

'Thanks be to God I can now legally marry Roda,' I replied. 'I thought they might have barred me after they saw I did not know how to pray.'

'Don't worry about that,' said Hanafi, beaming from ear to ear. 'There is so much you have to learn. This is only the beginning.'

The sun was setting in a fiery ball somewhere beyond Elephant and Castle and as we drove back I thought how strange it was that religion could ever be an obstacle to two people getting married. I realised that for months I had being trying to understand people's lives in Cairo, but somewhere along the way, leaning in closer to take a better look, I had passed through the looking glass and now found myself on the other side. Embracing Islam, changing the most basic attribute any human being can have – my name – I had reached the point where I no longer knew myself. At least, I thought consolingly, Jews and Christians living in Muslim lands have been doing what I had just done for hundreds of years.

Islam has always been a religion of conquest, sharing power only until an opportunity arises for control. Once a person or a place becomes Islamic, there is an unshakeable belief that it should stay that way. What choices more than a billion Muslims from Egypt to Chile make in the decades ahead is one of the central questions of our time. For non-Muslims the future may sometimes seem daunting, as if nothing can be done to influence which path will be taken, as if nothing can ever change, but religion is only an idea and ideas can change in a heartbeat.

In the West we often like to think of life as a game. We think of people as players, winning some days, losing others. But the rules I had played by in Britain did not work in Cairo. In Egypt life was no game; it was preparation for the afterlife. Social rules seemed topsy-turvy, the law of the land erratic. Only the rules of Islam remained immutable, though subject to a Pandora's box of possible interpretations. I knew that I had only scratched the surface of life in Egypt and I silently prayed that it would stay that way. Now a Muslim, I nevertheless dreaded being treated the way Egyptians treat each other. Egyptian journalists in particular face systematic harassment and arbitrary arrest.

While Hanafi drove, he animatedly described the rewards I could now expect in the next life. There is no greater achievement in Islam than converting an unbeliever so Roda he held up as a particular paragon of virtue, highly likely to receive bounteous rewards in the afterlife for having shepherded me into my new faith. As he spoke I surveyed Cairo's decaying glory and thought back over the stories I had heard in the course of that year and a deep sadness welled up inside me.

Cairo has become a cruel and neglectful mother, as if the grinding poverty and the weight of millions of people and cars have worn down her benevolence and her will to go on. How different it all might have been, I thought, if geology had handed Egypt Saudi Arabia's wealth. Perhaps then she might have been able to evolve from an agriculture-based nation and contain her urban population explosion, the way, say, Japan had done. But generations of misrule have sapped her spirit until today the air is no longer safe to breathe and the water so polluted even the fish suffer kidney problems. Corruption and stagnant bureaucracy pervade life's every corner, leaving Egyptians with nothing but faith to take them into the future.

Thomas Jefferson said, 'When the people fear the government you have tyranny . . . when the government fears the people you have liberty.' I had found that women in Cairo fear both the government and other people. In Muwazafeen I had come into contact with the richest, luckiest women in Egypt, who were many times better off than their country cousins, yet they still feared walking the streets because of harassment, feared their neighbours for spying on them and feared their families for their punishment. Their wings were clipped the day they were born.

Life in the Middle East is no longer traditional, in the sense that it is now not lived strictly according to the Koran but, even if PlayStations are replacing card games, nor is it fully 'modern' in the Western sense either. It is stranded somewhere between the two and changing all the time. In the flux between old and new individuals face internal conflicts over competing obligations and contradictory expectations.

Today Egyptian women are better educated than ever before, but they are still expected to do the child rearing and domestic chores, to abstain from social interaction outside their family and to compete on an unequal basis with men in the workplace. Though they can sometimes and to some extent choose a husband, family pressures are strong and their lives are blighted by discrimination, deprivation and violence. As Arab society moves towards a new equilibrium, it is women who are paying the highest price.

Some Cairenes seek solace in drugs, religion or endless rounds of cards. Others leave to work as indentured servants for their Gulf Arab cousins. Everyone clings to memories of better times, the days before Cairo became a monster to her people and a slave to foreign powers. They remember their beloved city when she was great: when Cairo was the cradle of Arab nationalism and Egyptians were the proud leaders of the Arab world.

Postscript

Egyptians have been marrying foreigners since the time of the pharaohs. Roda and I married the following July, when the summer heat was at its most unbearable and the streets were crowded with tourists. Normally weddings take place at home, in the mosque or at a designated government legal office, but by law foreigners may only get married in one place: an excruciatingly ugly fourth-floor concrete government office inside the Ministry of Justice.

The waiting room was jammed. The system was, you took a number on arrival before taking your place at the back of the line, like being served at the supermarket delicatessen counter.

Naturally everyone was in celebratory mood, smiling and laughing and taking pictures, and as each couple signed the contract in the marriage office the noise of women ululating and people clapping came echoing down the corridor. The assembled foreigners made a colourful sight. There were all kinds from every walk of life: African refugees, Palestinians, Western divorcees with their toy boys, a veritable United Nations. Each came accompanied by their little group of loved ones and witnesses, and despite the grim office setting everyone had turned out in their best clothes.

The brides were the ones who suffered most, trying to keep their hair, veils and make-up intact without knowing how much longer they would have to wait or even if they were going to get married that day, but by the time we finally made it to the front of the queue Roda still looked as beautiful as the first time I had seen her at Jerome's leaving party. Ultimately it did not matter one bit if the waiting room was grotty or that our wedding was a million miles from anything either of us had imagined. We were happy to have made it and overwhelmed by the feeling that just by being there that day we had already created something beautiful together.

When our turn came, we passed through three dingy offices in turn, presenting various photographs and other pieces of information at each desk. The last room was where the actual legal wedding took place. Our assembled relatives and friends crammed in as best they could between filing cabinets and other well-worn pieces of office furniture. Since we were having a civil marriage – the only kind foreigners in Egypt are permitted – no imam was present, just a sweaty, chain-smoking civil servant with a five o'clock shadow in a nylon suit. Roda's father and Nadia's husband were our two obligatory Muslim male witnesses.

Even religious Muslim weddings are not a sacrament but a straightforward legal agreement with a written contract. Business is conducted not between the bride and groom, but between the groom and the bride's father, so as the official registering us said a prayer and linked my hand in his, I found myself staring lovingly not at Roda but into the heavily browed brown eyes of my new father-in-law. Roda sat behind him. Then the official said another prayer as Roda's father and I took turns to read our parts of the contract out loud. Permission to marry now officially granted, responsibility for Roda's welfare duly passed from him to me. We signed and stamped the wedding contract with inky blue thumbprints, Roda's girlfriends ululated loudly making the office ring, and the women waiting down the corridor all joined in.

That night we cracked open the champagne to celebrate – not the most appropriate way to start my new life as a Muslim perhaps, but I had changed my religion not my culture and I wanted to drink a toast to love, marriage and Sami Hussein.

Now you can order superb titles directly from Abacus

☐ Al Jazeera   Hugh Miles   £9.99

The prices shown above are correct at time of going to press. However, the publishers reserve the right to increase prices on covers from those previously advertised, without further notice.

───────────────── ⟨ABACUS⟩ ─────────────────

Please allow for postage and packing: **Free UK delivery.**
Europe: add 25% of retail price; Rest of World: 45% of retail price.

To order any of the above or any other Abacus titles, please call our credit card orderline or fill in this coupon and send/fax it to:

Abacus, PO Box 121, Kettering, Northants NN14 4ZQ
Fax: 01832 733076   Tel: 01832 737526
Email: aspenhouse@FSBDial.co.uk

☐ I enclose a UK bank cheque made payable to Abacus for £ . . . . .
☐ Please charge £ . . . . to my Visa/Delta/Maestro

Expiry Date ☐☐☐☐   Maestro Issue No. ☐☐

NAME (BLOCK LETTERS please) . . . .

ADDRESS . . . .

. . . .

. . . .

Postcode . . . . Telephone . . . .

Signature . . . .

Please allow 28 days for delivery within the UK. Offer subject to price and availability.